was the 2004 presidential election stolen?

was the 2004 presidential election stolen?

EXIT POLLS, ELECTION FRAUD,
AND THE OFFICIAL COUNT

Steven F. Freeman and Joel Bleifuss

Foreword by U.S. Representative John Conyers, Jr.

Seven Stories Press
New York | Toronto | London | Melbourne

11/10/06
ww
$17.95

Seven Stories Press
140 Watts Street
New York, NY 10013
http://www.sevenstories.com/

In Canada: Publishers Group Canada, 250A Carlton Street, Toronto, ON M5A 2L1

In the UK: Turnaround Publisher Services Ltd., Unit 3, Olympia Trading Estate, Coburg Road, Wood Green, London N22 6TZ

In Australia: Palgrave Macmillan, 627 Chapel Street, South Yarra, VIC 3141

College professors may order examination copies of Seven Stories Press titles for a free six-month trial period. To order, visit www.sevenstories.com/textbook/ or send a fax on school letterhead to 212-226-1411.

Library of Congress Cataloging-in-Publication Data
Freeman, Steve.
Was the 2004 presidential election stolen? : exit polls, election fraud, and the official count / Steven F. Freeman and Joel Bleifuss.— 1st ed.
    p.   cm.
Includes bibliographical references.
ISBN-13: 978-1-58322-687-2 (pbk. : alk. paper)
ISBN-10: 1-58322-687-7 (pbk. : alk. paper)
1. Presidents—United States—Election, 2004. 2. Elections—Corrupt practices—United States. 3. Election forecasting—United States. 4. Voting—United States. I. Bleifuss, Joel. II. Title.

JK5262004 .F74 2005
324.973'0931—dc22   2005026943

Book design by Jon Gilbert

Printed in the USA.

10 9 8 7 6 5 4 3 2 1

Contents

Foreword

Dear Reader,

The Founders of the American republic were explicit in their desire that the voice of the people operate in the election of the President. More than simply reflecting the desires of the majority, Hamilton insisted that the electoral process afford a "moral certainty." Elections needed to convey a sense of fairness and finality if the fledgling democracy was to survive.

The United States has not always lived up to the notion of justice and equity at the ballot box. Much of the national story can be told as the grudging but certain extension of voting rights to every free American. But despite the obstacles of the past—and despite how very far we have to go to live up to the ideal—the principle of electoral justice remains sound. No event has a more profound impact on the contours of American citizenship than participation in a national election. No civic responsibility is more important than the duty of a citizen to challenge the wisdom of his or her elected leaders.

And when we have reason to doubt, when officials operate secretly under color of law or behind the veil of untested technologies, when the results of a national election cannot be trusted to reflect the ballots cast, no obligation could be greater than that of a citizen to question the electoral process itself.

The events of November 2004 gave us such reason to doubt. This book, *Was the 2004 Presidential Election Stolen?* by Steven F. Freeman and Joel Bleifuss, asks some very hard, very important questions about an electoral process that yielded anything but "moral certainty."

To be sure, aberrant results in exit polls are but one warning that something may have gone wrong—either with the statistical analysis or with the election itself—and that the election results warrant greater scrutiny.

Guided in no small part by Steve Freeman's original analysis of exit polls nationwide, I began my own investigation of the official results. My staff reviewed thousands of pages of primary source materials, copies of actual ballots, voter registration databases, and poll records. They conducted interviews with any number of individuals having firsthand knowledge of irregularities. We traveled all over the country in search of even more information, so much of it obscured by government failings and partisan motives.

What we found indicated problems in nearly every sphere of the electoral process—ranging from machine tampering and malfunction to the intimidation of minority voters in urban and rural areas, from the purposeful misallocation of voting machines to unjustifiably long lines in precincts with historically high turnout.

Without a doubt, most states did not experience the extent of problems uncovered in Florida in 2000 or Ohio in 2004. Most secretaries of state and local election authorities are competent and conscientious officials, men and women who faithfully execute a broad and complicated task. Unfortunately, the lesson of our past two presidential elections has become patently clear—poor decisions by election officials, whether motivated by political bias or stunning negligence, can result in the disenfranchisement of voters and the massive distortion of election results.

In these pages, Steve Freeman and Joel Bleifuss shape the raw data into an image of all that the Founders warned us against. Precious few polling sites can actually verify that votes are recorded as cast. Voting machines are unreliable and easily subject to tampering. Election officials acting in bad faith have little difficulty blocking the sparse opportunities to check the accuracy of the results. Theirs is a critique that warrants response.

As I commend this work to you, I reflect upon the sentiments of Martin Luther King, Jr., who believed that Americans "shall have to do more than register and more than vote; we shall have to create leaders who embody virtues we can respect, who have moral and ethical principles we can applaud with enthusiasm." Our elections are about more than the ballots we cast—the outcome must be shaped by decent men and women, in government and around it, who will neither be deterred by the frustrations of a broken system nor silenced by those who wield it.

—Congressman John Conyers, Jr.
Washington, D.C., October 2005

Preface

Driving to the University of Pennsylvania on the afternoon of the election, I turned on the radio. The host of a talk-radio show was lamenting that the exit-poll numbers looked impossibly grim. Unless the President found some way to turn this thing around, we were in for a bad four years. "Now we were going to see the real John and Teresa Heinz Kerry," he warned. For most of my brief commute, a caller from Florida complained about the huge turnout in his precinct. In the long line where he had waited to vote, he said, he was probably the only Bush voter. He could hardly believe all the derelicts, drug addicts, and other dregs that the Democrats had managed to drag out to the polls.

At 9:30 p.m. EST that evening, I went to my neighbor's home to watch election coverage. I was surprised by how little information was being transmitted, and there was not a word about the exit-poll results I had heard about earlier in the day. When the anchorman assured us that they would be giving us projections as soon as the network decision team was confident, but not a minute before, I bolted.

I picked up my friend's laptop and began to pore through CNN's Web site. Their data largely confirmed those earlier reports of a Kerry victory, and given that these were the numbers after the polls had closed, it appeared to me as though Kerry had won both the popular vote and in the electoral college. After about fifteen minutes of inspection, I announced this to the eight or so people in the room. They responded that that wasn't what was being reported on

TV. I looked up over the laptop to watch the television screen, puzzled by the contrasting stories. The laptop screen projected a Kerry victory in nearly every battleground state, in many cases by substantial margins. But on TV James Carville was saying that Kerry needed to "draw an inside straight" to pull off the win. The Slate Web site indicated a narrow edge to Kerry in Florida; the networks all had Florida solidly in the Bush camp. CNN's Web site data informed us of commanding Kerry victories in Pennsylvania and Minnesota; TV anchors told us these states were too close to call.

As a professor who has taught courses in research methods— earlier that semester I had taught a workshop on survey methods— it seemed inexplicable to me that exit polls could be so far off. Exit polls are not predictions of what might happen on Election Day; they are surveys of actual voters who have just cast their votes.

Eventually, the election came down to Ohio, where exit polls showed Kerry with a projected victory of more than 4%, based on a large sample that should have been accurate within 2% to 3% of the final tally. But although the networks were conservative in refusing to call the state, TV viewers were left with little doubt that Bush had won. I was perplexed and uncertain—there were voters still waiting in line in Ohio cities, uncounted provisional votes, and so on. How could the exit polls be that far off?

The next morning, I learned that Bush had prevailed and that Kerry was preparing his concession speech, but nothing was reported on why the exit polls were so far off—or even that they were far off. I went to the CNN site to study the numbers that I had seen the night before and saw instead an entirely different set of numbers with no explanation. I wondered if I had incorrectly remembered what I'd seen the night before.

Over the next two days, I listened to the news and read the papers, expecting an explanation, but there was little mention of the exit polls, except as the source of data used to inform us that Bush had won because of "moral values" and how the Democratic

Party was out of touch with America's heartland. When the exit-poll discrepancy did come up, the few meager explanations offered—there were "too many women in the sample," for instance—could not conceivably be correct. I asked a few colleagues if they had heard anything. None had. I was doubly baffled, not only by the exit-poll discrepancy itself, but that this fact had all but vanished from the face of the earth.

I spent much of the day Friday trying to find the original exit-poll data. Why was the exit-poll data carried on CNN, MSNBC, and other major Web sites so different from what they'd posted on the night of the election? And what was the explanation for the wide discrepancy between the original exit-poll data and the official count? That the outcome of the election might be invalid had not even occurred to me as a possibility, but why were the exit polls so far off? On the Web I came across widespread speculation that the election results were fraudulent. Much of it was clearly flawed. But there was a reasonably coherent 2004 presidential election theft thesis put forward by author Thom Hartmann on a Web site called Common Dreams.[1] I also found damning charges concerning issues of which I was only vaguely aware, notably electronic voting, Ohio vote suppression, and anomalies in the 2002 midterm elections.

Regarding what might have gone wrong with the polls, I found no reasonable answers, just deflections and vacuous reporting. Lead exit pollster Joe Lenski told the *Los Angeles Times*, "I'm not designing polls for some blogger who doesn't even understand how to read the data."[2] A *New York Times* article reported that the newspaper had obtained a report issued by pollsters that "debunked the possibility that the exit polls are right and the vote count is wrong," but the story did not explain beyond that declaration how the possibility was "debunked."[3] In fact, no evidence whatsoever was presented in the *Times* or anywhere else of skewed survey data or any problem at all with the polls other than the fact that "uncorrected" data had been released to the public, and that a technical glitch allowed that data to remain on the CNN Web site throughout election night.[4]

On the academic research methods listserv of which I am a member, I asked colleagues for explanations about the discrepancy. Few answers were forthcoming, but it turned out others had the same questions.

Trying to find the original data I'd seen on election night, I came across a post by Jonathan Simon on a surprisingly vast Web site, Democratic Underground. Simon's post recorded forty-six exit-poll projections and how far they deviated from the official counts.[5] I went to my neighbor's house to get the computer that I had been using on election eve. The election night screen shots from the national survey and sixteen states were still preserved, and they corroborated completely Simon's data.

I was more perplexed than suspicious. It seemed inconceivable that millions of votes could be stolen in a U.S. presidential election. What happened to those twenty thousand Democratic National Committee lawyers? Doesn't the party track the numbers? If there were something to this, why would Kerry concede? And why wouldn't reporters be jumping on the story? And why weren't political scientists speaking up? Florida 2000 was one thing, but a discrepancy of millions of votes that goes uncontested by the would-be victors, unchallenged by responsible professionals, unreported in the media, and undetected in academia in what was probably the world's most closely watched election in half a century—that was an entirely different matter.

All these questions led back to the more fundamental one: what had caused the large, unexplained discrepancy between the exit polls and the official count?

In the 2004–5 academic year, I held a special position as a research scholar at the University of Pennsylvania's Center for Organizational Dynamics, affording me unusual freedom to conduct interdisciplinary research of broad significance. So, when neither reporters, nor pollsters, nor the Democrats, nor political scientists raised the obvious questions, I thought that, well, perhaps this is my job as much as anyone else's. So, after some research, I sat down to write. I described what I was able to learn about exit-poll reliability, the statistical implausibility of their being so far off, and the inadequacy of the explanations offered thus far. On November 9, I circulated a first draft of "The Unexplained Exit-Poll Discrepancy" to colleagues and invited them to comment. On every page in big bold letters was this notice:

> DRAFT—Do not circulate, reproduce, post, or cite without the express consent of the author.

Despite the warning, the draft was widely circulated, and I received requests to post or circulate it even more widely. So I released it the next day with the qualifier that it was an early draft, again inviting comments and information and asking that I be informed if it were posted or cited so that I would at least know where to send revisions.

The conclusion I offered seemed to me fairly innocuous:

> Widespread assumption of misplay undermines not only the legitimacy of the President, but faith in the foundations of the democracy. . . . The election's unexplained exit-poll discrepancies make fraud or mistabulation . . . an unavoidable hypothesis, one that is the responsibility of the media, academia, polling agencies, and the public to investigate.

Over the next ten days I received a torrent of messages from across the country and around the world—hundreds of phone calls and more than two thousand e-mails, most of them extending thanks for asking the obvious questions that the media and everyone else with a public voice had been ignoring. Both my personal

Web page and the Web page of the University of Pennsylvania research center where I work went down. Mixed in with the letters of support were inquiries and suggestions on how to improve the paper, and various theories about what went wrong with the exit polls. I also received a good deal of hate mail: "looser" [sic], "sour grapes," a string of a hundred messages repeating "FOUR MORE YEARS," and indignant letters to the Dean demanding my resignation or censure, including one that said, "How dare he hypothesize mistabulation or fraud in a presidential election!"

The paper spread all over the Internet, and I began to be overwhelmed with media phone calls and interview requests. But although the story was widely covered in the independent media, my interviews with reporters from the *Washington Post* and *USA Today* never made it into print. I rushed out on last-minute notice to do a CNN studio interview that did not air. An MSNBC interview was canceled (because a verdict was reached that afternoon in the Peterson murder trial). Over the next few days, stories appeared in the *Washington Post*, the *New York Times*, and many other publications ridiculing "Internet conspiracy theory."[6] My article, as far as I know, was not mentioned in any of these stories; rather, they seemed to cherry-pick the weakest Internet allegations to debunk and, on that basis, dismiss any and all inquiry as "conspiracy theory." Despite the obvious importance of the subject, colleagues with impressive credentials who raised questions about the official election results, such as Fritz Scheuren, the president of the American Statistical Association, could not get op-eds published.[7] ABC resisted publishing on their Web site a column by their own columnist, mathematician John Allen Paulos—the winner of the 2003 American Association for the Advancement of Science award for the promotion of public understanding of science—when he, too, took notice of the discrepancy.[8]

In addition, my mail contained some eyewitness reports of malfeasance. Three precinct workers from Perry County in Appalachian Ohio wrote:

360 people signed the book and 33 absentee ballots were cast for a total of 393 votes. The Board of Election is reporting 489 votes cast in that one precinct. WE HAVE A COPY OF THE ENTIRE POLL BOOK for this precinct (other totals were hand checked).

They said they went to the FBI, who referred them to the secretary of state's office, despite the fact that the precinct workers believe that the secretary of state's office was the source of the alleged malfeasance. (Ohio Secretary of State Kenneth Blackwell served as an Ohio chairman of the 2004 Bush-Cheney Campaign.[9])

Unfortunately, I could not investigate these claims. I was unable to even look at most of the e-mails I received (sorry to those of you who wrote), and had to get a new, separate e-mail account so that my students could reach me. But nobody else was investigating either. Which itself was data. I looked at the problem as I would any other research question. I formulated the only two hypotheses that could explain the discrepancy—something was wrong with the exit polls or something was wrong with the official count. I then sought out theory and data that could substantiate either one of them.

Most public voices have been anxious to dismiss out of hand any inquiry into the possibility of a corrupted vote count.[10] But absence of scrutiny does not make a democracy function; democratic processes do. And among these processes is public scrutiny. Inquiry into the integrity of an election neither undermines democracy nor divides a nation. To the contrary, the only way to maintain democracy or unite a people is to ensure that election probity is beyond question. All the major political parties must be confident that they did, in fact, have a fair chance to prevail. And the only way to restore such confidence is by an honest probe into what really happened in the 2004 presidential election.

—Steven F. Freeman
Philadelphia, March 2006

NOTE ON TABLES, FIGURES, DATA, AND STATISTICAL ANALYSES

The tables and figures presented in this book use data that come from the indicated sources and, unless otherwise noted, are the creation of the authors and not reprinted directly from these sources.

Because of space limitations and the complexity of statistical analysis we were unable to present all the data compiled and all the analyses conducted in preparation for this book. Complete data sets and details of analyses, including statistical analysis, are available on Freeman's website, http://www.electionintegrity.org.

CHAPTER 1

Dateline
November 2, 2004

November 2, 2004, was shaping up as a day of celebration for Democrats.

In the closing days of the campaign, several factors had augured well for Massachusetts Senator John Kerry. Pre-election opinion polls indicated a final surge. The Democrats would benefit from an unprecedented get-out-the-vote effort and a fervor that exceeded any election in recent memory.[11] Most significant, President George W. Bush's approval ratings were low.[12] As the historical record of prior elections show, an incumbent job-approval rating below 50% indicates trouble ahead, and an election-eve survey in every battleground state gave Bush ratings below that figure—in most cases far below.[13] Sure enough, Election Day exit polls showed Kerry ahead in nearly every battleground state, in many cases by sizable margins. Kerry-Edwards campaign staffers met to draft an acceptance speech and Beltway Democrats began speculating about posts in the new Kerry administration.

President George W. Bush and his supporters, meanwhile, were despondent. That day, Bush cast his vote in Crawford, Texas, and then boarded Air Force One to fly back to Washington via Columbus, Ohio. En route he learned that exit polls indicated Sen. John Kerry would win the election. Clearly, Bush, a seasoned politician, took the numbers very seriously. His administration had helped pay for exit polls two days earlier, in the October 31, 2004, election in Ukraine, to ensure that any fraud committed would be exposed and to help the opposition candidate, whose candidacy the Bush administration favored. According to one source, Bush had one of his tantrums and canceled three scheduled phone-in television interviews in the key battleground state of Florida. In an attempt to calm the president, Karl Rove, the political operative who had guided Bush through previous elections, assured him everything would be okay.[14]

Bush wasn't alone in thinking he had lost. Many Americans, including most political observers, sat down to watch the evening television coverage convinced that John Kerry would be the next president.

But the counts that were being reported on TV bore little resemblance to these projections. In key state after key state, tallies differed significantly from the exit-poll survey projections. In *every* case, the shift favored Bush. Nationwide, exit-poll surveys projected a 51% to 48% Kerry victory, the mirror image of Bush's 51% to 48% margin of victory in the official count.

In the days after the election, the media largely ignored this exit-poll discrepancy. When it was mentioned, it was only to report that the exit polls were flawed.[15] The discrepancy, however, was real and way beyond the statistical margin of error.

COULD THE COUNT BE THAT FAR OFF?

Florida 2000 was one thing—a mix of vote suppression, miscounts, so-called errors, flawed technology, and recounts that were non-counts in the state governed by the winning candidate's brother. But the exit polls of 2004 suggest the possibility that large numbers of votes were actually deleted, added, or switched in jurisdictions throughout the country—enough to determine the outcome of the election. How could this have happened, given the wide geography, different administrative systems, and array of voting technologies?

Following Election Day 2004, the Internet was flooded with stories of election fraud and thwarted voter intent. Many of the accounts were poorly informed, wrong, or presented unsubstantiated theories that proved false upon further investigation. Other allegations, however, bear further scrutiny. Some painted a disturbing picture of Republican elected officials suppressing, discouraging, and preventing citizens from exercising their right to cast a vote that counts. Others raised valid concerns about the integrity of the vote-counting process once votes were cast.

Few people are as familiar with running fair elections as former President Jimmy Carter, whose Carter Center has monitored more than fifty elections worldwide. In September 2004, Carter predicted that the upcoming U.S. election would be as contentious as the one in 2000, with Florida again at the center of the storm. In a *Washington Post* op-ed column, he wrote that "some basic international requirements for a fair election are missing in Florida," the most significant of which are the following:

•A nonpartisan electoral commission or a trusted and non-partisan official who will be responsible for organizing and conducting the electoral process before, during, and after the actual voting takes place. . . . Florida voting officials have proved to be highly partisan, brazenly violating a basic need for an unbiased and universally trusted authority to manage all elements of the electoral process.

•Uniformity in voting procedures, so that all citizens, regardless of their social or financial status, have equal assurance that their votes are cast in the same way and will be tabulated with equal accuracy. Modern technology is already in use that makes electronic voting possible, with accurate and almost immediate tabulation and with paper ballot printouts so all voters can have confidence in the integrity of the process. There is no reason these proven techniques, used overseas and in some U.S. states, could not be used in Florida.

It was obvious that in 2000 these basic standards were not met in Florida, and there are disturbing signs that once again, as we prepare for a presidential election, some of the state's leading officials hold strong political biases that prevent necessary reforms. . . . It is unconscionable to perpetuate fraudulent or biased electoral practices in any nation. It is especially objectionable among us Americans, who have prided ourselves on setting a global example for pure democracy. With reforms unlikely at this late stage of the election, perhaps the only recourse will be to focus maximum public scrutiny on the suspicious process in Florida.[16]

As Carter predicted, in 2004 Florida featured prominently, if less publicly, as a state where incidents of vote suppression and alleged fraud again tilted the vote toward George W. Bush. But the big story in 2004 was the swing state of Ohio, with its 20 electoral votes, where the presidential election is thought to have been decided. In Ohio, Secretary of State Kenneth Blackwell, in the tradition of former Florida Secretary of State Katherine Harris, served both as cochair of the 2004 Bush-Cheney Campaign and the state's chief election official. According to the official count, Bush won the state by 118,000 votes, or 2% of the total vote.

On Election Day 2004, it was immediately apparent that the vote in Ohio was fraught with problems. Concerned about the difficulties voters encountered as they attempted to cast their ballot in Ohio, on November 5, 2004, Rep. John Conyers, Jr. (D.-Mich.), the ranking Democratic member of the House Judiciary Committee, along with Reps. Jerrold Nadler (D.-N.Y.) and Robert Wexler (D.-Fla.), wrote Comptroller General of the United States David M. Walker and asked that the General Accountability Office "immediately undertake an investigation of the efficacy of voting machines and new technologies used in the 2004 election, how election officials responded to difficulties they encountered, and what we can do in the future to improve our election systems and administration."[17] The three wrote:

> The essence of democracy is the confidence of the electorate in the accuracy of voting methods and the fairness of voting procedures. In 2000, that confidence suffered terribly, and we fear that such a blow to our democracy may have occurred in 2004.

In the following months investigators for both Democrats on the House Judiciary Committee and the Democratic National Committee's (DNC) Voting Rights Institute explored what happened in Ohio on Election Day 2004.

On January 5, 2005, under the leadership of Conyers, the Democrats on the Judiciary Committee (Republicans on the committee refused to participate) released a 102-page report, *Preserving Democracy: What Went Wrong in Ohio*. Those findings, commonly referred to as the Conyers Report, concluded:

> We find that there were massive and unprecedented voter irregularities and anomalies in Ohio. In many cases these irregularities were caused by intentional misconduct and illegal behavior, much of it involving Secretary of State J. Kenneth Blackwell.

The DNC began conducting its own investigation on December 6, 2004, releasing its report, *Democracy at Risk: The 2004 Election in Ohio*, on June 22, 2005, six months later.

That investigation found, in the words of DNC Chairman Howard Dean:

Our election system failed the citizens of Ohio in 2004, and in particular failed African Americans, new registrants, younger voters and voters in places using touch screen [electronic voting] machines. More than a quarter of all Ohio voters reported problems with their voting experience. Twice as many African American voters as white voters reported experiencing problems at the polls. Voters experienced incredibly long lines, some waiting as much as 8 hours. And African American voters reported waiting about twice as often. Nearly one quarter of all Ohio voters reported that their experience in 2004 has made them less confident about the reliability of elections in Ohio. And no wonder. This is not right. This is not the American way, and it's not good for our democracy when our citizens don't have confidence that their voice is being heard. Now this study focused on Ohio, but the truth is there was anecdotal evidence from around the country, that raised serious questions about the way elections are being conducted.

In her letter submitting the report to Dean, Donna Brazile, the 2000 campaign manager for Al Gore, who now chairs the party's Voting Rights Institute, wrote: "Voters across America voiced concerns which questioned the fairness and the accuracy of the 2004 general election. . . . Numerous irregularities characterized the Ohio election: We find evidence of voter confusion, vote suppression and negligence and incompetence of election officials." As the report noted, "More than one quarter of all voters in Ohio reported some kind of problem on Election Day, including long lines, problems with registration status and polling locations, absentee ballots and provisional ballots, and unlawful identification requirements at the polls."

The foremost election official in Ohio, Blackwell, an African American, is a controversial public figure. On October 20, 2004, he made national news when, at a Christian Right rally, he called on people of God to vote yes on issue 1, Ohio's anti–gay marriage constitutional amendment, saying, "I don't know how many of you have a farming background, but I can tell you right now that notion even defies barnyard logic . . . the barnyard knows better."[18] Dubbed by the *Chicago Tribune* as the "anti-Obama" candidate, he is running in the 2006 race for Ohio governor.

On December 2, 2004, Conyers and eleven other Democratic members of the House of Representatives sent a letter to Blackwell. They provided him with a detailed account of Election Day irregularities and asked a series of thirty-four questions related to their "ongoing investigation."

Blackwell has refused to respond to those who criticize his administration of Ohio's 2004 elections, saying he would only answer questions from Justice Department or Government Accountability Office investigators. When questioned by reporters, his spokesman, Carlo LoParo, said that Blackwell would not address questions that are "not based in reality." "These are conspiracy theorists and petty partisan people hell-bent on eroding public confidence in our election system," LoParo said.[19]

The problems Conyers's investigation uncovered can be divided into two broad categories: procedural irregularities that served to suppress the vote, and counting irregularities that raise doubts as to whether votes were tallied as cast.

LEGAL FRAUD: SUPPRESSING THE VOTE IN OHIO

There is little question but that a great deal of vote suppression occurred in 2004. While vote suppression is not the focus of our analysis, it is important to consider the extent of vote suppression in the 2004 election. Most suppression is legal or at least semilegal. Nonetheless, the practice provides insights into the nature of the U.S. electoral system, those who engage in antidemocratic actions, and the techniques they use to do so.

Obstacles to voting disproportionately affect the poor and transient. Democrats, who traditionally get support from these constituencies, advocate policies that permit their maximum inclusion in elections. Republicans maintain, however, that policies regulating voting access have at times been too inclusive—like the days when big-city Democratic machines could count on vital support from graveyard voters. More recently, in the 1996 election, Republicans charged that African Americans in New Orleans casting multiple votes gave Democrat Mary Landrieu the Louisiana Senate seat and that California's lax voter registration procedures allowed illegal aliens to vote, giving Democrat Rep. Loretta Sanchez her congressional victory over then-Rep. Bob Dornan.[20]

In response, Republicans have advocated strict procedures for voter verification, which, as a practical matter, have probably served to suppress legitimate votes at least as much as they have inhibited illegitimate ones. Identification requirements such as providing a tax or utility bill in one's name, for example, make it difficult for students or subtenants to prove residence, and exclude the homeless.

In recent elections, however, some Republican officials, particularly those in Florida and Ohio, have pursued suppression policies with vigor not seen since the days of Jim Crow.

In the case of Ohio, the Conyers Report documented "procedural irregularities" that served to suppress the vote. In the December 2, 2004 letter to Blackwell, Conyers and his eleven colleagues wrote:[21]

It appears that a series of actions of government and nongovernment officials may have worked to frustrate minority voters. Consistent and widespread reports indicate a lack of voting machines in urban, minority and Democratic areas, and a surplus of such machines in Republican, white and rural areas. As a result, minority voters were discouraged from voting by lines that were in excess of eight hours long. Many of these voters were also

apparently victims of a campaign of deception, where flyers and calls would direct them to the wrong polling place.
Once at that polling place, after waiting for hours in line,
many of these voters were provided provisional ballots after
learning they were at the wrong location. These ballots
were not counted in many jurisdictions because of a directive issued by some election officials, such as yourself.

The DNC report echoed Conyers's and quantified the disparity
of treatment between black and white voters. The report noted:
"African American voters had a starkly different Election Day experience than white voters. . . . There was a vast disparity in the level
of confidence in the election system among Ohio voters based on
race: 71 percent of whites are very confident their vote was counted
correctly versus 19 percent of African Americans." And the report
went on to document these findings:

> Twice as many African American voters as white voters
> reported experiencing problems at the polls (52 percent vs.
> 25 percent). . . . African Americans reported waiting an
> average of 52 minutes in line to vote while white voters
> reported waiting an average of 18 minutes. . . . Statewide,
> 16% of African Americans reported experiencing intimi-
> dation versus only 5% of white voters. . . . African American
> women and younger African Americans experienced the
> most registration problems.[22]

Prior to the election, the voter-registration process in Ohio was
explicitly manipulated by Blackwell. On September 7, 2004, he
instructed all county boards of elections to strictly adhere to an out-
dated regulation still part of Ohio election law and reject voter registration forms not "printed on white, uncoated paper of not less
than 80 lb. text weight."[23] After three weeks of public outrage, he

rescinded his order. In the interim, however, a number of county clerks had followed his directive and rejected otherwise valid registrations. Further, some county election officials only learned about the change in directives when informed by the media. In the letter that received no response, Conyers asked him, "Have you conducted an investigation to determine how many registration forms were rejected as a result of your September 7 directive?"

Even complying with the directive did not guarantee a person's registration would be accepted. Many Ohioans complained that their registration applications were lost or otherwise never processed. Others alleged that their absentee ballot applications were lost or never processed. In a double suppression, Blackwell did not allow Ohioans who had requested—but never received— absentee ballots to vote.

Many duly registered Ohio voters—particularly those who lived in heavily Democratic precincts—had trouble voting once they got to the polls. Conyers reported that "throughout predominately Democratic areas in Ohio on Election Day, there were reports of long lines caused by inadequate numbers of voting machines." Further, he noted that "in a number of locations, polling places were moved from large locations, such as gyms, where voters could comfortably wait inside to vote to smaller locations where voters were required to wait in the rain."

In the Knox County precinct serving Kenyon College, only two voting machines were available, requiring some voters to wait in line more than eight hours to vote.

In Franklin County, where there were 102,000 newly registered voters, many of whom were African American, either 81 or 125 voting machines (depending on which official source is to be believed) were never deployed to precincts. As a result, some voters in inner-city Columbus—mostly African American Democrats—had to wait in line up to seven hours to cast their ballot, while an unknown number gave up and went home.[24]

"In vote-rich Franklin County," says Conyers, "27 of the 30 wards with the most machines per registered voter showed majorities for Bush, while six of the seven wards with the fewest machines delivered large margins for Kerry."[25] No such troubles were reported in Republican, white, and rural areas, some of which had a surplus of machines.

Conyers asked Blackwell, "How much funding did Ohio receive from the federal government for voting machines?" and "What criteria were used to distribute those new machines?"

Manipulation of the rules for casting provisional ballots was another method used to suppress the vote. The Help America Vote Act mandate that voters be allowed to cast provisional ballots was mostly a success around the nation, allowing votes to be cast that would have been rejected in past elections.

In Ohio, Blackwell directed county election officials to count only provisional ballots that came from voters who had gone to the correct precinct for their home address. Yet one of the major reasons that provisional ballots were established was to allow voters who had gone to the wrong precinct to vote, with the provision that they were duly registered in another precinct. Conyers wrote, "In Hamilton County, officials have carried this problematic and controversial directive to a ludicrous extreme: they are refusing to count provisional ballots cast at the correct polling place if they were cast at the wrong table in that polling place." (In cities it is common for polling places to serve multiple precincts, with registration for each precinct at a different table.) In this way about four hundred voters in Hamilton County were disenfranchised.

In total, 24,000 provisional ballots were not counted in Ohio.[26]

For some Ohioans, finding out where to vote was not easy. Conyers wrote, "It has been reported that fraudulent flyers were being circulated on official-looking letterhead telling voters the wrong place to vote, phone calls were placed incorrectly informing voters that their polling place had changed, 'door-hangers' telling

African American voters to go to the wrong precinct and elections workers sent voters to the wrong precinct."

Even were it possible through a manual recount to obtain an official count in Ohio that accurately recorded the votes that were cast, that count would incompletely reflect the intent of the electorate because so many who were legally entitled to vote were prevented from doing so.

The voting-machine shortages in Democratic districts, the barriers to registration, the purges of supposed felons from voter rolls, and the unmailed, lost, or rejected absentee ballots all represent distortions to the vote count above and beyond what is measured by the exit-poll disparity. The exit polls, by design, sample only those voters who have already overcome these hurdles. Vote suppression affects neither exit polls nor vote recounts, because the thwarted voter never makes it to the election booth.

What happened in Ohio was a travesty of democracy. According to state and federal law, many of these practices were criminal in that they interfered with an individual's right to vote. Unfortunately, vote suppression is institutionalized in our election system, so much so that questions of legality are not necessarily considered relevant to the question of who won. If Bush won Ohio because of the number of votes lost and suppressed, but the election was otherwise fraud-free, many people would say that the election had been stolen in a fair fight and was in some sense legitimate. That would be the kind of stolen election Ken Blackwell and his county operatives could highlight on their Republican Party résumés.

The same would not be true if the election had been stolen by directly adding, deleting, or switching votes.

PALM BEACH COUNTY ALL OVER AGAIN

Among the many irregularities in Ohio were the impossibly high counts for third-party candidates in Cuyahoga County. For example, voters casting ballots at Benedictine High School in heavily Democratic precinct 4N gave Libertarian Party candidate Michael Badnarik 32% of the vote. Voters in another heavily Democratic precinct who also cast their votes at Benedictine High gave the Constitution Party—"God, Family, Republic"—candidate Michael Peroutka 40% of the vote.

In Cuyahoga County, Ohio's most populous and most important source of Democratic votes, the order in which candidates are listed on the ballots varies by precinct, including precincts located in the same polling place. Therefore, ballots with presidential candidates listed in different orders were available at the same polling place. And in Benedictine High and several other voting locations that served multiple precincts, poll workers apparently directed voters to place their cards in any machine, when they should have directed voters to use the machine assigned to their precinct. Thus, if Kerry was listed first on one ballot and second on another, a machine programmed to count the first vote for Kerry would miscount any ballot on which Kerry was listed second. According to the report from the Democrats on the House Judiciary Committee, *Preserving Democracy: What Went Wrong in Ohio*, "It appears that hundreds, if not thousands, of votes intended to be cast for Senator Kerry were recorded for a third-party candidate. At this point it is unclear whether these voting errors resulted from worker negligence and error, or intentional manipulation."

James Q. Jacobs, in a study published on the Web, "How Kerry Votes Were Switched to Bush Votes," documents that such vote-switching occurred throughout the county. Its effects are most easily identifiable in precincts where Badnarik and Peroutka received abnormally large vote totals, but the net effect was most severe in the many precincts where Bush and Kerry alternated ballot positions. In these precincts, Kerry received Bush's votes and vice versa. Given that Cuyahoga County is overwhelmingly Democratic, this resulted in large numbers of votes lost to Kerry and gained by Bush.[27]

THE SECRET COUNT IN WARREN COUNTY

In Warren County, a predominantly Republican Cincinnati suburb, the votes were counted according to law by representatives of both the Democratic and Republican parties.[28] However, on election night Republican officials locked down the county administration building. A reporter who had wanted to watch the count was prevented from doing so. Speculation immediately ensued that something fishy was going on.

According to county officials, the building was locked down after an FBI agent told them the bureau had received a terrorist threat that ranked ten on a scale of one to ten. Subsequently, county officials have declined to name the agent, while the FBI has stated that it has no information on any such threat.

It is unclear when the unnamed FBI agent told county officials of this supposed threat. The county commissioner has said that the decision to lock down the building was made at an October 28 closed-door meeting. However, e-mail messages dated October 25 and 26 show that preparations for the lockdown were already under way.

The House Judiciary Committee Democratic staff write:

It is important to view the lockdown in the context of the aberrant results in Warren County. . . . In the 2000 Presidential election, the Democratic presidential candidate, Al Gore, stopped running television commercials and pulled resources out of Ohio weeks before the election. He won 28 percent of the vote in Warren County. In 2004, the Democratic Presidential candidate, John Kerry, fiercely contested Ohio and independent groups put considerable resources into getting out the Democratic vote. Moreover, unlike in 2000, independent candidate Ralph Nader was not on the Ohio ballot in 2004. Yet, the tallies reflect John Kerry receiving exactly the same percentage in Warren County as Gore received, 28 percent [of the 95,512 ballots cast].[29]

In their letter to Blackwell, Conyers and his colleagues raised the following three questions: "If County officials were not advised of terrorist activity by an FBI agent, have you inquired as to why they misrepresented this fact? If the lockdown was not as a response to a terrorist threat, why did it take place? Did any manipulation of the vote tallies occur?"

Blackwell never responded, which led the House Judiciary Committee Democratic staff to conclude:

> Given the total lack of explanation by Mr. Blackwell or Warren County officials, it is not implausible to assume that someone is hiding something. . . . Given the statistical anomalies in the Warren County results, it is impossible to rule out the possibility that some sort of manipulation of the tallies occurred on election night in the locked down facility. The disclosure that the decision to lock down the facility was made the Thursday before the election, rather than on Election Day would suggest the lockdown was a political decision not a true security risk.

G.O.P. GHOSTS IN THE MACHINES?

The Conyers Report uncovered a number of other troubling irregularities.

House Judiciary Committee Democratic staff received many complaints from voters who said that when they voted on electronic DRE (Direct Recording Electronic) voting systems, they saw their vote for Kerry transferred to Bush. The *Washington Post* reported that in Youngstown in Mahoning County, twenty-five DRE machines transferred an unknown number of votes from Kerry to Bush. The Election Protection Coalition received a report from one voter who said, "Every time I tried to vote for the Democratic Party Presidential vote the machine went blank. I had to keep trying, it took five times."[30] Dorothy Fadiman, who was making a documentary on the election, captured the testimony of scores of Mahoning County voters who suffered the same experience.

In Perry County, House Judiciary Committee Democratic staff uncovered a number of precincts where the tabulated vote appears highly irregular. In "Reading S" precinct the sign-in book indicates that 393 people cast votes (including 33 by absentee ballot). Yet the official tally in the precinct indicates that 489 votes were cast. In "W Lexington G AB" precinct 350 people are registered to vote, yet 434 ballots were counted—a voter turnout of 124 percent, which is impossible. The Perry County Board of Elections later revised the vote for only that precinct, explaining that, due to a computer error, some votes were counted twice. In three precincts more signatures appear in the sign-in books than votes cast, indicating that some ballots somehow disappeared.

Perry County election officials also report that 91% of eligible voters in that county are registered, an extraordinarily high registration rate. Many of those voters were supposedly registered in 1977, a year in which there was no federal election. Indeed, on one day, November 8, 1977, about 3,100 voters were registered.

In Montgomery County, two traditionally Democratic precincts had an undervote rate of more than 25% each. Undervotes are recorded when a valid ballot is recorded, but no vote appears in the slot for president at the top of the ballot. In other words, in those two precincts almost six thousand voters stood in line to vote but purportedly declined to vote for president. Common sense suggests that very few voters intentionally decline to choose a presidential candidate, least of all after waiting in lines for many hours. This

25% undervote rate is in stark contrast to the 2% rate of undervoting nationwide.

In Butler County, an underfunded Democratic candidate for the Ohio Supreme Court, Ellen Connally, received 59,532 votes, while Kerry received 54,185 votes—or, more than 5,000 fewer votes than Connally. In five other Ohio counties, Connally received a total of 10,000 or more votes in excess of Kerry's total number of votes and she received 5,000 more votes than Kerry in another ten counties combined. All that in an election in which Republican judicial candidates were "awash in cash" and in which the victorious Republican candidate for the State Supreme Court received about 40,000 fewer votes than the Bush-Cheney ticket.

Conyers and his colleagues write, "It appears to be wildly implausible that 5,000 voters waited in line to cast a vote for an underfunded Democratic Supreme Court candidate and then declined to cast a vote for the most well-funded Democratic Presidential campaign in history." They went on to ask Blackwell, "Is there any precedent in Ohio for a down ballot candidate receiving on a percentage or absolute basis so many more votes than the Presidential candidate of the same party in this or any other presidential election?"

OHIO'S RECOUNT

With conventional voting systems, fraudulent activities are in principle traceable, but only if a secure chain of custody is maintained for the ballots, and a subsequent manual count is actually conducted. Such counts are rare, however, conducted only when a race is close and the vanquished party is able and willing to pay for it.

On December 7, 2004, the Libertarian and Green parties in Ohio requested that Ohio's eighty-eight counties recount the vote, paying $113,600, or $10 a precinct, to have it done. The funds were raised publicly, largely from an online campaign, and were donated by thousands of individuals, Democrats as well as Greens and Libertarians.

Referring to the myriad electoral irregularities that plagued the Ohio vote, Green Party presidential candidate David Cobb told reporters in Columbus that "when these sorts of things happen, we have to stand up. It's not as a Green Party member that I am standing up, it is as a citizen of this country. And citizens across this country, citizens across the state of Ohio, are demanding to know exactly what happened."[31]

Ohio law says that in a recount, a random 3% of a county's votes, from randomly selected precincts, must be counted by hand. In the case of punch cards, the ballots are hand counted and then run through a mechanical tabulator that is attached to a computer. In the case of optical-scan systems, the hand-marked ballots are counted by hand and then scanned. In the case of electronic voting systems, no recount is possible. If a discrepancy is found between the hand counts and the tabulator or optical-scan counts, the whole county must be recounted by hand. This is not possible in those counties that use DRE voting systems, because there is no paper ballot to count. Of Ohio's eighty-eight counties, some use punch cards, others use optical-scan systems, and still others use DRE touch-screen systems.

The December 2004 hand recount of votes in Ohio did little to allay concerns about the integrity of the punch-card and optical-scan voting systems. Indeed, the recounts in Clermont and Hocking Counties both raised questions about whether votes were counted as cast.

CLERMONT COUNTY'S OPTICAL-SCAN SCAM

In Clermont County, Bush did very well.

Clermont County was one of three contiguous Republican-controlled counties in southwest Ohio where Bush registered the greatest increase in votes from 2000.[32] Butler and Warren Counties were the other two. (Recall that Warren County was where the county officials, responding to a supposed terrorist threat, locked down the county administration building, and barred reporters from observing the vote count.) Those three counties combined gave Bush 37,109 more votes relative to his Democratic rival than he received in 2000.

In the 2000 election, Democrats had written off Ohio and Gore barely campaigned there. In 2004, Ohio was a Democratic priority. John Kerry and John Edwards spent more time there during the campaign than in any other state. Yet between November 2000 and November 2004, Bush's share of the vote in Clermont County increased from 67% (30% Gore, 2% Nader) to 71% (29% Kerry), and his margin of victory there had increased from 26,202 to 37,062 votes.

Some of Bush's vote increase can no doubt be accounted for by the overall increase in voter turnout, particularly among evangelical Christians who turned out to vote for the anti–gay marriage amendment to the state constitution. But in Clermont County, which uses an optical-scan voting system where voters fill in a circle next to the candidate's name and the ballot is then run through a tabulator, remarkable irregularities were observed during the recount.

On December 14, Clermont County began its recount. Problems immediately surfaced, according to three Democratic recount observers who filed affidavits for Conyers's office.[33]

First, the county's Board of Elections decided not to do a random recount of 3% of the ballots as required by Ohio law, but rather a recount of the thirteen smallest precincts and one of the larger precincts. Democratic Party recount observers challenged this apparently illegal procedure, but their challenge was denied by the board. "This will provide fewer errors on the recount," one of the Clermont County Board of Elections members explained.

One of the first things the observers noticed was that the optical-scan ballots were being kept under lax security. "When we arrived for the recount the ballot boxes were not sealed, nor did the doors to the Board of Elections offices meet the security criteria for ballot boxes," said Jeannine Tater, a Democratic recount observer, in her affidavit. "They each had a very small master key lock. The keys were not for a security lock, nor were they printed with the words 'do not copy.' Locks for all ballot boxes were identically keyed. There were at least two keys to these boxes. . . . One employee offered another employee her lock box key. However, the other employee said that she did not need the key since she had found the other key."

While watching the hand recount, Stephen Spraley, the Ohio Democratic Party's volunteer Recount Coordinator for Clermont County saw something strange—votes for Kerry were covered up with a sticker and a vote for Bush was marked. "I noticed that there were ballots with oval stickers over different candidates," said Spraley in his affidavit. "I concentrated on the presidential race and saw that there was a ballot with an oval sticker on the 'John Kerry and John Edwards' oval spot and it clearly had a darkened tone to it even though there was a white oval sticker over it. 'Bush and Cheney' was also marked with that oval filled in."

Spraley asked the board's deputy director, Kathy Jones, where the stickers came from and who placed them on the ballots, but before she could respond, Dan Bare, the director of the Clermont County Board of Elections, interrupted and said that questions about ballots must be addressed at a Board of Elections meeting. At the meeting Spraley again raised the issue of the stickers: "I asked who put stickers on the ballots, where did they come from and why were they put on? The Republican board member said the stickers were put on election night. Priscilla [O'Donnell, a Democratic member of the Board of Elections] said she knew nothing about the stickers. At that point there was a hush in the room and nothing more was said."

Tater also saw the stickers covering up the Kerry-Edwards mark on the ballot sheets. "When questioned all of the Board of Elections employees indicated that they did not use stickers on Election Day to 'correct' ballots," said Tater in an affidavit. "They 'also did not provide erasers to voters.' According to Dan Bare, 'If a voter made a mistake on a ballot, the ballot was returned to the precinct judge and a new ballot was issued; up to three ballots are permitted per voter. We did not use stickers to correct mismarked ballots.'"

Tater continued, "When questioned, all of the employees from the Board of Elections said they had 'never seen the stickers' and had no idea where they came from. All confirmed that stickers were not used on Election Day."

The recount observers noted that the same kind of oval stickers that covered up the Kerry-Edwards votes were used to label the buttons on the county's four tabulating machines. "The stickers were clearly from the Board of Elections," said Tater. One of the observers asked Bare if they could take a picture of one of the ballots that had a sticker covering up a vote for Kerry and Edwards, but Bare denied the request.

Bob Drake, a Green Party observer in Clermont, called Carolyn Betts, a Cincinnati attorney, who volunteered to observe the Hamilton County recount for the Green Party. "During the course of the discussions about the stickers, the story gradually changed and Board of Election staff admitted that the stickers had been used to 'fix' ballots for Bush that originally had been voted for Kerry and erased," said Betts in her affidavit. "I was skeptical of this explanation because in my readings about Ohio election law, I had learned that instructions to voters for optical scan ballots were that if the voter made a mistake, the voter was to turn in the incorrectly-marked ballot and get a new one, and could do that up to a total of three or four ballots. I knew that voters are not given erasers to change their ballots, so if they were to erase a mistaken blackening of a bubble, they would have to have brought an eraser with them, or borrowed one."

Betts drafted a letter requesting that the Clermont Board of Elections meet several demands before certifying the recount. That letter read in part, "We ask each member of the Board to disclose publicly what knowledge he or she has of the 'stickers' found on certain ballots selected for the 3% hand count in Clermont County. Who affixed such stickers, what was their purpose and what statutory or regulatory authority can be cited in support of such practice?" The letter went on to say, "Irregularities exist that justify a 100% recount in accordance with the Secretary of State's guidelines. We hereby exercise our right to demand a 100% hand recount of the votes of Clermont County." The Clermont County Board of Elections denied their requests and on December 16, 2004, voted to certify the recount.

In late January 2005, when Conyers learned about the irregularities in Clermont County, he wrote to the FBI about the "strong evidence of vote tampering if not outright fraud in Clermont County, Ohio. . . . Ballots clearly marked for Kerry/Edwards appear to have been fraudulently obscured by stickers and counted as votes for Bush/Cheney. Given the seriousness of these allegations, I urge your office to investigate this."

HOCKING COUNTY'S TAINTED PUNCH-CARD RECOUNT

Hocking County is a rural county of 18,378 registered voters in southeastern Ohio, fifty miles south of Columbus. In the 2004 election, Bush recorded 53% of the voters and Kerry recorded 47%.

In the week before the county was to undertake its vote recount, a field representative of Triad Governmental Systems, the company that services the county's tabulator that counts punch-card ballots, visited the Hocking County election offices to adjust the tabulator and the computer that provides the commands. The visit troubled Sherole Eaton, a Democrat and the deputy director of elections, according to an affidavit she provided to Conyers.[34]

Triad Governmental Systems, of Xenia, Ohio, wrote and services the vote-counting software for the punch-card counting machines in forty-one of Ohio's eighty-eight counties. Triad and its affiliates at Rapp Systems Corporation are the industry leader in supplying the machines and software that are used to count punch cards and optical-scan paper ballots in Ohio and Florida. Rapp Systems' Psephos Corporation supplied the infamous butterfly ballot to Palm Beach County that cost Al Gore the election in 2000. The company's founder, Tod A. Rapp, has contributed $2,650 to the national Republican Party and George W. Bush since 1996.[35]

On December 10, 2004, Michael Barbian Jr., a Triad field representative, came to the Hocking County elections office, said Eaton in her affidavit.

> I asked him why he was visiting us. He said, "to check out your tabulator, computer." . . . He proceeded to go to the room where our computer and tabulation machine is kept. . . . He stated that the computer was not coming up. I did see some commands at the lower left hand of the screen but no menu. He said that the battery in the computer was dead and that the stored information was gone. He said that he could put a patch on it and fix it. . . . He proceeded to take the computer apart and call his offices to get information to input into our computer. Our computer is 14 years old and as far as I know had always worked in the past. . . . [He] then asked me which precinct and the number of the precinct we were going to count. I told him, Good Hope 1 # 17. He went back into the tabulation room. Shortly after that he stated that the computer was ready for the recount. . . . He said not to turn the computer off until after the recount. . . . He advised Lisa and I on how to post a "cheat sheet" on the wall so that only the board members and staff would know about it and what the codes meant so the count would come out perfect and we wouldn't have to do a full hand recount of the county. My faith in Triad and the Xenia staff has been nothing but good. The realization

that this company and staff would do anything to dishonor or disrupt the voting process is distressing to me and hard to believe.[36]

As Eaton understood it, the "cheat sheet" was a way to insure that the 3% recount of Hocking County ballots would validate the original official count and thus prevent ballots from the whole county from being recounted.

In a letter to Triad president Brett A. Rapp and the technician Barbian, Conyers wrote: "The purpose of the Ohio recount law[37] is to randomly check vote counts to see if they match machine counts. By attempting to ascertain the precinct to be recounted in advance, and then informing the election officials of the number of votes they need to count by hand to make sure it matches the machine count is an invitation to completely ignore the purpose of the recount law." He then asked Rapp and Barbian to answer a number of questions, but received no response.

Douglas W. Jones, an election computer expert at the computer science department of the University of Iowa, Iowa City, was also concerned. He reviewed Eaton's affidavit and said in an affidavit of his own:

> I have reviewed the Affidavit of Sherole L. Eaton . . . as well as the letter of Congressman John Conyers. . . . In light of this information, and given my expertise and research on voting technology issues and the integrity of ballot counting systems, it is my professional opinion that the incident in Hocking County, Ohio, threatens the overall integrity of the recount of the presidential election in Ohio.[38]

Barbian said in an interview with documentary filmmaker Lynda Byrket that he had also adjusted the tabulating software in Lorain, Muskingum, Clark, Harrison, and Guernsey Counties. Other Triad field representatives worked on machines in Greene and Monroe Counties during the recount.

In addition, in some counties, including Fulton and Henry, Triad was able to "dial up" its vote-tabulating computers over phone lines, and prior to the start of the recount, instruct the computers to recount just the presidential vote.

In the interview, Byrket asked Barbian, "You were just trying to help them so that they wouldn't have to do a full recount of the county, to try to avoid that?" To which Barbian responded, "Right."

Byrket also filmed the meeting of the Hocking County Election Board at which Barbian's visit to the election offices was discussed. Conyers describes what transpires in the video this way:

> Among other things, a police officer present at the hearing notes that there has been no explanation as to why Mr. Barbian provided a "cheat sheet" of the election day results to election officials and why he requested information about what precinct would be counted. Because of repeated attempts to ascertain such an explanation and despite repeated interruptions from the Triad President [Brett Rapp] designed to squelch the explanation, an answer to these questions is scattered throughout the tape, but is rather simple: the purpose of the "cheat sheet" was to cheat.[39]

Eaton's affidavit and the video of the Hocking County meeting spurred Conyers to write the FBI on December 15 and ask that it "immediately investigate this alleged misconduct" and "consider the immediate impoundment of election machinery to prevent any further tampering."[40] On January 12, 2005, the FBI responded, saying that their investigation did not uncover "any credible evidence that anyone engaged in any conduct which violated federal election laws."

The Democratic staff members of the House Judiciary Committee concluded:

Triad and its employees engaged in a course of behavior to provide "cheat sheets" to those counting the ballots. The cheat sheets told them how many votes they should find for each candidate, and how many over- and under-votes they should calculate to match the machine count. In that way, they could avoid doing a full county-wide hand recount mandated by state law. . . . By ensuring that election boards can conform their test recount results with the election-night results, Triad's actions may well have prevented scores of counties from conducting a full and fair recount.

The controversy in Hocking County continued in 2005. In May, the Hocking County Board of Elections fired Sherole Eaton without stating a reason. In addition to alerting Conyers to the suspicious recount procedures, Eaton had gone public with the fact that the Hocking County director of elections, Republican Lisa Schwartze, had organized a Republican fund raiser out of her office and unlawfully shredded voter-registration documents. Eaton, who was close to retirement, maintains she was fired in retaliation for speaking out. She told the local *Logan Daily News*, "They are targeting me as a whistle-blower and that is wrong. I have rights."

The Hocking County prosecutor has said his office would investigate the document shredding.[41]

Coming to Eaton's defense, Conyers wrote a letter to the elections board. "Absent any other explanation, and having been told at the time of the incident [when the Triad representative provided 'cheat sheets'] that Ms. Eaton was an excellent employee, I can only conclude that Ms. Eaton's firing was solely out of retaliation. In my view, Ms. Eaton should be rewarded, not punished, for honestly and ethically fulfilling her duties."

ABUSES OF POWER

On January 18, 2005, Ohio's Republican attorney general Jim Petro asked the Ohio Supreme Court to sanction and fine four lawyers who had brought two lawsuits to the Ohio Supreme Court contesting the outcome of the 2004 election—suits he described as "the worst type of lawsuit abuse." The lawyers had withdrawn their suits a few days earlier, realizing that their case would be dismissed as moot since Bush was going to be inaugurated on January 20.[42]

In his petition, which would be denied by the Ohio Supreme Court four months later, Petro, representing Blackwell and Ohio's twenty Republican members of the Electoral College, charged that the four lawyers were motivated by "partisan political purposes." He wrote, "Instead of evidence, they offered only theory, conjecture, hypothesis, and invective. A contest proceeding is not a toy for idle hands. It is not to be used to make a political point, or to be used as a discovery tool, or be used to inconvenience or harass public officials, or to be used as a publicity gimmick."

Clifford O. Arnebeck, one of the attorneys in question, said that in trying to pursue their case, they had received no cooperation from Blackwell's attorneys. "What they did was stonewall. They recognized the guy [Blackwell] could not withstand cross-examination," Arnebeck said. "It's improper, putting himself out as some kind of a king."[43]

For his part, Blackwell does not see himself as a king; he serves the king of kings.

Paul Weyrich, the brilliant right-wing political strategist, has described Blackwell as "someone who is God-centered and who prays to do God's will rather than his own."[44]

As Blackwell sees it, there are two types of laws, those of men and those of God. In defying an October 20 directive from a federal judge that he not unduly restrict the use of provisional ballots, Blackwell invoked Gandhi, Martin Luther King and St. Paul, all of whom went to jail for what they believed. In Blackwell's case this was the belief that people can only cast provisional ballots in the precinct where they should be registered, rather than in any precinct in the county in which they live. "He believes God wanted him as Secretary of State during 2004. It is difficult to disagree with that proposition," wrote Weyrich, referring to Bush's victory.

And Blackwell makes no apologies for doing the Lord's work and swinging the Ohio election to Bush. Indeed, on his Web site Blackwell dismisses his critics and boasts, "Last time I checked, Katherine Harris wasn't in a soup line, she's in Congress."

BEYOND OHIO

The investigations presented by the House Judiciary Committee Democratic staff's *Preserving Democracy* (the Conyers Report), and by the DNC's Voting Rights Institute's *Democracy at Risk* document electoral malfeasance in Ohio that goes beyond institutionalized suppression. Moreover, the investigations suggest that fraud was widespread. These findings are supported by numerical and statistical data in addition to exit-poll numbers indicating that the count was off by more than enough to swing the election.

Similar activities occurred across the nation. We only know about it in Ohio because that is the one state that has been investigated and that was forced to undertake at least a pretense of a recount. On Election Day, MSNBC's voter hotline was besieged with 100,000 calls. The Election Protection Coalition (a group launched by the People for the American Way and composed of sixty organizations, including the Electronic Frontier Foundation and the Verified Voting Foundation) established an Election Day hotline and a Web-based "Election Incident Reporting System." All told, the coalition received 40,002 reports of election irregularities, 2,242 of which involved voting machines.[45]

Indeed, the variety of incidents reported on Election Day led

Ralph Nader to say that "this election was hijacked from A to Z."
He told journalist Ritt Goldstein he believed the Republican Party
was able to "steal it before Election Day."[46]

On October 28, 2005, New York University professor Mark
Crispin Miller met Kerry at a political event and gave him a copy of
his book *Fooled Again: How the Right Stole the 2004 Election & Why
They'll Steal the Next One Too (Unless We Stop Them)*. In a
November 4, 2005, interview on Amy Goodman's *Democracy Now!*
radio show, Miller said:

> He [Kerry] told me he now thinks the election was
> stolen. . . . He said he doesn't believe that he is the person
> who can go out front on the issue because of the sour
> grapes . . . question. But he said he believes it was stolen.
> He says he argues about this with his Democratic col-
> leagues on the Hill. He had just had a big fight with
> [Connecticut Democratic senator] Christopher Dodd.

Miller said that Kerry was persuaded to concede the election
by his top advisers, particularly longtime political consultant Bob
Schrum, who, beginning with George McGovern, has worked for
eight Democratic presidential candidates, all of whom have lost.
However, Miller says John Edwards wanted to hold off on a concession until they had more information. According to Miller,
Kerry called Edwards and said, "They [Kerry's advisers] say that if
I don't pull out, they [Kerry's political opponents] are going to
call us sore losers." To which Edwards replied, "So what if they call
us sore losers?"

According to Kerry spokeswoman Jenny Backus, none of the
conversation Miller reported on *Democracy Now!* occurred. She told
Raw Story, "I know Mr. Miller is trying to sell his book and he feels
passionately about his thesis, but his recent statements about his
conversation with Senator Kerry are simply not true. The only thing

true about his recollection of the conversation is that he gave Senator Kerry a copy of his book."

Yet, Miller isn't the only person to whom Kerry is reported to have voiced concerns about the integrity of the election. Robert Parry, who as a reporter for *Newsweek* in 1987 helped break the Iran-contra story, reported on ConsortiumNews.com that Kerry "suspects that the election was stolen, but that he didn't challenge the official results because he lacked hard proof and anticipated a firestorm of criticism if he pressed the point."

Jonathan Winer, a longtime Kerry adviser and a former deputy assistant secretary of state, told Parry, "Kerry heard all the disquieting stories, but he didn't have the evidence to do more." Winer said that the "disquieting stories" included Republican election officials in Ohio providing an inadequate number of voting machines to heavily Democratic precincts and reports from voters who said that when they cast their ballots on DRE electronic voting machines they saw their vote for Kerry transferred to Bush. On top of that, Winer said, Kerry was mindful of what had happened in 2000, when Gore won the popular vote but lost the election after five Republicans on the Supreme Court stepped in and stopped the recount.

"Do you think they're too ethical to steal an election?" Winer said. "In 2000, they did steal an election."

According to Winer, Kerry didn't believe evidence existed that could prove the 2004 Bush-Cheney Campaign committed election fraud in 2004. Further, Kerry knew he would be harshly criticized if he challenged the election results without compelling proof that a crime had been committed.

"The powers in place would have smashed him," said Winer, who in the 1980s experienced how hard it was to go up against the GOP establishment and its media support network when he worked for Kerry's Foreign Relations Subcommittee investigation into the connections between the CIA-funded contras and cocaine traffickers.[47]

Both Miller and Winer reported that Kerry suspects that there was tampering with the electronic voting machines.

Winer, who is now an attorney specializing in information security, told Parry that it is conceivable that Republican operatives hacked the DRE electronic voting systems in 2004, but that without the confession of a credible witness such a crime would be hard to prove. "There are systems for one-time use that erase themselves afterwards," Winer said. "You'd have to have a confession and anyone who would confess would look psychotic."

Parry observes: "Kerry appears to have weighed how he would look if he made accusations about possible hi-tech hi-jinks affecting the outcome of a presidential election. Pundits surely would have put him on the couch as a delusional conspiracy theorist. But Kerry's decision not to fight has left millions of Americans wondering if their democratic birthright has been stolen—along with the last two presidential elections."

CHAPTER 2

Florida Sets the Stage in 2000

Unlike the 2004 election, the 2000 election prompted major investigations by U.S. news organizations. Hundreds of journalists in investigative teams descended on the southern part of the state and stayed there for months. The information that resulted from that reporting spike has provided a context in which to view the 2004 election and the allegations of election fraud—and by election fraud we mean an organized effort to alter the actual vote count to the benefit of one candidate or another—surrounding it.

The 2000 presidential election in Florida has been was widely viewed as a blemish on American democracy, an anomalous confluence of an uncannily close contest and an unusual assortment of errors in a highly atypical state. Palm Beach County bumper stickers from the period help recall the public assessment:

"We put the 'duh' in Florida."

"If you think we can't vote, wait till you see us drive."

"Honk if you voted for Gore. That's the big button in the middle of your steering wheel."

"It ain't over 'til your brother counts the votes."

But Florida 2000 was not an anomaly. Rather, it exposed the willingness and ability of Bush-Cheney Campaign officials to subvert the will of the electorate.

The lengths to which the state Republican Party, board-of-elections officials, and a major data-gathering company went prior to the election to remove voters likely to support Gore should have served as evidence that something was afoot. If we think that it's inconceivable that a significant number of people in positions of civic and political responsibility would resort to fraud on a scale that could change the outcome of a presidential election, we should just remember what happened in Florida 2000 with the felon scrub list.

In 2000, Florida legally deprived more than 800,000 citizens who had been convicted of felonies of the right to vote.[48] This represents more than 7% of the Florida voting-age population—a larger percentage than in any other state. And that figure happens to include 31% of the state's voting-age African American males.[49]

Loss of voting privileges in Florida is not simply a collateral consequence of a felony conviction. Historically, the denial of voting privilege has been used as a means to suppress black political power. Like many states, Florida first adopted a felon disenfranchisement statute during Reconstruction when the Fifteenth Amendment and its extension of voting rights to African Americans were ardently contested.[50]

Racial motivations were openly admitted throughout the South. At the 1901 Alabama Constitutional Convention, John B. Knox, president of this gathering, warned the assembled white people of "the menace of negro domination."[51] As a remedy, he advocated "manipulation of the ballot" by expanding the state's disenfranchisement law to include crimes of "moral turpitude," crimes that included misdemeanors, and even actions that were not punishable by law. And in 1916, the Mississippi Supreme Court upheld the state's felon disenfranchisement law and ruled, "Restrained by the federal constitution from discriminating against the negro race, the convention discriminated against its characteristics and the offenses to which its criminal members are prone."[52]

Most states subsequently have repealed such restrictions. Florida is one of fourteen that has not, and one of ten that disenfranchise ex-felons for life.[53] Although a few other countries deny voting rights to prison inmates, the United States is unique in restricting the rights of nonincarcerated former felons.

The United States is also exceptional for the rate at which it issues felony convictions. In Florida, an offender who receives probation for a single sale of drugs can face a lifetime of disenfranchisement.[54] Further, felon disenfranchisement has increased dramatically as sentencing rates have surged. The United States presently has the highest incarceration rate in the world; 7 out of every 1,000 Americans are in prison, compared with 1 out of every 1,000 Canadians and less than .5 of every 1,000 Japanese.[55] Indeed, sociologists Christopher Uggen and Jeff Manza calculate that if former felons had been disenfranchised in 1960 at 2000 rates, John F. Kennedy's 119,000-popular-vote victory margin in the 1960 presidential election would have disintegrated, and Richard Nixon would have won with a plurality of more than 100,000 votes.

Uggen and Manza calculate that in 2000, Florida disenfranchised 827,200 felons and ex-felons—7.03% of a voting-age population of 11,774,000. Based on felon voting rates in other states and the voting behavior of Floridians matching felons in terms of gender, race, age, income, labor-force status, marital status, and education, they estimate that 155,000 of these felons would have voted for Gore in 2000 and 70,000 would have voted for Bush, resulting in 85,000 net votes for Gore in Florida.[56]

FAUX FELONS DISENFRANCHISED

In 1999, shortly after Jeb Bush became governor and Katherine Harris took over as secretary of state, Florida embarked on a project to produce a master list of former felons who would then be scrubbed from voter rolls. Florida devoted unprecedented resources to the task. In 1998, under the purview of Katherine Harris's predecessor, the Florida Department of Elections gave Database Technologies Inc. (DBT) a contract for a first-year fee of $2,317,800 to scrub the voter rolls. (The firm previously doing the work for the Florida Board of Elections had been awarded the job for a bid of $5,700.) The terms of this contract were not publicly disclosed.[57]

Greg Palast reports that even for an ambitious effort, this payment on a per-record basis was more than ten times industry norms.[58] The state and DBT justified this unusually high figure based on contract requirements that called for "manual verification using telephone calls and statistical sampling."[59] However, it appears that DBT was paid such a grand sum precisely *not* to verify names. One list from DBT included 8,000 names from Texas supplied by George Bush's state officials. These 8,000 Florida voters were all listed as having been felons in Texas. As it turns out, almost none were felons. Nearly all had committed only minor violations and misdemeanors. Typical was Reverend Willie Whiting, who was removed from the voting rolls for a speeding ticket twenty-five years earlier.[60]

Under orders from Harris's office, DBT provided matches of anyone with a close name. Thus, for example, John Jackson is a black man who had served time in Texas, so Johnny Jackson Jr., a black man in Florida with the same birth date, was purged from the registration rolls.[61] DBT used lists of former felons that included names and birth dates and race, but counted as a "match" names that were only approximate. DBT specifically wrote Harris's office to say that their name-match criteria would include a lot of nonfelons, and Harris's office advised them in writing to lower the name-match criterion further to 85%. All told, DBT generated a list of 82,389 voters to purge from registries.[62]

DBT subsequently tried to defend their lists by claiming they were 85% accurate.[63] But that would still mean that well over 10,000 mostly minority, poor, and Democratic Floridians were illegally disenfranchised—more than twenty times Bush's margin of victory in the state. Plus, where verification was attempted, the accuracy of the list was nowhere near 85%. Officials in Leon County, Florida, tried to verify the 694 names on the list from Tallahassee and found only 34 to be a match—a 5% accuracy rate.[64]

Robert E. Pierre reported in the *Washington Post* that responsibility for this faulty voter purge lies with Harris's office, not DBT.

> From the beginning, Database Technologies raised serious concerns that non-felons could be misidentified. . . . "Obviously, we want to capture more names that possibly aren't matches," said Emmett "Bucky" Mitchell, who headed the state purge effort, in a March 1999 e-mail to Database Technologies product manager Marlene Thorogood, who had warned him of possible mistakes. . . . Clay Roberts, director of the state's division of elections, confirmed the policy. . . . "The decision was made to do the match in such a way as not to be terribly strict on the name." "We warned them," said James E. Lee, vice president of communications for the company. "The list was exactly what the state wanted. They said, 'The counties will verify the information, so you don't have to.'"

Florida officials neither sought reimbursement nor penalty, but rather awarded DBT another contract renewal, bringing total fees to over $4 million.[65]

EFFORTS TO SUPPRESS THE AFRICAN AMERICAN VOTE

Following the election, the United States Commission on Civil Rights (USCCR) and the National Association for the

Advancement of Colored People (NAACP) issued reports that documented a wide variety of vote-suppression measures targeting black voters.[66]

In south Florida in 2000, the state's most Democratic region, early voting was hampered by a lack of preparation and staffing.[67] Polling places did not open on time, equipment did not work, and the systems could not handle the volume of voters. Predominately white precincts got laptop computers to correct bureaucratic errors; black precincts did not. In Tampa, ten white precincts got laptops; none went to districts with large black populations. Clerks trying to call the office of the state supervisor of elections were often unable to get through.[68]

Those voters whose names did not appear on the registration rolls because of felon scrub lists should have been offered affidavit ballots, but testimony indicates that voters who requested the provisional ballots were often denied them.[69]

The Leadership Conference on Civil Rights reported that poll workers in minority neighborhoods "were instructed by elections officials to be particularly strict in challenging voter qualifications because of 'aggressive' voter registration and turnout efforts."[70] In Osceola County, for example, Hispanic voters were told to produce two forms of identification, even though under state law only one is required. A Palm Beach County resident testified that black voters were asked to show photo identification while she and other white voters were waved through with no such requests. Stacy Powers, a news director at Tampa's WTMP, challenged the poll manager's actions to prevent those without such identification from voting. "She told me not to get snippy with her," said Powers, who was forced to leave the polling place.[71]

The USCCR report documents polling places moving without notification and closing early, and people in line by 7:00 p.m. not being permitted to vote. Julian Borger of the *Guardian* of London reported several forms of police harassment, subsequently corroborated by USCCR hearings, including a police vehicle-inspection blockade near a polling place in a black precinct outside of Tallahassee.[72]

BAD BALLOTS

In 2000 Florida had a significant exit-poll discrepancy, and as it did in 2004 the discrepancy favored Bush. Suppressed votes aside, 2000 Florida exit polls projected a 7.3% Gore victory. What happened to that projected victory margin? As in 2004, we see questionable practices involving ballots and voting technologies, and an exit poll whose data has never been fully reviewed or explained. The problems in Florida with the butterfly ballots, punch-card ballots, and the incompletely detached chads were reported at length. But the real issue both then and now is not about technology alone, but rather how public officials can use their power to manipulate technology and thereby the vote counts.

In *Jews for Buchanan*, John Nichols notes the sad irony of elderly Holocaust survivors miscasting their votes for a politician whose politics are tinged with anti-Semitism. Republicans subsequently denied the butterfly ballot had any impact. Karl Rove claimed that Buchanan's Reform Party had 16,695 registered voters in Palm Beach County, when it had only 700.[73] Bill O'Reilly dismissed the voters as "morons." "Are you supposed to go in and pull the ballot for them?" he asked.[74] Of course, lever "pull" ballots are only used in the Northeast, and poll workers are, in fact, supposed to help confused voters. Ann Coulter presented another Bush-team spin:

> I love these jackasses claiming they meant to vote for Gore but—whoops!—slipped and pulled the lever for Buchanan instead! Oh really. Let's pretend that's true. Sorry, but that's one of the disabilities of being a political party that preys on

the stupid. Sometimes your "base" forgets it's Election Day, too. Live by demagoguing to the feeble-minded, die by demagoguing to the feeble-minded.[75]

The problem wasn't the voter. Don A. Dillman, who has researched the design of paper questionnaires, made the following observation the day after the election:

> I've never seen one set up like this. It's very confusing the way they have put things on the right side together with things on the left side. . . . If you passed over the first candidate to go for the second candidate, it's logical that you'd punch the second hole.[76]

The butterfly ballot cost Al Gore more than 15,000 net votes. It cost him more than 2,000 votes attributed to Buchanan, whose punch hole was located between that of Bush and Gore, and to Socialist candidate David McReynolds, whose punch hole was located to the right of and below Lieberman's name. Buchanan was awarded 3,407 Palm Beach County votes; he himself estimated his true vote to be 300 to 400.[77] Buchanan's estimate corresponds with statistical analyses comparing his Palm Beach vote with other Florida counties and projections based on his absentee votes, which did not use the butterfly ballot. McReynolds received almost as many votes in the county (302) as in the whole rest of the state put together (320), even though Palm Beach County represented only 7% of the Florida electorate.

Although Palm Beach County punch-card instructions read, "Vote for Group" (meaning the presidential and vice presidential candidates), if a voter made two punches this would result in a rejected ballot. In the county, 15,371 ballots contained votes for Gore and another candidate; 3,751 contained Bush and another candidate. Thus, the poor design of the ballot cost Gore between 11,000 and 12,000 net overvotes in rejected ballots, in addition to the votes miscast for Buchanan and McReynolds.

UNCOUNTED VOTES

When Harris certified a 537-vote victory for George Bush in the Florida presidential election, 175,010 Election Day ballots were still uncounted. These uncounted ballots were rejected by tabulating machines as having no vote cast for president (undervotes) or as having more than one vote cast for president (overvotes). And they remained uncounted despite Florida law and legal precedent[78] because the U.S. Supreme Court intervened to stop the manual count ordered by the Florida Supreme Court.

The uncounted ballots have since been analyzed independently, most thoroughly by the National Opinion Research Center (NORC), a nonprofit research group based at the University of Chicago. The NORC data reveals that despite all the legally and illegally disenfranchised voters, and despite the other obstacles faced by Democratic voters, including the butterfly ballot and blockades, Gore would not only have won, but would have done so by a large margin, almost 50,000 votes.

TABLE 2.1: THE UNCOUNTED VOTES

	BUSH	GORE	OTHERS, UNMARKED OR UNATTRIBUTABLE	TOTAL
UNDERVOTES	13,055	14,332	33,803	61,190
OVERVOTES	24,288	70,020	19,512	113,820
TOTALS	37,343	84,352	53,315	175,010

Source for the data: See tables 2.2, 2.3, 2.4.

The numbers in table 2.1 indicate a net gain of more than 47,000 votes for Gore based on a liberal standard for attributing votes; that is, any indication of a vote for either Gore or Bush.

But no matter what standard is used, Gore would have emerged victorious.

Consider first the undervotes, ballots for which, according to the machines that tabulated the votes, a choice for president was not properly entered. These ballots were the ones that were the focus of so much media attention in the weeks after the 2000 election.

The accounting firm BDO Seidman conducted an audit of the undervotes for the *Miami Herald, Knight Ridder,* and *USA Today.* According to the audit, 54,350 of the undervotes came from punch-card ballots. Of these ballots, 23,856 indicate no mark for president or partial marks for more than one candidate (the latter were subsequently reclassified as overvotes); the remainder fall into the categories indicated in tables 2.2 and 2.3.

TABLE 2.2: MARKED PUNCH CARD BALLOT UNDERVOTES IN FLORIDA,

2000 PRESIDENTIAL ELECTION

	DIMPLE	PINPRICK	DETACHED 1 CORNER	DETACHED 2 CORNER	DETACHED 3 CORNER	PUNCHED CLEANLY	TOTAL BALLOTS
BLANK	322	115	16	66	60	3,275	3,854
BUSH	10,004	750	132	304	512	456	12,158
GORE	10,745	807	79	255	297	970	13,153
OTHERS	991	230	7	11	9	81	1,329
TOTAL	22,062	1,902	234	636	878	4,782	30,494

Source for the data: *The Miami Herald Report,* p. 231. See Further Readings.

The remainder of the undervotes, 6,761, came from optical-scan ballots; 4,419 of these ballots indicate no mark for president. The rest fall into the categories indicated in table 2.3.

TABLE 2.3: MARKED OPTICAL-SCAN BALLOT UNDERVOTES IN FLORIDA,

2000 PRESIDENTIAL ELECTION

	CIRCLED OR MARKED CANDIDATE OR PARTY	UNDER-LINED CAND-IDATE	CIRCLED OR PARTIALLY FILLED BUBBLE OR ARROW	MARKED X OR CHECKED	ERROR WITH WRITING INSTRU-MENT	WRITE-INS	TOTAL BALLOTS
BLANK	0	0	0	1	0	7	8
BUSH	198	32	105	274	216	35	860
GORE	369	40	161	367	187	55	1,179
OTHERS	33	1	5	23	14	219	295
TOTAL	600	73	271	665	417	316	2,342

Source for the data: *The Miami Herald Report,* p. 232.

The reason so few people know the degree to which the failure to count the votes distorted the official certification numbers is that politicians, litigants, and the press incorrectly focused exclusively on these undervotes. Undervotes, in particular incompletely punched chads, were the subject of most of the media coverage, many of the lawsuits, and the Florida Supreme Court ruling.

Two ballot studies completed before the NORC study focused exclusively on undervotes. The *Miami Herald* recount examined 10,000 undervotes in Miami-Dade County, counting missed "clean punches," and found that Gore would have gained no more than 49 votes if a recount of Miami-Dade ballots had been allowed. "That would have been 140 too few to overcome Bush's lead, even when joined with Gore gains in Volusia, Palm Beach and Broward counties—the three other counties where Gore had requested manual recounts," the *Herald* reported.[79] The *Miami Herald* erred, however, in the conclusions it drew from its Miami-Dade recount. The *Palm Beach Post* completed a manual recount of undervotes in Palm Beach County on January 27, 2001, and reported a net gain of 682 votes for Al Gore. Along with the 49 votes found in Miami-Dade, Bush's 537-vote victory turns into a 194-vote defeat.

As mentioned above, the *Miami Herald* also sponsored, along with *Knight Ridder* and *USA Today*, a statewide study of undervotes conducted by the accounting firm of BDO Seidman. These BDO Seidman findings were reported in much the same way. Newspapers presented several scenarios. In some of them, Gore would have failed to make up the 537-vote certified Bush margin of victory. This is especially true in scenarios in which manual counts take place only in the four counties in which Gore sued.

Most newspapers tended to emphasize this scenario. But it's difficult to see why, other than to provide an excuse to legitimize the election. After all, the four-county recount requested by Al Gore was rejected by the Florida Supreme Court's ruling on December 8, 2000, which instead ordered a statewide recount.

Lance deHaven-Smith, a professor of public policy at Florida State University, observed that, under any of the five most reasonable interpretations of the Florida Supreme Court ruling, Gore does, in fact, more than make up the deficit:[80]

➤Prevailing statewide standard—for punch cards, accept a single-corner-detached chad; for op-scan, any affirmative mark, as indicators of voter intent. Gore wins by 9 votes.

➤County-by-county standards, which were in use at the time. Gore wins by 56 votes.

➤Two-corner-detached statewide—requires at least two corners detached as indicator of voter intent. Gore wins by 146 votes.

➤Most restrictive. Accepts only perfect ballots that machines missed or ballots with unambiguous expressions of voter intent, including punch-card ballots where voters made choices with pencil markings. Gore wins by 156 votes.

➤Most inclusive. Applies a uniform standard of dimple or

better to punch cards statewide; for op-scan, any affirmative mark, as indicators of voter intent. Gore wins by 148 votes.

The story that was really missed, however, is the ignoring of the overvotes. Neither logic nor Florida law suggest why overvotes should not be assessed for determining voter intent. And, in fact, Judge Terry Allen, the judge authorized to oversee the state count, issued a ruling to that effect hours before the U.S. Supreme Court shot down the effort. In interviews, Allen reiterated his position: "Logically, everything the Florida Supreme Court said was, 'You have to look at the clear intent of the voter.' Lewis said, 'Logically, if you can look at a ballot and see, this is a vote for Bush or this is a vote for Gore, then you would have to count it. . . . Logically, why wouldn't you count it?'"[81]

Unlike the earlier studies, NORC, which was commissioned to do the work by a media consortium of eight news organizations (*New York Times*, *Wall Street Journal*, *Tribune Company*, *Washington Post*, *Associated Press*, *St. Petersburg Times*, *Palm Beach Post*, and CNN) focused equally on overvotes. They found that 19,512 of the 113,820 rejected overvotes contained no marks for either Bush or Gore, or marks for both. The remaining 94,308 fall into the categories reported in table 2.4.

TABLE 2.4: ALLOCABLE OVERVOTES IN FLORIDA, 2000 PRESIDENTIAL ELECTION

	UNCOUNTED WRITE-IN VOTES	TWO-MARK OVERVOTES	MULTIPLE-MARK OVERVOTES	ALL ALLOCABLE OVERVOTES	
BUSH	697	15,236	8,355	24,288	26%
GORE	1,544	39,148	29,328	70,020	74%
TOTAL	2,241	54,384	37,683	94,308	

Source for the data: National Opinion Research Center. "NORC Florida Ballots Project." See Further Readings.

Write-ins are ballots on which there is a mark for either Bush or Gore, and that candidate's name is also written in. Two-mark overvotes are ballots on which either Bush or Gore is marked and one other mark for president is also on the ballot. Multiple-mark over-votes are ballots on which either Bush or Gore is marked and more than one other mark for president is also on the ballot.

While it's possible that in some cases these allocations may not represent the intent of the voter, the great bulk undoubtedly do. In most cases, it's easy to understand both the intent and why the "error" was made. On the butterfly ballots in Palm Beach County, for example, it said "vote for the group," so punches were made both next to the presidential candidate and below, next to the vice presidential candidate. In others, the ballot itself gave incorrect instructions. More than 20% of ballots in black precincts of Duval County were rejected because the listing of presidential candidates was split over two pages, and on the sample ballot, voters were instructed to mark every page. Had the most reasonable interpre-tation for the broad majority of overvotes been accepted, Gore would have won by more than 40,000 votes, despite all the other problems with ballots that cut into his totals. Even had only those ballots been counted in which the voter emphatically tried to ensure the vote by writing in Gore's name as well as marking it, Gore still would have won.

Unfortunately, most news organizations reporting on the audit chose to bury the story about overvotes. Deep within the *New York Times* article, "Study of Disputed Florida Ballots Finds Justices Did Not Cast the Deciding Vote," reporters Ford Fessenden and John M. Broder write, "More than 113,000 Florida voters cast ballots for two or more presidential candidates. Of those, 75,000 chose Mr. Gore and a minor candidate; 29,000 chose Mr. Bush and a minor candi-date. Because there was no clear indication of what the voters intended, those numbers were not included in the consortium's final tabulations."[82]

As part of the historical context in which the 2004 election took place, it's important to highlight the nonrandom nature of the "errors." If the missed votes were a function of clerical error or out-dated technology, errors would be distributed almost equally, in the same percentage as the counted votes. But they're not. Counties and precincts more likely to support Bush disproportionately had technologies where errors would be brought to voters' attention so that they could be corrected and votes would be counted. Counties and precincts with large African American populations, which were more likely to support Gore, had technologies where ballots would predictably go uncounted. The U.S. Commission on Civil Rights (USCCR) study concludes that although blacks made up 11% of Florida's voting population, they cast 54% of the uncounted ballots.[83]

ILLEGALLY COUNTED ABSENTEE BALLOTS

Bush also picked up votes, and Gore lost votes, because of the dis-parate ways in which absentee ballots were counted. In Republican-majority counties, absentee ballots cast by the military and by Republicans (in Florida, party identification is displayed on the outside of envelope) were much more often accepted than absentee ballots cast by civilians and by Democrats in Democratic-majority counties.

Jeffrey Toobin, in his book on the Florida recount, *Too Close to Call: The Thirty-Six-Day Battle to Decide the 2000 Election*, reports that lawyers for the 2000 Bush-Cheney Campaign successfully pres-sured county officials to accept illegal absentee ballots that lacked valid postmarks, witness signatures, proof of date, or other errors on expected Bush votes while urging rejection of those same types of ballots when on suspected Gore votes.

In an analysis of 2,500 overseas absentee ballots, the *New York Times* found that 680 were questionable. Of those, 80% came from voters registered in counties carried by Bush. In Bush counties, 62% of ballots that provided no proof they were mailed before Election

Day were counted, while in Gore counties only 18% of ballots that lacked such proof were counted.

As for domestic absentee ballots, in Bush counties, 71% of ballots with domestic postmarks that were received after November 7 were counted, compared to 31% of those received in Gore counties.

While Secretary of State Harris and the 2000 Bush-Cheney Campaign representatives insisted that the election had to be certified seven days afterward, Florida election officials continued to count absentee ballots received up to ten days after the election. Indeed, half of the 4,256 overseas ballots that were received after November 7 were received on November 16 and 17, raising the question of whether they were illegally cast after Election Day.[84]

Absentee ballots have long been recognized as vulnerable to fraud because it is difficult to ensure that the ballots are cast by the voters who are identified as casting the ballots and because the secrecy of the ballot can be compromised.

Indeed, absentee ballots were the source of the fraud in the 1998 Miami election of Xavier Suarez as mayor. Investigative reporting by the *Miami Herald* uncovered forged signatures, fake addresses, paid vote brokers, ballot tampering, and absentee ballots filed on behalf of dead people, which prompted investigation into the accusations and the removal of mayor-elect Xavier Suarez from office. Suarez was forced to step down after 111 days in office and the *Miami Herald* would go on and win a Pulitzer Prize for investigative reporting.

Suarez, who had been a Democrat, switched party affiliation and in 2000 worked in Florida to elect George W. Bush. On November 8, 2000, he told Evan Shapiro of Feedmag.com that he "helped fill out absentee ballot forms and enlist Republican absentee voters in Miami-Dade County" for the 2000 presidential election. "Dade County Republicans have a very specific expertise in getting out absentee ballots. I obviously have specific experience in this myself," he said.[85]

HOW ACCURATE WERE THE MACHINES THAT
TABULATED THE BALLOTS?

A final, important, remarkably overlooked set of questions concerns the ballots that the machines did count: were they accurately tabulated?

The exit polls indicated a 7.3-point Gore victory. Voter News Service (in 2000 VNS was the predecessor to NEP) explained away the error as due to a combination of overstating Democratic voters and other errors, but Mitofsky, who worked that election as an analyst on the CBS/CNN decision team, said, "Of the thousands of races I have participated in, this is only the second time I have seen this much solid evidence for a projection that turned out wrong."[86]

Commentators like Jeffrey Toobin, who have looked at the uncounted and problematic ballots, have presumed that they are the cause of the discrepancy between the exit polls and the official count.[87] Accounting for the documented, but uncounted ballots, leads to a 50,000 vote victory for Gore, but that 50,000 represents a small part of the 7.3-point exit-poll discrepancy. Even if we suspect that as many as 10,000 Bush-Cheney absentee ballots are illegitimate, that still amounts to a victory margin of only 60,000, or less than 1 percentage point. A victory margin of 7.3% of Florida's electorate would represent 435,000 votes.

Four days after the election, James Baker and the Bush team began to state dismissively that the votes had already been counted and recounted, and that Bush was the winner of both counts.[88] But this was a lie. The only thing "recounted" was the lie itself. The automatic machine recount to which Baker referred was never completed. Rather, one quarter of the votes—sixteen counties, representing 1.25 million votes—were never even retabulated.[89]

TABLE 2.5: ADDING IN THE LOST VOTES

	BUSH CHENEY	GORE LIEBERMAN	OTHERS	TOTAL
CERTIFIED RESULTS	2,912,790 48.85%	2,912,253 48.84%	138,067 2.32%	5,963,110
BUTTERFLY BALLOTS		3,300	(3,300)	5,963,110
UNDERVOTE— PUNCH CARDS	12,158	13,153	1,329	5,989,750
UNDERVOTE— OPTICAL SCAN	860	1,179	295	5,992,084
OVERVOTES WITH INTENT	23,802	68,620	1,886	6,086,392
SUM	2,948,982 48.46%	2,998,505 49.27%	138,277 2.27%	6,085,764

Source for the data: See tables 2.2, 2.3, 2.4.

Manual counts were performed in only three out of sixty-two counties. Elsewhere, there was no systematic check of the machines against paper ballots to ensure that they were, in fact, tabulating the votes accurately. In Miami-Dade, the Democratic county with the most suspicious results, the manual count was stopped and never completed, having been halted by the infamous "Brooks Brothers" mob of Republican congressional staffers.[90] It is disturbing that in an election so close no one demanded to verify the accuracy of the tabulating machines, given the exit-poll discrepancy and some particularly suspicious numbers. For example, a VNS memo stated, "The exit poll in Tampa was off by 16% due to an overstatement of the vote for Gore."[91]

Two "errors" caused the networks to call the election for Bush, which in turn led Gore initially to concede. These errors involved mistabulations by machines manufactured by Global Elections Management Systems, Diebold Election Systems' predecessor. One apparent data-entry error in Brevard County led to 4,000 votes being lopped off the Gore total. The other, larger error subtracted 16,022 votes from Gore's total in Volusia County and distributed it to other candidates, including Bush. The *Washington Post* and CBS reported that this was due to a "faulty memory card."[92]

Based on these numbers, the Fox News election decision team, led by John Ellis, first cousin of George W. and John Ellis (Jeb) Bush, called Florida for Bush at 2:16 a.m. Other networks soon followed, and Gore called Bush to concede, setting up the post-election media portrayal of Bush as the president-in-waiting and Gore as the tarrying loser unwilling to get off stage. Computer scientists say, however, that a faulty memory card would be extremely unlikely to cause the Volusia County subtraction of Gore votes. A memory card is like floppy disk. When a disk goes bad, your computer will fail to read the file, and will crash or give you an error message. It won't replace one number with another. Bev Harris, author of *Black Box Voting*, obtained Diebold internal memos that cast doubt on this "explanation." For example, Ken Clark, Diebold's manager of research and development, in a January 18, 2001, 1:41 p.m. e-mail, wrote:

> My understanding is that the card was not corrupt after (or before) upload. They fixed the problem by clearing the precinct and re-uploading the same card. So neither of these explanations washes. That's not to say I have any idea what actually happened, it's just not either of those. . . . The problem is, it's going to be very hard to collect enough data to really know what happened. The card isn't corrupt so we can't post-mortem it (it's not mort).[93]

PARTISAN USE OF POWER

According to Senator Richard Lugar, the 2004 U.S. exit-poll discrepancy is not comparable to the Ukraine exit-poll discrepancy that was decried as evidence of fraud, because the United States is a mature democracy, whereas Ukraine is a "nascent democracy" where we have concrete physical fraud such as voter intimidation.[94]

But for a blunt, blatant disruption of the democratic process, one need look no further than the "Brooks Brothers" mob that stopped Miami-Dade's 2000 vote recount. In the early morning of November 22, as Broward completed a manual count and Palm Beach plodded forward erratically, Miami-Dade's recount had just gotten started. By midmorning, that count had yielded a net gain for Gore of 157 votes.[95] The party officials doing the recount were prevented from continuing their work, however, by a mob subsequently identified as congressional staffers organized by then–Republican House majority whip Tom DeLay of Texas. Rep. John Sweeney (R.-N.Y.), himself indebted to DeLay for campaign and assignment support,[96] helped lead the charge, screaming, "Shut [the count] down!"[97] As John Nichols reported, cameras captured the scene that followed:

> Dozens of neatly attired, carefully coiffed "radicals" stormed through the hallways of the Clark Building, punching and kicking local Democrats, trampling people, and ultimately crowding into a narrow hallway outside the glass doors of the office of the Miami-Dade supervisor of elections. . . . "Stop the count" they screamed as their leaders banged fists on the glass. Rumors came from the mob that a thousand angry Cuban Americans were massing outside the building to storm it—no idle threat in Miami, a town still raw with tension from the Elian Gonzalez clashes of earlier in the year.[98]

The county-canvassing board then terminated the count in Miami-Dade, and Katherine Harris ruled that the official vote would revert to the machine tallies, discarding even the votes already counted—the 157 net gain for Gore.

SUPREME DECISION

Despite a month of Bush team bullying and Gore team prevaricating, the Florida court system fashioned a plan for a reasonable, statewide count of ballots the machines missed. Under the direction of Leon County Circuit Court Judge Terry Lewis, the entire state was on target for a statewide count of Florida's undervotes. Then the U.S. Supreme Court intervened.

When the Bush campaign initiated proceedings in federal court, few legal scholars thought there was any chance that the U.S. Supreme Court would take up the case. Solicitor General Theodore Olsen represented Bush before the Supreme Court only because no one of higher stature would accept the case. James Baker's first choice had been John Danforth, the highly regarded former senator from Missouri. Jeffrey Toobin in *Too Close to Call* writes, "Danforth was appalled. . . . He predicted that Bush's chance of winning in federal court was 'close to zero.' Federal courts just don't tell states how to run their elections, especially before a candidate has proved that the process harmed him in a particular way."[99]

The reasons the court should not have taken the case go well beyond Danforth's reservations. Justice John Paul Stevens wrote in his dissent on stopping the count, "The Florida court's ruling reflects the basic principle, inherent in our Constitution and our democracy, that every legal vote should be counted." Justice David Souter in his dissent of the final decree wrote, "The Court should not have reviewed either *Bush v. Palm Beach County Canvassing Board* . . . or this case, and should not have stopped Florida's attempt to recount all undervote ballots." And Justice Stephen Breyer added, "And whether, under Florida law, Florida could or could not take further action is obviously a matter for Florida courts, not this Court, to decide."

But the Supreme Court did take up the case, overruled the Florida court, and stopped the recount, awarding the presidency to

George W. Bush. The decree stopped a fair and orderly count, based on a painful twisting of the equal-protection clause of the Fourteenth Amendment, a bitter irony given the disenfranchisement of the black Americans the amendment was originally passed to protect. Alan Dershowitz of Harvard Law School called it "the single most corrupt decision in Supreme Court history," a decision based not on law but on the desire for "partisan advantage" and "personal gain."[100]

Indeed, the ruling was so bizarre it stumped the correspondents who were reporting the decision. They couldn't understand for whom the court had ruled. Bush himself, watching CNN, complained of the terrible ruling until Rove informed him that the court had ruled for him.[101]

Jamin B. Raskin, professor of constitutional law at American University, wrote, "[The decision was] demonstrably the worst Supreme Court decision in history. *Bush v. Gore* changes everything in American law and politics. . . . Dred Scott was, by comparison, a brilliantly reasoned and logically coherent decision."[102] Salon summed up the high court's attitude in its headline: "Supreme Court to Democracy: Drop Dead."[103]

But no one summed up the majority's ruling better than Justice Stevens. He wrote:

> Although we may never know with complete certainty the identity of the winner of this year's Presidential election, the identity of the loser is perfectly clear. It is the Nation's confidence in the judge as an impartial guardian of the rule of law.

CHAPTER 3

Electronic Voting: An Invitation for Fraud

As serious as conventional election fraud is, electronic voting takes the potential for election tampering to a whole new level. Conventional fraud may occur and not be detected, but it is, in principle, detectable, and flagrantly egregious behavior can usually be limited through the courts and public pressure. If legal procedures are pursued or if an investigative team is dogged, as they were not fully in Florida in 2000 and have yet to be in investigating Ohio in 2004, cases of conventional fraud can be exposed and justice served. After all, the *Miami Herald* won a Pulitzer Prize for investigative reporting on vote buying and ballot tampering by the campaign of Xavier Suarez, who had been elected mayor of Miami the previous November. As a result, Suarez was forced to step down after 111 days in office.

With electronic voting systems, however, fraud may be undetectable, and those who have been declared the losers are left with no recourse to verify results. When we use the term "electronic voting," we are talking about direct-recording electronic (DRE) voting machines that utilize touch-screen terminals to record votes. A typical DRE machine works like this: A voter signs in at their precinct, is given an access card, enters the voting booth, swipes the card on the DRE voting machine, votes using a touch screen, and the vote is electronically recorded.

"Electronic voting" can also refer to optical-scan voting systems, where the voter blackens an oval next to the candidate's name on the ballot and then feeds the ballot through a machine that scans the mark and electronically records the vote. In 2004, about 35% of voters cast their ballots on optical-scan systems and, as we have mentioned, 29% on DRE. But while most voting machines are vulnerable to programming fraud, we distinguish between machines that count paper ballots (such as optical-scan), which can in principle be manually recounted, and machines that directly record votes electronically, in which no verification is possible.

WHOM WOULD YOU TRUST WITH YOUR VOTE?

Stanford University computer scientist David Dill, an outspoken critic of electronic voting, is the founder of the Verified Voting Foundation (VerifiedVoting.org), an organization whose mission is to "champion reliable and publicly verifiable elections in the United States."

At a hearing before the Senate Committee on Rules and Administration in June 2005, Dill testified:

> Suppose voters dictated their votes, privately and anonymously to human scribes, and that the voters were prevented from inspecting the work of the scribes. Few would accept such a system, on simple common-sense grounds. Obviously, the scribes could accidentally or intentionally mis-record the votes with no consequences. Without accountability, a system is simply not trustworthy whether or not computers are involved. [But such a] system can be made trustworthy by having the voter fill out his own ballot or by allowing each voter to check the ballot filled out by the scribe. We can have a trustworthy voting system if, instead of a futile effort to ensure that the voting equip-

ment is error-free by design, we empower each voter to verify that his vote has been accurately recorded. In other words we need voter-verified paper ballots.

Because of their intensely competitive nature, voting and elections are predicated on the idea that you don't trust any one person or any particular group. Fair elections are set up with representatives from competing parties monitoring the polling place together. No vote, no machine, no ballot is ever supposed to be controlled by one person or one party. And if questions arise as to whether the vote has been fair, the losing candidates have recourse. They can ask to inspect the ballot box, the machine, the votes, and so on. They can, in principle, request a manual count of the votes and observe this count.

But with DREs, the people who program the machines are in the same position as Dill's hypothetical scribes. We have to trust them and there's no accountability. You touch the screen and the machine makes a record. You hope it's right, but there's no way of knowing or checking; there is no paper trail.

Americans think of Florida 2000 as a nightmare, but at least in Florida we have a partial accounting of what happened. In 2002 and 2004 we had elections that in general seemed to go smoothly but produced unexpected results. DRE voting systems made it impossible to know whether voters behaved unpredictably or the count was tainted by electronic glitches or vote fraud.

The concept of e-voting is so flawed that when the Association for Computing Machinery (ACM), the computing industry's principal professional society, polled its 75,000 members, 95% responded that voters should demand voting systems that provide a physical record.[104]

Computer scientist and election integrity activist Bruce O'Dell, one of the founders of U.S. Count Votes, put it this way: "The ACM is a large group of professionals of very diverse political backgrounds. Outrage is essentially universal across my profession. Imagine, if 95% of a group of structural engineers said a bridge will fall down if you drive on it, would anyone in their right mind still drive on it?"

THE ELECTRONIC VOTING MACHINE INDUSTRY

About 80% of DRE electronic voting systems used in the United States are manufactured by one of three companies: Diebold Election Systems of Austin, Texas; Election Systems & Software (ES&S) of Omaha, Nebraska; and the British-owned Sequoia Voting Systems of Oakland, California.[105] In November 2004, about 50 million voters—29% of all voters—cast their ballots on DREs, according to Election Data Services, Inc. Diebold boasts on its Web site that "over 75,000 Diebold electronic voting stations are being used in locations across the United States." And, according to ES&S, its forty thousand DRE voting machines record votes in twenty states.

The voting machine company Datamark, which became American Information Systems and is now known as ES&S, was founded in 1980 by two brothers, Bob and Todd Urosevich. Today, Todd is a vice president at ES&S and Bob is CEO of Diebold Election Systems. Diebold Election Systems is an Austin, Texas–based subsidiary of Diebold Inc.

Walden "Wally" O'Dell, chairman and CEO of Diebold Inc., is a longtime Republican activist. In 2004 he was a member of the Bush "Pioneers," a group of supporters who each pledged to raise $100,000 for the presidential race and were honored for their work at a party at Bush's Crawford, Texas, ranch. Most famously, in September 2003, O'Dell held a packed $1,000-per-head Bush fund-raiser at his 10,800-square-foot home in Upper Arlington, a suburb of Columbus, Ohio. In the invitation to that party O'Dell said he was "committed to helping Ohio deliver its electoral votes to the president."

O'Dell isn't the only Diebold partisan. One of the longest-serving members of the Diebold board of directors was W. R. "Tim" Timken, a Republican loyalist and a major contributor to GOP candidates. Since 1991 the Timken Company and members of the Timken family have contributed more than a million dollars to the Republican Party and to GOP presidential candidates such as George W. Bush.[106] Timken resigned from the board in June 2005, after Diebold amended its corporate ethics policy and barred company executives from contributing to political candidates.

Diebold has also been tainted by charges that a convicted felon wrote the computer code that is used to count votes.[107] In January 2002, Diebold acquired Global Election Systems, an electronic-voting-machine company where Jeffrey Dean, a senior vice president, wrote the vote-counting systems code. Prior to being employed by Global Election Systems, he had done time in a Washington state prison. He had been convicted of twenty-three counts of felony theft in the first degree, for a scheme that, according to a court document, "involved a high degree of sophistication and planning" and included planting back doors in his software that allowed him to skim and reallocate monies from his clients' accounts to his accounts (a process similar to vote transferring).[108]

Controversy has also swirled around ES&S. What are we to make of a situation in which a U.S. senator who, unbeknownst to the general population, owns a share of the voting-machine company whose machines are used to count the votes in his own elections and who had been the acting president of that company (American Information Systems, which was to become ES&S) until a few weeks before he announced his intention to run for the Senate in 1996?

We are referring to the Republican senator from Nebraska, Chuck Hagel. In 1992, Hagel, then an investment banker and president of the holding company McCarthy & Co., became chairman of American Information Systems, which was to become ES&S in

1999. Sen. Hagel reportedly still owns more than $1 million in stock in McCarthy & Co., which owns a quarter of ES&S.

In the 1996 elections, Hagel launched his political career with two stunning upsets. He won a primary victory in Nebraska against Republican attorney general Don Stenberg, despite the fact that he was not well known. Then, in the general election, Hagel was elected to the Senate in what *Business Week* described as "an unexpected 1996 landslide victory over Ben Nelson, Nebraska's popular Democratic governor."[109]

At the start of the race Nelson was leading in the polls 65% to 18%, but in the November election Hagel won with 56% of the vote—an election in which machines made by American Information Systems (ES&S) tallied 85% of the vote.[110] The *Washington Post* called Hagel's 1996 win "the major Republican upset in the November election."[111]

In the 2002 election, Hagel's opponent, Charlie Matulka, charged conflict of interest and requested that the Senate Ethics Committee investigate. The request was denied. Matulka also asked Nebraska's Republican secretary of state John A. Gale for a hand recount of the paper ballots that could then be matched against the computerized results. (Nebraska uses optical-scan systems manufactured by ES&S that provide an auditable paper trail.) Matulka was told that Nebraska has no provision in the law allowing a losing candidate to verify vote tallies by counting the paper ballots.[112] "This is the stealing of our democracy," Matulka told the *New York Times*.[113]

Electronic-voting-machine maker Sequoia Voting Systems, the third-largest DRE manufacturer, has faced questions about its marketing strategies. Phil Foster, a Sequoia sales representative and vice president, has been implicated in a scam involving the purchase of Sequoia voting machines that resulted in several felony convictions. In January 2001, he was indicted for "conspiracy to commit money-laundering and malfeasance" in a case that involved kickbacks to a Louisiana election official and cost Louisiana taxpayers an estimated $48 million. (A Louisiana state judge later dismissed the charges against Foster, ruling that the case against him was based on testimony he had given to a grand jury for which he had been granted immunity.)[114]

Sequoia has also been criticized for its refusal to allow independent examinations of its operating systems. The March 2002 Palm Beach County election was conducted using newly purchased Sequoia Voting Systems DRE machines that were purchased through Phil Foster. In a case challenging that election, Theresa LePore testified that under the county's purchase contract with Sequoia, it was a third-degree felony to disclose specifications of the how the machines operate. (LePore was the Palm Beach County supervisor of elections who in 2000 thrice undermined the public vote: first as the designer of the infamous butterfly ballot; then by adopting an arbitrarily strict guideline for accepting ballots as valid in the November 2000 court-ordered hand count; and finally by delivering to Tallahassee the results of that manual count two hours late, thereby giving Katherine Harris grounds for denying the hand count.) Professing wonder as to why anyone would want to take the machines apart, she told the court, "There's not much inside." LePore added that Sequoia would cancel the warranty on the machines if they were opened for inspection.[115]

ELECTRONIC VOTING — EASY TO MANIPULATE

Avi Rubin, a professor of computer science at Johns Hopkins University and an expert in computer security, has examined the machines of DRE manufacturer Diebold Election Systems and found them to be "poorly designed, with lax security and programming errors."

Six days before the 2004 election, in an op-ed article in the *Baltimore Sun*, he warned of the dangers of DRE systems:

Without paper ballots that can be physically examined, the only recount possible is a review of the votes recorded by the DRE system itself. And if those votes were recorded incorrectly, no recount will fix the error. The incorrect result could never be detected, much less corrected. . . . Technical glitches and malfunctioning machines—the kinds of problems that occur with any computer system—could result in the loss of votes in unrecoverable ways. Worse, these fully electronic machines could be rigged—undetectably, because of the complexity of the software that runs them. . . . While we can never eliminate the possibility of tampering with elections, the impact of an attack on a DRE system would likely be more serious than the results of tampering with traditional mechanical voting machines or paper-based systems, such as optically scanned ballots. This is because a bug in the software of an electronic voting system, whether accidental or intentional, has the potential to skew results in more than an isolated polling place or two. It could impact the vote totals on many thousands of machines in hundreds of precincts.[116]

Rubin was part of a Johns Hopkins Information Security Institute research team that examined Diebold's DRE voting machines and found both serious security shortcomings[117] and a propensity for errors.

In an incredible lapse in security, for example, the "source code repository" for Diebold's AccuVote-TS DRE was found on an unsecure Web site and downloaded by Bev Harris, author of *Black Box Voting*. The Johns Hopkins researchers used this source code in their examination of the Diebold AccuVote-TS, and they concluded that "this voting system is unsuitable for use in a general election," does not meet "even the most minimal security standards," and could be exploited "by unscrupulous voters."

They write, "We show that voters, without any insider privileges, can cast unlimited votes without being detected by any mechanisms within the voting terminal software." Not to mention "malicious insiders," about whom the researchers had this to say:

> Such insiders include elections officials, the developers of the voting system, and the developers of the embedded operating system on which the voting system runs. If any party introduces flaws into the voting system software or takes advantage of pre-existing flaws, then the results of the election cannot be assured to accurately reflect the votes legally cast by the voters.

In May 2004, Rubin testified before the U.S. Election Assistance Commission, which was created by the Help America Vote Act, to, among other things, establish voluntary standards for voting systems. He said in part:

> With respect to the Diebold AccuVote TS and TSx [DRE voting machines] we found gross design and programming errors, as outlined in our attached report. The current certification process resulted in these machines being approved for use and being used in elections. We do not know if the machines from other vendors are as bad as the Diebold ones because they have not made their systems available for analysis.

Concerned about reports of election fraud and vote suppression in the 2004 election, Rep. John Conyers, Jr. (D.-Mich.), the ranking Democrat on the House Judiciary Committee, asked the Government Accountability Office (GAO), the investigative arm of Congress, to examine the allegations. In September 2005, the GAO released a report that found electronic voting systems "have caused local problems in federal elections—resulting in the loss or miscount of votes."

The GAO highlights one major problem with electronic voting systems: they can be hacked because of woefully inadequate security systems. The report notes, "Regarding key software components, several evaluations demonstrated that election management systems did not encrypt the data files containing cast votes (to protect them from being viewed or modified). . . . If exploited, these weaknesses could damage the integrity of ballots, votes and voting system software by allowing unauthorized modifications."

The report goes on to say that flaws in electronic voting-security protections "could allow unauthorized personnel to disrupt operations or modify data and programs that are critical to the accuracy and the integrity of the voting process." The report cites these examples:

➤In some cases, other computer programs can access voting system files that contain records of cast votes, and alter files without a record of hacking showing up in the system's audit logs.

➤On Diebold's AccuVote-TS, a DRE, it "might be possible" to alter ballot-definition files—so votes on the touch screen for one candidate would actually be recorded and counted for another.

➤Computer security experts working with a Florida local-elections supervisor demonstrated that someone with physical access to an optical-scan system can use altered memory cards, falsifying election results without any record of the deed.

➤In one DRE model, the same personal identification number was programmed into all election-supervisor cards nationwide—meaning the number was widely known.

➤Several reviews reported that smart cards (which activate touch screens on DREs) and memory cards (which program an optical-scan system's terminals) were not secured by some voting systems. Reviewers exploited this weakness by altering such cards to improperly access administrator functions, vote multiple times, change vote totals, and produce false election reports in a test environment.

Because elections are overseen by the states, the federal government is unable to mandate electoral procedures. So the GAO called on the Election Assistance Commission (EAC), the four-member presidential commission established by the Help America Vote Act (HAVA), to implement voluntary reforms and safeguards such as establishing security standards and a national program to certify electronic voting systems. However, the GAO notes that "important initiatives are unlikely to affect the 2006 election due, at least in part, to [Bush administration] delays in appointment of EAC commissioners and in funding the commission."

The GAO concluded: "Until these efforts are completed, there is a risk that many state and local jurisdictions will rely on voting systems that were not developed, acquired, tested, operated, or managed in accordance with rigorous security and reliability standards."

Rep. Conyers responded to the report this way: "I am shocked at the extent and nature of problems that GAO has identified. . . . It is incumbent upon Congress to respond to this problem and to enact much needed reforms such as a voter verified paper audit trail that protects all Americans' right to vote."

EASTER EGGS

Diebold and ES&S say that they test their machines, but that's the equivalent of allowing professional athletes to administer their own drug tests. Bev Harris documents the almost total failure of municipalities to independently verify the accurate functioning of their machines. But even if they were diligent in conducting pre- and post-election tests, that would still be insufficient. Ted Selker, a computer-science professor affiliated with the Cal Tech/MIT Voting Technology Project, points out that general testing cannot possibly reveal all bugs or vote-altering code.[118] Selker explains that these are undetectable pieces of code known as "Easter eggs." He writes:

> In a voting machine, such code would do nothing until Election Day, when it would change how votes were recorded. Such code could be loaded into a voting machine in many ways: in the voting software itself, in the tools that assemble the software (compiler, liner and loader), or in the tools the program depends on (database, operating system scheduler, memory management and graphical-user-interface controller).

Easter eggs could be activated by the clocks that are part of many of the voting machines. Selker writes, "Tests must therefore be conducted to catch Easter eggs and bugs that occur only on election day."

ELECTRONIC VOTING MACHINES COMPARED TO LAS VEGAS SLOT MACHINES

In 2004, the *New York Times* ran a series of editorials called "Making Votes Count." One of those editorials, "Gambling on Voting," compared electronic voting machines to Las Vegas slot machines. We highlight some of those key distinctions in table 3.1.

TABLE 3.1: ELECTRONIC VOTING MACHINES COMPARED TO LAS VEGAS SLOT MACHINES

	LAS VEGAS SLOT MACHINES	ELECTRONIC VOTING MACHINES
SOFTWARE	The state of Nevada has access to all gambling software. It is illegal for casinos to use software that is not on file.	Electronic voting machine software is a trade secret.
SPOT-CHECKING	Board inspectors show up unannounced at casinos to compare computer chips to those on file. If there is a discrepancy, the machine is shut down and investigated.	No checks are required and, even if an election official wanted to, he or she wouldn't have a chip to compare to the one found in the machine.
STANDARDS	Rigorous standards are constantly updated. For example, the machine must work when subjected to a 20,000-volt shock.	Voting machine standards are three years old and gaping security holes still exist.
BACK-GROUND SCRUTINY	Manufacturers are subject to background checks that last six months or more, and any uncovered criminal record is investigated.	No scrutiny. Citizens have no way of knowing, for example, if e-voting programmers or industry executives have been convicted of fraud.
EQUIPMENT CERTIFICATION	Certification by a public agency that maintains an arm's-length relationship with manufacturers. Public questions are invited.	Certification is done by for-profit companies chosen and paid by the manufacturers. No public information is available on how the testing is done.
DISPUTES	If a gambler believes she or he has been cheated, the casino is required to contact the Gaming Control Board, which has investigators on call around the clock. Investigators can open up machines to inspect their internal mechanisms and their records of recent gambling outcomes.	If voters believe a voting machine has manipulated their votes, in most cases their only recourse is to call a Board of Elections number to lodge a complaint that may or may not be investigated.

Defenders of DRE electronic voting machines say that there has not been a single verified incident of tampering with an electronic machine under real-world conditions.[119] Unfortunately, that's the point. How can we verify tampering? Given the lack of an auditable paper trail and the refusal of DRE companies to allow their voting machines to be inspected, how do we know if electronic votes are accurately recorded and tabulated? We don't. An exit poll that closely matched machine counts would be about the only reason to have confidence in official results from these machines. And a large discrepancy between the exit polls and the official count should be cause enough for suspicion.

Take the case of Florida, where in 2004 there was a 4.9 percentage-point difference between the exit polls and the official tally.

FLORIDA 2004: PALM BEACH REDUX

Although Ohio was the most scrutinized state in the 2004 presidential election, it may not have been the worst. What happened on Election Day in Florida, because of Bush's larger margin of victory in the official count, has gone relatively uninvestigated.

Recall that in 2000, Florida Secretary of State Katherine Harris helped Bush win by purging voting rolls of some 57,700 alleged felons, 90% of whom were purged incorrectly.[120] The majority of those purged were African American or Hispanic nonfelons who happened to share a name with someone on a felons list somewhere.[121]

Harris's successor, Glenda Hood, tried the same thing again in 2004. She attempted to cut 47,000 supposed felons from Florida's voter rolls. After a judge ordered that her list of felons be made public, it turned out that the list contained hardly any Latino names, which, given Florida's demographics, immediately threw the accuracy of the list into question. She had excluded hundreds of Latino felons (Latinos of Cuban origin in Florida often back Republican candidates). And the list did include hundreds of African Americans who had won restoration of their voting rights. The list was soon scrapped owing to public outcry.

The 2004 election also saw a repeat performance by Theresa LePore, the election supervisor in Palm Beach County, one of the three large and Democratic-voting counties in the state. In 2000, LePore had fully cooperated in using the flawed felon list to scrub voters from the rolls. (Officials in other counties didn't cooperate.) LePore's action resulted in the disenfranchisement of thousands of voters, most of them African American. She was rewarded for her work in the 2000 election by Governor Jeb Bush, who named her to the bipartisan Select Task Force on Election Procedures, Standards and Technology.[122]

In March 2001, the task force issued its report and recommended that the state install "a uniform voting system for use throughout the state . . . that meets both Florida's 'Voting Systems Standards' and 'user standards' such as . . . documentation for vote-auditing purposes." DRE voting machines clearly did not meet that standard, since they do not produce an auditable paper trail that would allow ballot recounts.[123]

One of DRE touch screen's foremost proponents was Florida Secretary of State Katherine Harris. "The touch-screen technology appears to be a significant leap forward," she said in August 2001. "We hope we are going to see a lot more of these opportunities materialize."[124] She was joined in her enthusiasm by fifteen county election supervisors, including LePore, who subsequently went out and purchased DRE machines for their counties.

DREs have one big advantage for election officials. "There's really no such thing as a recount," says Doug Lewis, executive director of the Elections Center, a national organization of about one thousand election officials. "You can flip that switch 48 times and 48 times it's going to come out the same way."[125]

In Palm Beach County, LePore spent $14.4 million buying a DRE touch-screen system from Sequoia Voting Systems for Palm Beach County.

The county commissioners approved the purchase in September 2001, but LePore had not informed them that Phil Foster, the Sequoia vice president involved in the kickback scams, had overseen the contract negotiations with Palm Beach and other counties. In addition to the taint of corruption, mechanical problems with the DREs surfaced immediately.

The Sequoia DREs were first used in March 2002 in two Palm Beach County municipal elections. In Boca Raton, Mayor Emil Danciu came in third in a race for a seat on the city council, even though a pre-election opinion poll had him the front-runner by 17 points. He went to court and sued to gain access to the Sequoia source code in order to see if it was flawed. LePore told the court that the code was a trade secret, and his suit was thrown out.

"She's defended the system almost to the point where it's been ridiculous," said Danciu's daughter Charlotte, who worked on his campaign. "She treated us as though we were sore losers, and as though we were imbeciles. The tenor of what she told us was that if people were too dumb to vote on electronic machines, they shouldn't be voting."[126]

In the city of Wellington, a runoff election was held that involved one race with only two candidates. The final vote tally was 1,263 to 1,259, but 78 ballots for some reason had no vote. LePore explained the discrepancy this way: "They knew there was an election. Everybody said, 'Go vote.' They got there and decided there was nobody they wanted to vote for and cast their ballot anyway [for nobody], for whatever reason, maybe to maintain voting history."[127]

BROWARD COUNTY: FOLLOWING THE
PALM BEACH MODEL

Unlike Palm Beach County, in 2000 Broward County conducted a no-nonsense manual count, the results of which were delivered promptly to Tallahassee and included in the official count. They had no ballot-design issues that led to thousands of miscast votes. But whereas Palm Beach's LePore was rewarded with appointment to a state commission, in November 2003, Florida Governor Jeb Bush took the highly unusual step of using his executive powers to remove Broward's elected elections supervisor, Miriam Oliphant, for "incompetence." He replaced her with Brenda Snipes, a retired elementary school principal with no elections experience. Although Snipes, like LePore, is a nominal Democrat, she had the support of some of the governor's close Republican advisers in the county.

Since then, Broward County has followed the trajectory of Palm Beach, its neighbor to the north. Using a new $12.7 million ES&S DRE system purchased by Oliphant, Broward held a special election on January 6, 2004, for an open seat in the Florida House of Representatives. Republican Ellyn Bogdanoff was elected with a 12-vote margin of victory.

As in the Wellington election, it was the only race on the ballot, and as in Wellington many voters—134—supposedly came to the polls but cast no vote. But since there is no paper trail, it is impossible to go back and verify whether those ballots were intentionally left blank or fell victim to faulty or malicious code.

Because the margin of victory was less than one-quarter of 1%, the state canvassing board, chaired by Gov. Jeb Bush, was required by Florida law to conduct a manual count, but of course with DREs no manual count is possible. Snipes's Deputy Election Supervisor Gisela Salas put it this way, "Very simply, some people choose not to vote. That could be a legitimate choice of the voter. There's no way to tell."[128]

The *St. Petersburg Times* observed, "The solution, everyone agrees, is to stop having close elections. 'We just pray for large margins,' said [Gisela] Salas, the [Broward County] deputy election supervisor, 'we definitely have to do some heavy praying for the fall elections.'"

That fall, on Election Day 2004, Snipes proceeded to "lose" 76,000 absentee ballots that were requested by voters, including 58,000 supposedly mailed on October 7 and 8.[129] Five days before the election the county resent the 76,000 ballots. It is not known how many voters received them in time to return their ballots by the deadline.

In the 2004 election, both Broward and Palm Beach counties also rejected large swaths of absentee ballots because of what they deemed unacceptable signatures. In doing so, they refused to use certified handwriting experts. And while election officials did not know for certain which candidate's votes they were rejecting, they did know the voter's party affiliation. These were printed on the outside of each return envelope.[130]

In general, the debate in Florida over an auditable paper trail breaks down along party lines, with Republicans opposing it and Democrats supporting it. In fact, the state's Association of Elections Supervisors is on record opposing an auditable paper trail. Republican Kurt Browning, the elections supervisor in Pasco County, said he didn't see the need for "spending millions of dollars to keep a relatively small number of people happy."[131] His view is shared by the Republican state legislature, Governor Bush, and Secretary of State Hood.

Writing in the *Independent* of London, reporter Andrew Gumbel observed, "The Republicans can only be thrilled that those southern counties have opted for electronic voting machines, without an independent paper trail, because they make meaningful re-counts essentially impossible."[132]

But that didn't stop the state Republican Party from playing to

Floridians' fears of vote fraud. In the 2004 election, the party sent out a mailing that featured a photograph of President Bush and urged party faithful to make sure their vote counts by voting absentee since the new DRE voting machines don't produce an auditable paper trail.

ELECTRONIC VOTE FRAUD IN FLORIDA?

When you combine this lack of an auditable paper trail with the fact that DRE voting systems are vulnerable to hacking, you have a recipe for large-scale electoral fraud.

Following the 2004 general election, a team of researchers at the University of California, Berkeley, led by Michael Hout, the chair of the university's Sociology and Demography graduate program, analyzed the vote in Florida.

The Berkeley researchers compared 2000 to 2004 county-voting results in Florida and found that Bush's vote gains in counties that used Sequoia or ES&S DRE voting machines far exceeded his gains in counties with auditable paper ballots. After controlling for the effects of income, number of voters, change in turnout and size of the Hispanic/Latino population, they concluded that "electronic voting raised President Bush's advantage from the tiny edge he held in 2000 to a clearer margin of victory in 2004." The researchers calculate that in Florida, DRE voting machines gave Bush between 130,000 and 260,000 more votes in Florida than he should have received based on voter-demographic and voter-turnout data. Bush won Florida by 360,000 votes, so these additional votes would not have made the entire difference. However, Hout's research is only part of the picture.

At a press conference announcing the study, Hout said, "No matter how many factors and variables we took into consideration, the significant correlation in the votes for President Bush and electronic voting cannot be explained."[133]

Hout's study was widely criticized, but as Columbia University Professor Andrew Gelman observes, "They have found an interesting pattern, which closer study suggests arises from just two of the e-voting counties: Broward and Palm Beach, which unexpectedly swung about 3% toward Bush in 2004."[134]

Normally, scientists are reluctant to make statistical claims on the basis of one or two outliers (data that deviate greatly from the norm), and are often inclined to throw away anomalous readings. But in investigating the possibility of electoral fraud, outliers are the most important place to look.

The 2004 Republican vote swing in Palm Beach and Broward—two counties with DRE voting systems—was also inconsistent with increases in Republican and Democratic voter registrations between 2000 and 2004. Florida does not provide new registration figures by party, but it does provide total registrations. Between 2000 and 2004, Palm Beach Democratic Party registrations increased by 34,047, a figure that is more than fifteen times greater than the 2,262 increase in Republican registrants. Assume, for the sake of argument, that the Palm Beach County electorate voted for Kerry and Bush by the same percentage they voted for Gore and Bush in 2000. Were that the case, one would expect that the differential between Kerry and Bush would stand at 146,565 votes in Kerry's favor. However, according to the official count in Palm Beach County, Kerry beat Bush by 115,975 votes. To put it another way, in 2004 Kerry got 2 percentage points less of the total vote Gore received in 2000, despite an unprecedented increase in Democratic registration, rigorous get-out-the-vote efforts, minimal loss of votes to Ralph Nader, and no confusing butterfly ballot to siphon off thousands of votes to the Reform Party candidate.

SNOHOMISH COUNTY'S PARALLEL SYSTEMS AND DIVERGENT RESULTS

One way to test the hypothesis that DRE voting systems were used to conduct election fraud in 2004 would be to examine the election results from a county that used parallel voting technologies—one electronic and one nonelectronic, and then tested the results in a recount.

Snohomish County, Washington, a suburban county north of Seattle, fits that bill. Snohomish citizens who vote absentee fill out paper ballots that are counted with an optical-scan system. Those who vote at their precincts on Election Day use Sequoia-manufactured DRE electronic voting machines. Voters who have an absentee ballot can drop it by their polling place on Election Day, an option chosen by about 10% of Snohomish voters in 2004. Washington has long been encouraging early voting, and absentee ballots currently constitute about two-thirds of the overall vote.

On Election Day 2004, a curious thing happened in Snohomish County. According to the official election results, a vote cast on a Sequoia DRE was much more likely to be for a Republican than a vote cast by an absentee ballot and then counted on an optical-scan machine.

The gubernatorial contest between Democrat Christine Gregoire and Republican Dino Rossi is a particularly good race to examine closely because it was subjected to two recounts that generated an extraordinary quality and quantity of data about the two different voting systems.

The close vote count, which had Rossi winning the state by 126 votes, triggered an automatic machine recount. This first recount resulted in an even narrower, 42-vote lead for Rossi. Democrats requested a statewide hand recount, which Gregoire won by 129 votes and she was sworn in. Legal challenges mounted by Rossi led to a trial in which the judge ruled that Gregoire's victory should stand.

In Snohomish County, Gregoire led the absentee vote 97,044 to 95,228, or 51% to 49%; however, she lost the DRE electronic vote 42,143 to 50,400, or 46% to 54%, and ended up losing the county 139,189 to 145,628, or 49% to 51%—the first time a Democrat has not carried Snohomish since 1992. (Kerry carried the county.)

How does one explain the 5-percentage-point discrepancy between Rossi's and Gregoire's absentee ballot counts and their DRE counts? Or the similar but lesser 3-percentage-point discrepancy between Bush's and Kerry's absentee counts and their DRE totals?

That this discrepancy might have been due to problems with the auditable optical-scanning machines was ruled out by the election's hand recount, which confirmed the scanned numbers. No such independent corroboration is available for DRE machines, as there is no physical way to recount DRE votes by hand.

This Snohomish anomaly is the subject of a study published on VotersUnite.org by Paul R. Lehto, an attorney in Everett, Washington, who has been active in local Democratic politics, and Jeffrey Hoffman, a professor of mechanical engineering at Northern Michigan University in Marquette.[135] (Hoffman, Lehto's brother-in-law, provided the statistical analysis.) Lehto and Hoffman examine the discrepancy between the two types of votes—absentee on optical scan and Election Day votes on DRE machines—from a variety of angles.

DRE touch-screen voting systems were introduced in Snohomish County in 2002, replacing the previous optically scanned paper ballot system, which remained in use for absentee ballots. However, with the change in technology came an apparent change in voting patterns in Snohomish County; prior to 2002, Democrats generally did better at the polls on Election Day than they did with absentee ballots, which as a general rule are used more often by Republicans. That changed when the county switched to Sequoia's DRE touch-screen voting systems. Lehto and Hoffman write, "Starting in 2002, in all county-wide races pitting Democrats against Republicans,

Republicans have gained in excess of 2% on election day in every race." One can imagine three explanations that could account for this discrepancy between the two types of voting systems.

First, maybe Republicans tended to vote on Election Day and Democrats tended to vote absentee. Not likely. Not only in past Snohomish elections, but throughout the nation, Republicans are more likely than Democrats to vote absentee.

What's more, infrequent voters, who would be particularly unlikely to vote absentee, trend Democratic. And the 84% turnout in the county suggests that there were many infrequent voters voting Democratic on Election Day 2004.

Second, perhaps Rossi benefited from a late surge in support. According to the NEP statewide exit polls, this didn't happen. Of those polled, 91% said they had made up their mind about whom to support for governor by October 26. Those who made up their mind in the three days before the election supported Gregoire over Rossi 54% to 34%.

Third, the possibility that this discrepancy might have been due to problems with the auditable optical-scan machines is ruled out by the election's hand count, which confirmed the optical-scan numbers. No such independent corroboration is available, or possible, for the votes cast on DRE machines.

The problems in the 2004 election go beyond the general e-voting numbers. On Election Day, voters at 58 of Snohomish County's 148 polling places reported three types of problems on the county's DRE machines: vote-switching after ballots are cast, ballots that were pre-voted, and freezing up. In these 58 precincts, Rossi beat Gregoire by 13 percentage points. At 14 polling places where Sequoia technicians made changes or repairs to the machines' Central Processing Units (CPUs) within three weeks prior to election, Rossi beat Gregoire by 16 percentage points. And on the nineteen Sequoia machines that had to be taken out of service on Election Day because of breakdowns, Rossi won by an inexplicable 21 percentage points. In total, overtly malfunctioning electronic DRE machines gave Republican Rossi 50% more votes than they gave his Democrat opponent. All of which raises one question: were Snohomish County's DRE machines programmed to steal the election?

TABLE 3.2: COMPARING ELECTRONIC VOTES WITH PAPER BALLOTS

A NATURAL EXPERIMENT IN THE SNOHOMISH COUNTY, WASHINGTON GUBERNATORIAL ELECTION

VOTING TECHNOLOGY	REPUB. CANDIDATE DINO ROSSI		DEM. CANDIDATE CHRISTINE GREGOIRE		WINNER/ MARGIN
	VOTES	PCT.	VOTES	PCT.	
PAPER/OPTICAL SCAN	95,228	49.5%	97,044	50.5%	Gregoire 1.0%
ELECTRONIC VOTING MACHINES	50,400	54.5%	42,145	45.5%	Rossi 9.0%
SPECIAL CONDITIONS					
POLLING PLACES WITH ELECTION DAY PROBLEMS	21,847	56.1%	17,100	43.9%	Rossi 13.2%
PRECINCTS WITH CPU CHANGES	4,237	58.1%	3,050	41.9%	Rossi 16.2%
MALFUNCTIONING DREs	155	60.5%	101	39.5%	Rossi 21.0%

Source for the data: Paul Lehto, Snohomish County Board of Elections.

A request by Lehto to conduct a complete audit, one that would include computer forensics of the Sequoia machines used in Snohomish County was met by a strong response from Sequoia. "Let me reiterate that under no circumstances, without Sequoia's approval, will you be allowed to run any kind of testing on the machines," said Bob Terwilliger, the Snohomish County auditor. Sequoia's contract with the county prohibits outside examination of Sequoia's electronic voting system.

On April 7, 2005, Lehto and Wells filed a lawsuit in King County Superior Court against Sequoia Voting Systems, Inc., and Snohomish County, Washington.

Their suit states, "[We] object to the provision of the contract [that attempts] to shield from public view and verification the means by which votes are recorded, counted, tabulated and reported on the grounds that they contain 'trade secret,' 'confidential,' or 'proprietary' materials. . . . Access to Sequoia Voting Systems, Inc. information is essential to insure the transparency and verifiability of elections." And they argue that the contract that prohibits outside examination of Sequoia equipment violates article I, section 1 of the Washington Constitution that states "all political power is inherent in the people."

DISCREPANCIES IN GEORGIA, AN E-VOTING STATE, IN 2002

Shortly after the 2000 election, Georgia's Democratic secretary of state Cathy Cox announced that her state would adopt a single statewide system for the 2002 midterm election, which it subsequently did—choosing a Diebold DRE machine, and thus putting the state in the vanguard of electronic voting.[136] Noting that the Diebold machine violated Georgia law, which requires that "any election system purchased and used by the state of Georgia 'shall be required to have an independent audit trail for each vote cast,'" Denis Wright, a founder of Count the Vote, tried to learn the basis on which the Diebold standard was chosen. He found out, however, that "the bids, and the deliberations and decisions of the committee in charge of recommendations, were exempted from Georgia's Open Records laws."[137] He also discovered that Diebold's chief lobbyist in Georgia was Lewis Massey, former Democratic secretary of state—and the former boss of Cathy Cox.

The 2002 federal election in Georgia had discrepancies between the polls and the official count similar to those seen in the 2004 presidential election. In the 2002 race for U.S. Senate, incumbent Democrat Max Cleland, a Vietnam vet and a triple amputee, was leading Saxby Chambliss 49% to 44% in an *Atlanta Journal-Constitution* opinion poll. Yet four days later, Cleland lost to Chambliss, a conservative U.S. congressman from rural Georgia,

46% to 53%—a 12-percentage-point discrepancy between the opinion poll and the official count.

The discrepancy in the 2002 race for Georgia governor was more extreme, with Republican Sonny Perdue beating incumbent Democrat Roy Barnes by a margin that had a 16-percentage-point discrepancy between the *Atlanta Journal-Constitution* poll and the official count.

Computer technician Rob Behler believes that the election "could have been manipulated" through electronic voting fraud. Behler spent the summer of 2002 in a warehouse helping prepare thousands of Diebold DRE machines for the November election. He told the *New York Times* that the Diebold hardware and software exhibited constant problems. While he was working on the machines, he said that Diebold sent three secret computer "patches" that were installed to update the DRE voting machines. And he said he heard of a fourth patch. Diebold and the State of Georgia say there was only one patch, which, according to Diebold, was installed "prior to the election but not last minute." Georgia elections officials concede that the one patch that they admit to having installed was only partially examined by the private company that certifies voting machines for the manufacturers.[138]

Other 2002 races also merit a close look. In 2001, the Republicans lost control of the Senate when Jim Jeffords left the party because, as he put it, Republicans no longer "stood for moderation, tolerance, fiscal responsibility."[139] Be that as it may, the G.O.P. bucked historical patterns of off-year elections, when the President's party typically loses seats. Republicans regained control of the U.S. Senate with victories in four of the five most competitive races, with only Tim Johnson in South Dakota surviving. As indicated in table 3.3, in each of these races the Democratic candidate had an edge in the pre-election telephone polls.[140] And, as we will show in Chapter 6, in all likelihood these poll averages overstate actual Republican support.

TABLE 3.3: FIVE BIG REPUBLICAN SURPRISE WINS IN 2002

RACE	DEM. LOSER	REPUB. WINNER	FINAL TELEPHONE POLLS/ CONDUCTED BY:	POLL MEAN	SWING
COLORADO SENATE	Strickland 46%	Allard (i) 51%	Zogby/MSNBC 49-44; USA/CNN/Gallup 45-47; *Denver Post* 42-41; *Rocky Mountain News* 42-38	Dem 2	Rep 7
GEORGIA SENATE	Cleland (i) 46%	Chambliss 53%	Zogby/MSNBC 46-44; *Atlanta Journal Constitution* 49-44	Dem 3	Rep 10
MINNESOTA SENATE	Mondale (i) 47%	Coleman 50%	Zogby/MSNBC 49-44; *Mason Dixon-St. Paul Pioneer* 41-47; *Minnea- polis Star-Tribune* 46-41	Dem 1	Rep 4
NEW HAMPSHIRE SENATE	Shaheen 47%	Sununu 51%	Amer. Research Group 44-48; Univ. New Hampshire/CNN/*USA Today* 45-46; Research 2000/*Concord Monitor* 47-46; Franklin Pierce College/ WNDS-TV 45-40; Becker Institute 48-42	Dem 1	Rep 5
GEORGIA GOVERNOR	Perdue (i) 46%	Barnes 51%	*Atlanta Journal Constitution* 51-40	Dem 11	Rep 16

Source for the data: National Council on Public Polls: 2002 Poll Performance.
Incumbents are denoted with (i). Walter Mondale replaced incumbent Senator Paul Wellstone, who was killed in a plane crash days before the election.

Unfortunately, for the 2002 general election we must rely on telephone-based opinion polls rather than exit polls. We don't have exit-poll data from 2002, reportedly because the computers of Voter News Service (VNS), the predecessor of NEP, malfunctioned on Election Day.

A CALL FOR ACTION

Pollster John Zogby, who has seen his opinion polls diverge from the official counts in the last two federal elections, is concerned about the nation's growing reliance on electronic voting systems. "We're ploughing into a brave new world here, where there are so many variables, aside from out-and-out corruption, that can change elections, especially in situations where the races are close," he says. "We have machines that break down, or are tampered with, or are simply misunderstood. It's a cause for great concern."[141]

Stanford University computer scientist Dill is more blunt. "If you look at the consequences for democracy, it's terrifying," says Dill. "If we had a way to make [computerized voting] safe, believe me, we would. There's no way to run a reliable election without a verifiable paper trial—that's what these machines don't have."[142]

Similar concerns were voiced by Jimmy Carter and James Baker, who cochaired the Commission on Federal Election Reform, which released its report in September 2005. In their introduction to the report, Carter and Baker write, "We propose ways to give confidence to voters using electronic voting machines that their votes will be counted accurately. We call for an auditable backup on paper at this time."

The report states: "Congress should pass a law requiring that all voting machines be equipped with a voter-verifiable paper audit trail.... This is especially important for direct recording electronic (DRE) machines for four reasons: (a) to increase citizens' confidence that their vote will be counted accurately, (b) to allow for a recount, (c) to provide a backup in cases of loss of votes due to computer malfunction, and (d) to test—through a random selection of machines—whether the paper result is the same as the electronic result."

Given the documented problems associated with DREs and their susceptibility to fraud, it is inexplicable that the Bush administration and Congress have not insisted that the electronic voting industry be tightly regulated. Testifying before HAVA's U.S. Election Assistance Commission on July 20, 2004, Johns Hopkins computer security specialist Rubin scolded policy makers:

> I do not know of a single computer security expert who would testify that these machines are secure.... At first I was puzzled by the lack of attention to the security critiques of DREs. Today I am outraged. At this point the failures of current DREs have been documented in four major studies by leading computer security experts.... Yet computer security experts, myself included, find ourselves routinely referred to as Luddites and conspiracy theorists.... Given the gravity of the security failings the computer security community has documented in current DRE systems, it is irresponsible to move forward without addressing them.[143]

CHAPTER 4

Biased Polls or Biased Count?

Given the myriad problems associated with electronic voting technology, the current national trend toward relying on electronic voting systems to record our votes inspires little faith in the official count. The vulnerability of voting systems is compounded by the documented examples of illegal or quasi-legal efforts to suppress votes by partisan election officials in key states, as we've seen in Ohio and Florida. It would seem that a well-conducted exit poll that confirmed the official count would be about the only reason we would have to believe the results of election systems that used electronic voting and other unverified machine counts. Considering the vulnerabilities of U.S. voting technologies to hacking and the widespread reports of voting problems, the discrepancy that occurred between the exit polls and the official count on Election Day 2004 should have raised a Chinese May Day of red flags.

CRIES OF FOUL PLAY

In the weeks after the election—and before the pollsters released their official report on the discrepancy—a variety of explanations were offered for why the official count deviated so significantly from the exit polls.

At first the only ones screaming foul within the mainstream

media were Bush supporters. "Exit polls are almost never wrong," wrote Republican pollster Dick Morris in the November 4 issue of *The Hill.* "So reliable are the surveys that actually tap voters as they leave the polling places that they are used as guides to the relative honesty of elections in Third World countries. . . . To screw up one exit poll is unheard of. To miss six of them is incredible. It boggles the imagination how pollsters could be that incompetent and invites speculation that more than honest error was at play here." Because he didn't believe the exit polls could be wrong, Morris saw a conspiracy: the Kerry-Edwards campaign had fixed the exit polls in order for Kerry to be declared the winner by the networks and thereby discouraging potential Bush voters in the West.

Like Morris, Michael Barone, a senior writer at *U.S. News & World Report,* also speculated that the Democrats had fixed the exit polls so that the networks would declare Kerry the victor.[144]

> My own suspicion is that some Democrats—at the command level, or somewhere below—had an election-day project of slamming the results. . . . If somebody had slipped some Democratic operative the list of exit poll sites—40 to 50 sites in each critical state—he or she could have slipped several hundred operatives into the polling places to take the exit poll ballots and vote for Kerry. The results would have shown Kerry much farther ahead than he actually was and, broadcast through drudgereport.com and other sources, could have heartened Kerry supporters during the afternoon and disheartened Bush supporters.

We asked Warren Mitofsky, one of the two lead NEP pollsters, whether there might be any merit to these suspicions. Mitofsky said that over several months he investigated both his own organization and talked to many local and national Democratic officials. Neither he nor his Democratic contacts could find evidence of any such activity. Besides, why would Democrats want to do this? No network was about to call any contested state early. Even if they were to, there's no evidence that early calls deter turnout. And even if calls did deter turnout, why wouldn't those voters whose candidate was projected the winner be equally likely to ask, "Why bother voting?"

Regardless of the merits of their theories, Morris and Barone understood that the exit-poll discrepancy indicated that something was amiss. Others looked for more mundane reasons for the discrepancy. To the degree an exit-poll problem was reported in the press, it was nearly always attributed to "early exit polls." For example, *The Nation*'s David Corn wrote:

> Clear away the rhetoric, and what's mainly left are the odd early exit polls (which did show Kerry's lead in Ohio and Florida declining as Election Day went on and which ended up with the current national Bush-Kerry spread) . . .[145]

But Kerry's lead in the exit polls did not decline as the day went on. The discrepancy prevailed throughout the day. And the exit polls never came close to matching the count.

So why was such an explanation so easily accepted and widely disseminated? The source for this misinformation appears to be pollster Joe Lenski, the cofounder of Edison Media Research, who partnered with Mitofsky to conduct the 2004 exit polls. The day after the election, he spoke with the *New York Times*.[146] The paper of record reported:

> [Lenski said] that it was possible that more Democrats and more women were voting earlier, perhaps skewing the data in the afternoon. But, he said, by the end of the night the system's polling data basically tracked with the actual results. "Sophisticated users of this data know the limitations of partial survey results," he said.

Apparently Lenski felt he had to come up with a reason for the exit-poll discrepancy and this was the best he could do. But the facts are these. Kerry's lead in the polls did not decline as the day went on, as Lenski and his partner in polling, Warren Mitofsky, would acknowledge eleven weeks later when they released their report on the exit-poll discrepancy. The system's polling data never tracked with the official results until the polls closed and the pollsters "corrected" their exit-poll data to conform to the official count. Had the system worked as intended, NEP would have posted these adjusted numbers rather than the actual exit-poll results, effectively erasing without a trace the exit-poll discrepancy.

Corn's article, which was widely reprinted, including on CBSNews.com, was typical of the misleading reporting about the exit-poll discrepancy. *U.S. News & World Report*'s Barone, after abandoning the Morris conspiracy thesis, also turns to the time-of-day bias:

> Love is stronger than hate. That is the lesson of the 2004 election results. Millions of Democrats and leftists have been seething with hatred for George W. Bush for years, and many of them lined up before the polls opened to cast their votes against him—one reason, apparently, that the exit-poll results turned out to favor Democrats more than did the actual results. But Republicans full of love, or at least affection, for George W. Bush turned out steadily later in the day.[147]

Like Corn's analysis, Barone's tribute to the president, however touching, is wrong. It too relies on the fallacious Early Exit-Poll Theory.

For Barone, it would seem, exit polls are only reliable elsewhere, like Venezuela. In August 2004, after the failure of the attempt to recall Venezuelan president Hugo Chavez, Barone wrote an impassioned piece about how the exit polls, which Chavez's opponents conducted, were right and the official count, observed by numerous election monitors, was wrong:

> It's something of a scandal that American news media have been taking the official vote count in Venezuela at face value. There is very good reason to believe that the exit poll had the result right, and that Chavez's election officials— and [Jimmy] Carter and the American media—got it wrong. . . . Independent exit polls are one of the guarantors of democracy in countries emerging from or under authoritarian rule.[148]

Other explanations for the discrepancy were floated. The *Washington Post* reported that pollsters may have included too many women, too few Westerners, not enough Republicans, and so on. Prominent Republicans appeared on television to offer similar theories. And Martin Plissner, former executive political director of CBS News (and self-described close friend of the pollsters), identified two problems that have been widely used to dismiss the exit-poll results:

> The pollsters who work outside the polling stations often have problems with officials who want to limit access to voters. Unless the interviews have sampled the entire day's voters, the results can be demographically and hence politically skewed. Finally, it is of course a poll, not a set of actual recorded votes like those in the precinct samples collected after the polls close.[149]

Mitofsky and Lenski have been doing exit polls for decades. We have little reason to suspect that they suddenly could not manage relations with local election officials or train their workers to do so.

Moreover, even if pollsters did experience difficulties accessing voters, as Plissner intimates, no suggestion was offered for how access issues might systematically skew exit-poll results so dramatically, since errors caused by lack of access ought to have favored each candidate roughly equally, whereas in this case only Bush was favored.

THE RELUCTANT BUSH RESPONDENT THEORY

Mitofsky and Lenski intimated their explanation for the discrepancy within a week of the election, although it would take them another eleven weeks to release their official report.

On November 9, Gallup Poll senior editor David W. Moore, in an article titled "Conspiracies Galore," reported Mitofsky and Lenski as saying that "Kerry voters apparently were much more willing to participate in the exit poll than were Bush voters." Based on their review of the numbers, "Mitofsky and Lenski dismiss the idea that in fact Kerry won—that the exit polls were right and the vote count wrong," Moore wrote. "Many voters simply refuse to participate in the poll. If the refusers are disproportionately for one candidate or another, then the poll will be biased." And for Moore, that settled it.

But where was the evidence to support—much less prove—the Reluctant Bush Respondent Theory? There wasn't a shred of supporting documentation, not even anecdotally. The only thing that was "apparent" about the Reluctant Bush Respondent Theory was that it was nothing more than conjecture.

On the other hand, arrayed against the Reluctant Bush Respondent Theory lay an impressive assortment of facts, circumstances, and common sense. First, pollsters routinely make adjustments for nonrespondents. Interviewers, as a matter of course, denote the race, sex, and estimated age of any respondents who refuse to participate in the poll. So, if a particular demographic group disproportionately refuses to respond, the other members of that group are overweighted to account for that.

We can imagine that some Bush voters may well have been reluctant to answer pollsters' questions owing to personal biases such as a distaste for the media's coverage of Bush, but we can also imagine why Kerry voters would have been reluctant to participate in the exit polls:

➤Except where poll workers happened to speak their language, non-English speakers were de facto "refusers." Among non-English speakers, Kerry was the heavy favorite.

➤The poor and poorly educated often feel intimidated in the presence of a more educated poll worker, and often consider themselves less entitled to express their opinion freely than those of higher economic status. Again, Kerry was the heavy favorite among the poor.

➤Single parents and low-wage workers are among the most harried members of society. If any group doesn't have time to talk to a pollster, it is these people. And again, Kerry was the heavy favorite among low-income workers and their families.

In fact, what circumstantial evidence there is about differential response rates would suggest the exact opposite of the Bush Reluctant Respondent Theory—higher-income, college-educated voters—a group that is disproportionately Republican—are more likely to speak to pollsters.[150]

And yet, by force of repetition and with dissenting voices being excluded from the conversation, the Reluctant Bush Respondent Theory took hold, in both conservative and liberal camps. No one bothered to investigate whether it could reasonably account for an exit-poll discrepancy that so strongly favored Kerry. Eventually, one blogger built a case that amounted to an elaboration of the Bush Reluctant Respondent Theory, still without explaining why we should consider it credible. Mark Blumenthal, a blogger who calls himself the Mystery Pollster, went from being an unknown opinion pollster who on Election Day was beseeching his colleagues for explanations about exit polls to the expert who appeared on *Nightline* on the eve of the inauguration to discuss the exit-poll discrepancy. Since the election, Blumenthal's much-cited blogging has been influential in quelling public doubts about the discrepancy between the exit-poll results and the official count, effectively providing justification for mainstream reporters not to examine the discrepancy.

On his Web site, www.MysteryPollster.com, Blumenthal laid out three basic points to bolster his argument that the discrepancy between the exit polls and the official count can be easily explained. One, Republicans are more suspicious of news media and less likely to respond to pollsters. Two, given that exit-poll response rates are at around 50%, this discrepancy is minor—not enough to make a big difference. And three, exit-poll discrepancies historically favor Democrats.

The arguments sound plausible, unlike those made in the first week after the election. But just because a theory sounds plausible does not mean it is correct. Let's examine each one closely. However, before we do, we need to better understand how exit polls work and what they can tell us.

HOW EXIT POLLS WORK

When done right, exit polls are able to predict election results with a high degree of reliability. Unlike telephone opinion polls that ask people which candidate they intend to vote for should they vote, exit polls are surveys of voters conducted after they have cast their votes at their polling places. In other words, rather than a prediction of a hypothetical future action, they are a record of a just-completed action.

Around the world, exit polls have been used to verify the integrity of elections. The United States has funded exit polls in Eastern Europe in order to detect fraud. Discrepancies between exit polls and the official vote count have been used to successfully overturn election results in Ukraine, Serbia, and Georgia. Properly conducted, they remove nearly all of the sources of potential polling error. Unlike telephone polls, an exit poll will not be skewed by the fact that some groups of people tend not to be home in the evening or don't own a landline telephone. Exit polls are not confounded by speculation about who will actually show up to vote, or by voters who decide to change their mind in the final moments. Rather, they identify the entire voting population in representative precincts and ask respondents immediately after voting to fill out a confidential questionnaire.

Moreover, exit polls can obtain very large samples—well over 100,000 voter-respondents in the 2004 election, as compared to the typical telephone poll of 1,500 or so respondents—thus providing even greater degrees of reliability.

The difference between conducting a pre-election telephone poll and conducting an Election Day exit poll is like the difference between predicting snowfall in a region several days in advance of a snowstorm and estimating the region's overall snowfall based on observed measures taken at representative sites. In the first case, you're forced to predict future performance on present indicators, to rely on ambiguous historical data, and to make many assumptions about what may happen. In the latter, you simply need to choose your representative sites well. So long as your methodology is good and you read your measures correctly, your results will be highly accurate.

THE ELECTION DAY EXIT POLLS

The national exit polls are conducted in two stages. The exit pollster begins by drawing a representative sampling of precincts that collectively mirror the ethnic and political diversity of the entire state. If these precincts are properly chosen, the sample can be used to produce a profile similar to the state as a whole with roughly the same proportion of blacks and whites and Asians and Hispanics, the same distribution of income, the same age profile and the same proportions of urban, suburban, and rural voters.

On Election Day, one or two interviewers report to each sampled precinct. From the time the polls open in the morning until shortly before the polls close at night, the interviewers select exiting voters at spaced intervals (for example, every third or fifth voter), giving each a confidential written questionnaire to complete. The interval between voters is chosen so that approximately one hundred interviews will be spread evenly over the course of the day. The voting preferences of absentee and early voters are accounted for with pre-election telephone polls.

Participation in the exit polls is voluntary and anonymous. The interviewer gives respondents a questionnaire asking for whom they voted, what issues influenced their vote, basic demographic characteristics (gender, race, age, income, and religion), and political attitudes, such as political philosophy, candidate job approval, views on the war in Iraq, and so on. Respondents fill out the survey privately, then put the completed survey in a clearly marked "ballot box" so they know that their identities cannot be tracked and that their answers will remain confidential. When a voter refuses to participate, the interviewer records the voter's gender, race, and approximate age. This data allows the exit pollsters to do statistical corrections for any bias in gender, race, and age that might result from refusals to participate. For example, if more men refuse to participate than women, each man's response will be given proportionally more weight.

The exit poll for the 2004 federal elections was conducted by the National Election Pool (NEP), a consortium of six news organizations (ABC, AP, CBS, CNN, Fox, and NBC) that pooled resources to conduct a thorough survey of each state and the nation. NEP, in turn, contracted two respected firms, Joe Lenski's Edison Media Research and Warren Mitofsky's Mitofsky International, to conduct the polls.

All told, 114,559 respondents participated in the 50 state exit polls conducted by NEP. Interviewers conducted the 50 state exit polls on November 2, 2004, at 1,480 precincts throughout the nation.

A subsample of the state samples was selected to provide a sample representative of the U.S. electorate for the national exit poll: 11,719 Election Day voters and 500 absentee and early voters were surveyed to provide demographic data on who voted for whom and for what reasons.[151]

The 2004 exit poll was a well-funded effort conducted by the most experienced pollsters in the business, and it represented a broad spectrum of media interests, from the more conservative-leaning Fox Network to the more liberal CBS. In all, the 2004 federal election poll satisfied all the criteria for obtaining a highly accurate and credible result.

THE HISTORY AND HISTORICAL ACCURACY OF EXIT POLLING

Exit polls were first developed in the 1960s, born of a competition among the networks to rapidly project election results, and advances in computer technology that enabled the analysis of large amounts of data.[152] The first exit polls were conducted independently by NBC and CBS in the June 1964 California Republican primary. NEP pollster Warren Mitofsky, then a young survey researcher, was hired by CBS from the U.S. Census Bureau to help with that poll.

From the outset, the polls performed well. Until the 2000 election, the only significant controversy about exit polls occurred in 1980, when exit polls allowed NBC to project a victory for Ronald Reagan three hours before the close of voting on the West Coast. Critics blasted the polls and NBC for calling the election before everyone had voted. In 1984 this was repeated with all three networks declaring victory for Reagan over Walter Mondale hours before the polls closed in the West. During a subsequent House Subcommittee hearing, executives from the three networks agreed not to project races until everyone had voted.

No one, however, debated the accuracy of exit polls. Scholars and practitioners, supporters and critics all agreed. In 1987, *Washington Post* columnist David Broder wrote that exit polls "are the most useful analytic tool developed in my working life."[153] And according to Albert H. Cantril, a leading authority on public opinion research, "As useful as preelection polls may be for measuring the evolving disposition of the electorate, they are not nearly as powerful as exit polls in analyzing the message voters have sent by the ballots they cast."[154] While political scientists George Edwards and Stephen Wayne put it this way: "The problems with exit polls lie in their accuracy (rather than [in their] inaccuracy). They give the press access to predict the outcome before the elections have been concluded."[155] That the press could trust the accuracy of exit polls was held as common wisdom. Exit-poll results were considered money in the bank.

As illustrated in figure 4A, anyone believing in Bush's Election Day prospects on the afternoon of November 2 could have obtained long odds on the Iowa Electronic Market. The chart shows that Bush's odds spiraled downward and reached a low at 4:32 p.m. on Election Day, and soared that night, after the official results had been announced. Financial markets, especially in politically sensitive sectors such as pharmaceuticals, similarly moved sharply down on Election Day. Then, the next morning, once a Bush victory seemed assured, even more sharply up.[156]

FIGURE 4A: GAMBLERS BELIEVED THE EXIT POLL

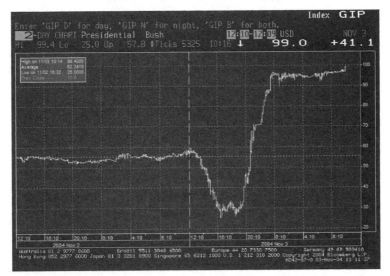

A chart from the Iowa Electronic Market, http://www.biz.uiowa.edu/iem/, where one can wager on election outcomes. The 2004 U.S. Presidential Winner Takes All Market is a real-money futures market where contract payoffs were determined by the popular vote cast in the 2004 U.S. presidential election. The chart illustrates that on Election Day, especially between 4:00 p.m. and 8:00 p.m., anyone believing in the president's re-election prospects could have obtained long odds.

USING EXIT POLLS TO INSURE ELECTION INTEGRITY

Exit-poll results do not always match up with official numbers. Sometimes exit polls are methodologically flawed. For example, in 1990 a Mason-Dixon Polling & Research exit poll predicted Douglas Wilder would win Virginia's gubernatorial election in a landslide when in fact he narrowly defeated his Republican opponent. However, the exit poll involved face-to-face interviews rather than anonymous questionnaires, and pollsters attributed that discrepancy to reluctance on the part of white voters, particularly white Democrats, to admit to interviewers that they voted against Wilder, an African American.

More often than not, however, we attribute discrepancies to corrupted official numbers, particularly when looking at overseas elections. Indeed, a highly transparent exit poll is one of the best means available to help insure an honest election.

When Mexico sought legitimacy as a modernizing democracy in 1994, Carlos Salinas instituted reforms designed to ensure fair elections. A central feature of those reforms was exit polls.[157] In the 2000 election, the Televisa television network, partly in an attempt to ensure against vote fraud, hired Mitofsky to conduct Mexico's exit polls.[158] Perhaps not coincidentally, this was the first time in the Mexican Institutional Revolutionary Party's (PRI) seventy-two-year history that it lost an election.[159]

In established democracies, exit polls play a central role both in ensuring election integrity and in quickly projecting results. In Germany, a nation that knows the dangers of a government that cannot be voted out, the entire process is totally transparent. The minute the polls close, television stations publish exit-poll projections conducted by independent firms, including Mitofsky International. The exit-poll results provide independent data that can be compared to the official tallies. They also provide the nation with an immediate projection of the winner and mitigate the need for a rapid count. Like most democracies, Germany, despite its technological prowess, votes by hand-marked ballots, counted in full public view by volunteer representatives of the political parties. This highly transparent system provides good evidence of just how reliable exit polls are. In three recent years for which data is available, exit polls for both the German national elections and the German elections for the European parliament have averaged results within 0.44 percentage points of the official results. (See Appendix A.)

Such accuracy is not unique to Germany. In the May 2005 British national election, a first-time exit-poll initiative was right on the mark. The poll predicted Labour would have a 37% share of the vote, against the Tories with 33% and Liberal Democrats with 22%.

The official count was Labour 35.3%, Tories 32.4%, and Liberal Democrats 22%.[160]

The United States and international agencies have funded exit polls throughout the former Soviet Union and elsewhere in Eastern Europe as a way to ensure clean elections. When exit polls in March 2000 and again in March 2004 closely matched the official count in Russia, the international community and Russians themselves were reassured that, whatever their feelings for Putin, the electoral system worked; he had gone before the people to approve of his presidency, and they had ratified it.

On the other hand, discrepancies between exit polls and the official vote count have been used to successfully overturn election results in Serbia, the former Soviet Republic of Georgia, and most recently in Ukraine.

In 2003, George Soros's Open Society Georgia Foundation hired Global Strategy Group to conduct an exit poll for Georgia's parliamentary election. The exit poll projected a victory for the main opposition party. When the sitting government announced that its own slate of candidates had won, supporters of the opposition stormed the parliament. With support from both the United States and Russia, they forced President Eduard A. Shevardnadze to resign.[161]

Using exit polls to help expose fraud is so generally accepted that the Bush administration helped pay for them during the 2004 elections in Ukraine. In Ukraine, exit polls in the November 22, 2004, runoff election indicated that Viktor Yushchenko would defeat the incumbent Viktor Yanukovych. Yet in the official count Yanukovych prevailed with a narrow victory.[162]

Following international protests and a national uprising, a new election was called. In testimony before the House International Relations Committee, Senator Dick Lugar (R.-Ind.) called on the State Department to help ensure that the new election would be fair. "I urge the Department to provide the funds necessary, as quickly as possible, to assist the Ukrainian people in their goal of free and fair elections. Specifically funds will be used to support election observers, exit polling, parallel vote tabulations, training of election commissioners, and voter education programs."[163]

In testimony before the same committee, Ambassador John Tefft, deputy assistant secretary for European and Eurasian Affairs, said the Bush administration helped fund exit polls because they could be used to expose fraud. "The United States government has worked consistently throughout 2004 to promote a free, fair campaign and election in Ukraine," he said. "We have tried to 'raise the bar' for fraud by focusing our assistance in ways that would help to expose large-scale fraud (such as parallel vote counts and independent exit polls)."[164] And he pointed to the discrepancy between exit polls and the official vote count to argue that the November 22, 2004, Ukraine election was stolen. He said, "It is impossible to know what the real numbers were, but a large-scale (20,000 respondents), nation-wide anonymous exit poll conducted by a consortium of three highly respected research organizations (partially funded by the United States Government) projected Yushchenko the winner with 53 percent versus 44 percent for Yanukovych." The results of the December 23, 2004, repeat election bore Tefft out, as a victorious Yushchenko, battling the effects of an assassination attempt by poisoning, was elected to office.

THE RELIABILITY OF THE NATIONAL ELECTION POOL (NEP) EXIT POLL

The 2004 exit poll in the United Sates was a generously funded effort by an independent news media consortium conducted by Warren Mitofsky, the man widely credited with its development. Since he designed his first exit poll for CBS in 1967, Mitofsky has directed exit polls in almost three thousand elections, including elections in Japan, Austria, Finland, Italy, Russia, Mexico, and Germany.[165]

Unlike exit polls in start-up democracies in Eastern Europe, exit polling in the United States has had a long continuous history in presidential elections beginning in 1968, and Mitofsky has had a hand in all of them.

Surveys are most difficult the first time they are conducted; each time they are repeated, additional sources of error can be eliminated. For example, workers can be trained to deal with specific obstacles faced in previous elections. As with any repeated complex process, each cycle tends to produce more accurate results. Having done these polls over the course of many election cycles, NEP pollsters have had extensive opportunity to learn from experience.

Political scientist Kenneth Warren is an exit pollster of more than twenty years and the author of *In Defense of Public Opinion Polling*. In documenting the historical accuracy of polling in the United States and of exit polls in particular, Warren concludes, "Exit polling has become very sophisticated and reliable, not only because pollsters have embraced sound survey research techniques, but because they have learned through experience to make valid critical adjustments."[166] Warren says that he has only once had an error greater than 2 percentage points—a 1982 St. Louis primary, in which mass vote fraud was subsequently uncovered.[167]

THE EXIT-POLL DISCREPANCY

On election night 2004, in state after state, the official vote counts showed numbers very different from what the NEP exit polls had predicted. The differences were all in the same direction. In ten of the eleven consensus battleground states,[168] the tallied margin of victory differed from the predicted margin of victory, and in every case, the shift favored Bush.

In table 4.1, the first shaded column shows the difference between the candidates' percentages of the vote as predicted by the exit polls; the next shaded column shows the difference between their tallied percentages of the vote. The rightmost column reveals the "shift," or deviation, between the predicted and the official count.[169]

TABLE 4.1: PREDICTED VS. TALLIED PERCENTAGES IN BATTLEGROUND STATES

	BUSH PRED.	KERRY PRED.	PRED. DIFF.	BUSH TALLIED	KERRY TALLIED	TALLIED DIFF.	TALLIED VS. PRED.
COLORADO	49.9%	48.1%	Bush 1.8	52.0%	46.8%	Bush 5.2	Bush 3.4
FLORIDA	49.8%	49.7%	Bush 0.1	52.1%	47.1%	Bush 5.0	Bush 4.9
IOWA	48.4%	49.7%	Kerry 1.3	50.1%	49.2%	Bush 0.9	Bush 2.2
MICHIGAN	46.5%	51.5%	Kerry 5.0	47.8%	51.2%	Kerry 3.4	Bush 1.6
MINNESOTA	44.5%	53.5%	Kerry 9.0	47.6%	51.1%	Kerry 3.5	Bush 5.5
NEVADA	47.9%	49.2%	Kerry 1.3	50.5%	47.9%	Bush 2.6	Bush 3.9
NEW HAMP.	44.1%	54.9%	Kerry 10.8	49.0%	50.3%	Kerry 1.3	Bush 9.5
NEW MEX.	47.5%	50.1%	Kerry 2.6	50.0%	48.9%	Bush 1.1	Bush 3.7
OHIO	47.9%	52.1%	Kerry 4.2	51.0%	48.5%	Bush 2.5	Bush 6.7
PENN.	45.4%	54.1%	Kerry 8.7	48.6%	50.8%	Kerry 2.2	Bush 6.5
WISCONSIN	48.8%	49.2%	Kerry 0.4	49.4%	49.8%	Kerry 0.4	No diff.

Source for the data: CNN website, November 3, 2004, 12:21 a.m.

Although these exit-poll numbers were available on CNN.com, they were never broadcast on TV (see figure 4B). Moreover, exit-poll data available on the Web site on November 3, 2004, and thereafter showed numbers very different from those released on Election Day (see figure 4C). This is because the survey results the NEP originally collected and presented to its subscribers were subsequently "corrected" to conform to official tallies.

Pollsters justify this adjustment of the exit-poll data to conform to the official count as a natural procedure. "Uncorrected" data were preliminary; however, once the counts come in, the numbers are adjusted to conform to the count. Mitofsky and Lenski have argued that their polls were not designed to verify election results, but rather to provide election-coverage support to subscribers. The exit polls are, they say, one set of data that the networks could use to project winners, to explain voting patterns, to discuss voter demographics, and to explain why people voted as they did.[170] Unlike the examples given above in Eastern Europe and elsewhere, in the U.S. pollsters take the official count as inviolable. They describe exit-poll results that differ dramatically from the official count as "errors," and the adjusting of the exit-poll results to conform with the official count as "correcting." We believe such terminology is counterproductive. We speak of "disparity" rather than "error," and for purposes of determining whether the count is, in fact, a measure of votes cast, in place of "corrected" and "uncorrected," we'll use the terms "adjusted" and "unadjusted," not words that pollsters use, but words that better describe the process.

FIGURE 4B: CNN WEB PAGE WITH UNADJUSTED EXIT-POLL DATA,

12:21 A.M., WEDNESDAY, NOVEMBER 3, 2004

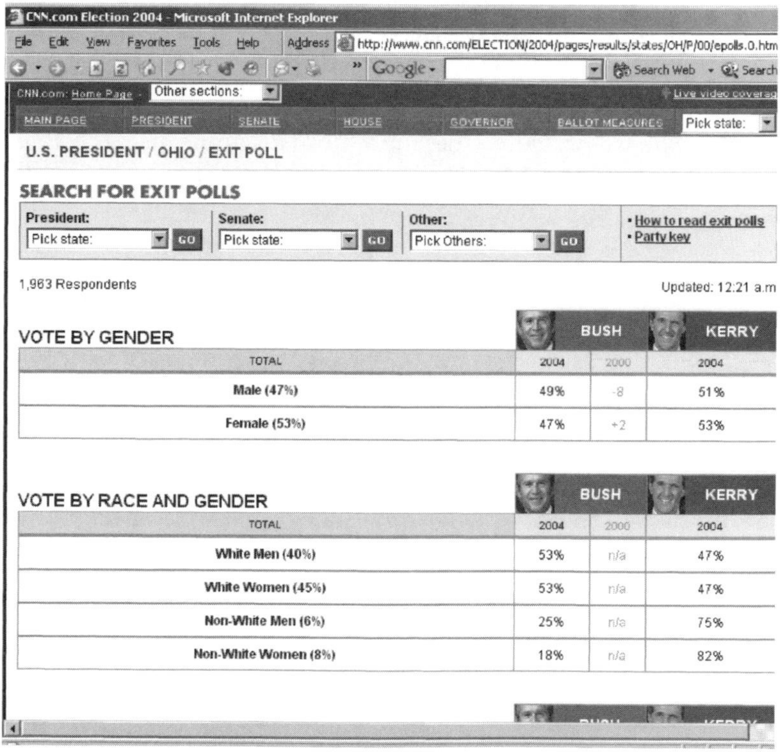

CNN.com Election 2004 - Microsoft Internet Explorer

File   Edit   View   Favorites   Tools   Help   Address http://www.cnn.com/ELECTION/2004/pages/results/states/OH/P/00/epolls.0.htm

Google ▾   Search Web ▾ Search

CNN.com: Home Page   Other sections: Live video coverage

MAIN PAGE   PRESIDENT   SENATE   HOUSE   GOVERNOR   BALLOT MEASURES   Pick state:

U.S. PRESIDENT / OHIO / EXIT POLL

SEARCH FOR EXIT POLLS

| President: | Senate: | Other: | • How to read exit polls |
| Pick state: GO | Pick state: GO | Pick Others: GO | • Party key |

1,983 Respondents   Updated: 12:21 a.m

VOTE BY GENDER		BUSH		KERRY
TOTAL		2004	2000	2004
Male (47%)		49%	-8	51%
Female (53%)		47%	+2	53%

VOTE BY RACE AND GENDER		BUSH		KERRY
TOTAL		2004	2000	2004
White Men (40%)		53%	n/a	47%
White Women (45%)		53%	n/a	47%
Non-White Men (6%)		25%	n/a	75%
Non-White Women (8%)		18%	n/a	82%

Had it not been for leaks from the media and a technical glitch on the CNN site that caused the unadjusted data to be aired, the unadjusted exit-poll data would never have been collected and preserved, and we might never have known about the exit-poll discrepancy at all. These data were not intended for public release. As Slate editor Jack Shafer put it, the six NEP members "signed a blood oath not to divulge it to unauthorized eyes."[171] Early releases of the data were available during the day because the numbers were leaked to bloggers and journalists. And then in the late evening the data became available to election watchers only because a computer problem prevented the NEP from making updates sometime around 8:30 p.m. EST on Election Day, and because one viewer had the awareness and presence of mind to systematically download and preserve the data.[172] The data used by coauthor Steve Freeman to originally document the discrepancy were screen shots (see figures 4B and 4C) collected from CNN's Web site by Jonathon Simon, a former political survey research analyst and voting verification activist who was watching that night from his home in Cambridge, Massachusetts. The data is corroborated and complemented by screen shots saved by the authors.[173]

A STATISTICAL ANOMALY?

A poll is a sample. A well-designed exit poll will closely approximate the underlying reality of how many votes each candidate got within a defined range of certainty. In science, especially in social science, the first analysis that we do when we see what appears to be an unusual pattern is to determine statistical significance, that is, the likelihood that the observed outcome could have occurred by chance.

One can look at the deviation between the count and exit-poll projections in a number of ways. Consider first the battleground states in which the election was fought. In each case, if the polls and

FIGURE 4C: CNN WEB PAGE WITH ADJUSTED EXIT-POLL DATA,

1:32 A.M., WEDNESDAY, NOVEMBER 3, 2004

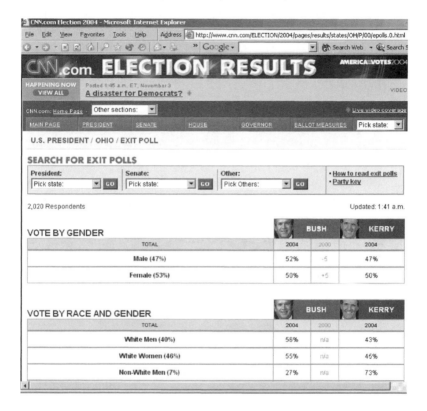

counts were unbiased, there would be an equal likelihood that the count would deviate toward the challenger as toward the incumbent.

In ten of the eleven battleground states there was a shift—that is, the official count differed from the exit-poll results—and in all ten that shift favored Bush. The likelihood that ten out of ten states would deviate toward the incumbent is equivalent to the likelihood that a fair coin tossed ten times will land heads each time. It can happen, but it doesn't happen often (1 out of 1,024 times). If we witness such a streak, we may reasonably suspect the coin might be "fixed," especially if the stakes are high and we are not permitted to inspect the coin. In science, the most common standard for saying that a phenomenon is not the product of chance alone is a likelihood of 1 in 20; a more rigorous standard is 1 in 100; the most rigorous standard typically used in science is 1 in 1,000. On this basis alone, we can reject the hypothesis that the exit-poll discrepancy could have occurred by chance.

THREE CRITICAL BATTLEGROUND STATES

Another way to look at the discrepancy is to focus attention on exactly where the presidency was decided. Conventional wisdom going into the election was that three critical states—Ohio, Pennsylvania, and Florida—would likely determine the winner of the presidential election. Prior to the election, CBS News' David Paul Kuhn reported, "Since Election 2000, Republicans and Democrats have banked their aspirations on an electoral trinity: Florida, Pennsylvania, and Ohio. As the Big Three goes, so goes the nation."[174] The numbers and logic were straightforward. Among the other battleground states, Michigan and Minnesota leaned Democratic, and Colorado and Nevada leaned Republican. Iowa, New Hampshire, and New Mexico don't have many electoral votes. Wisconsin has a long tradition as a liberal state, and only 10 electoral votes compared to 20, 21, and 27 for the big three. Campaign activities were also consistent with this logic. Ohio, Pennsylvania, and Florida were the three states the candidates visited most and in which they spent the most money. Conventional wisdom proved correct. Bush won two of the three and ascended to electoral victory as a result. In each of these states, however, the vote as predicted by exit polls deviated significantly from recorded tallies (table 4.2).

TABLE 4.2: PREDICTED VS. TALLIED PERCENTAGES IN THE THREE
CRITICAL BATTLEGROUND STATES, NOVEMBER 2004 ELECTION

	SAMPLE SIZE	BUSH PRED.	KERRY PRED.	PRED. DIFF.	BUSH TALLIED	KERRY TALLIED	TALLIED DIFF.	TALLIED VS. PRED.
FLORIDA*	2,846	49.8%	49.7%	Bush 0.1*	52.1%	47.1%	Bush 5.0	Bush 4.9
OHIO	1,963	47.9%	52.1%	Kerry 4.2	51.0%	48.5%	Bush 2.5	Bush 6.7
PENN.	1,930	45.4%	54.1%	Kerry 8.7	48.6%	50.8%	Kerry 2.2	Bush 6.5

*Exit poll data released by *Slate* at 7:28 p.m. EST, November 2, 2004, twenty-eight minutes after 95% of the Florida polls closed, showed Kerry leading 51% to 49%.

Source for the data: CNN Web site, November 3, 2004, 12:21 a.m.

A DISCREPANCY OUTSIDE THE MARGIN OF ERROR

Probability calculations depend on three factors: the size of the observed discrepancy, sample size, and sample characteristics. For statistical purposes, the NEP samples are quite large. Two thousand or so respondents is roughly the size of most national polls. (Readers who want to know more about such statistical inference can see Appendix B for an explanation of how small samples can accurately portray large populations.) In the absence of polling bias, each of these states' exit polls should have been accurate to within three percentage points.

It is important to note that pollsters take into account the fact that exit polls are not simple random samples. Polling margins of error are affected by two counterbalancing processes—stratification and clustering. Stratified sampling, that is, choosing representative precincts, can improve sampling efficiency by assuring that all strata, that is, all demographic groups, are appropriately represented.[175]

To avoid prohibitive expense, exit-poll samples are also clustered, which means that individuals from selected precincts are polled, rather than individuals from throughout the entire state. This increases the margin of error because of the possibility that precinct voters share similar characteristics that distinguish them from the rest of the state in ways that past voting behavior would not predict.[176] For example, voters in a precinct that has suffered a major plant closing might be disproportionately more likely to support a change in administrations than voters in otherwise comparable precincts.

FIGURE 4D: LIKELIHOOD OF EXIT-POLL RESULTS FOR KERRY IN OHIO

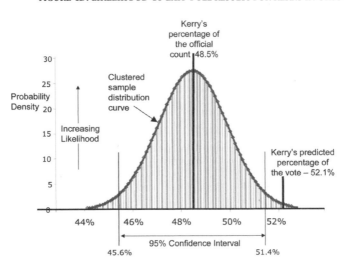

The distribution curve in figure 4D depicts the results from 1,963 randomly selected respondents from 49 randomly selected precincts in Ohio, the clustered sample of exit-poll respondents. The horizontal double arrow below the curve indicates the poll's 95% confidence interval. If this poll were conducted 20 times using this same population, we would expect that 19 times, Kerry would poll between 45.6% and 51.4%. It turns out that the likelihood that Kerry would poll 52.1% from a population in which he receives only 48.5% of the vote falls outside the 95% confidence interval and is less than 1 in 100 (.0073).

Conducting the same analysis for Florida, we find that Kerry's poll prediction of 49.7% of the vote is, as in Ohio, outside the 95% confidence interval. Given a population in which Kerry receives only 47.1% of the vote, the chances that he would poll 49.7% out of 2,846 respondents in an exit poll with no systematic error is less than two in 100 (.0164 percent).

In the third critical battleground state, Pennsylvania, Kerry's poll numbers are also outside the 95% confidence interval. Although he did carry the state, the likelihood that an exit poll would predict that Kerry would get 54.1% when he only managed to win 50.8% of the tallied vote is slightly more than one in one hundred (.0126).

Assuming that these state exit polls had no systematic bias, the likelihood of three such statistical anomalies—the dramatic differences between the official count and the exit-poll projections in Ohio, Florida and Pennsylvania—occurring together and all favoring the incumbent, Bush, is about one in 660,000. These odds are calculated by multiplying the three individual likelihoods: .0073 x .0164 x .0126. It is true that a properly conducted poll may, by chance, produce anomalous results. But even if in Ohio every nth voter in the surveyed precincts repeatedly happened to be a Democrat, there is no reason at all why that should have also been the case in surveyed precincts throughout Florida and Pennsylvania.

Thus, as much as we could say in social science that something is impossible, it was impossible that the discrepancies between predicted and actual vote counts in the critical battleground states of Florida, Pennsylvania and Ohio could have been due to chance or random error.

DO VOTERS' OPINIONS OF THE MEDIA AFFECT EXIT-POLL PARTICIPATION?

So how does one explain the discrepancy between the exit-poll results and the official count? Returning now to Blumenthal's

Reluctant Bush Respondent Theory, he writes that Republicans are less likely to respond to pollsters because consistently and increasingly they view the news media as biased and that perceptions of news media bias are consistently higher among Republicans and rising. He cites a January 2004 study by the Pew Research Center for People and the Press, which found "42% of Republicans believe news coverage of the campaign is biased in favor of Democrats compared to 29% of Democrats [who] believe news coverage is biased in favor of the Republicans. The overall percentage that believes the news is free of any form of bias has declined dramatically over the last seventeen years: 67% in 1987, 53% in 1996, 48% in 2000 and 38% this year."[177]

Blumenthal writes that NEP interviewers use the following pitch when asking voters to participate in the exit poll:

> I am taking a public opinion survey only after people have voted and it is completely anonymous. It is being conducted for ABC, the Associated Press, CBS, CNN, Fox and NBC, not for any political candidate or party.

He then asks his readers to consider that the NEP exit-poll interviewers wore an identifying badge with this brightly colored logo:[178]

Were Bush voters really less likely to talk to pollsters? If Blumenthal is correct that conservative voters would have been put off by a badge that included the Fox News logo among others, then we should see evidence in past elections and a trend in recent elections. All facts, however, point in the opposite direction. Although more Republicans than Democrats believe that news coverage is biased against their party, the gap is narrowing. Moreover, Blumenthal surely knew this, since it's right there in the title of the Pew study he quotes from, "Perceptions of Partisan Bias Seen as Growing—Especially by Democrats." As the report says:

> The growing sense of biased campaign coverage crosses party lines, but is most notable among Democrats. Four years ago, most Democrats (53%) said there was no bias in news coverage of the campaign; today just 40% of Democrats take this position, and those who do see bias overwhelmingly see it as favoring the other party. Republicans, too, are less apt to see campaign coverage as balanced today (33% say there is no bias, down from 41% four years ago).[179]

So, if conservatives were put off, we should have seen a considerably greater discrepancy as a result of media-wary Republicans avoiding the pollsters in past years. But there was only a marginal effect in the 1994, 1996, 1998, and 2000 elections (exit-poll results from 2002 were never made public). Prominent exit pollster Daniel Merkle, who has worked with both NEP and its predecessor, Voter News Service (VNS), told us that in 2000 VNS, "did a randomized experiment in some states specifically testing the logos on the questionnaires. This study found no effect of the logos."[180]

55% VS. 45%: NOT A BIG DIFFERENCE?

Blumenthal not only asserts that exit-poll response rates have been declining, but suggests that this decline goes a long way to explaining the 2004 exit-poll discrepancy. He writes on mysterypollster.com:

Given the overall 50% [response] rate, differences in response between Bush and Kerry supporters would not need to be very big to skew the results. Let me explain: I put the vote-by-party results into a spreadsheet for Ohio. I can replicate the skew in Ohio (one that makes Kerry's vote 3 percentage-points higher than the count and Bush 3 percentage-points lower) by assuming a 45% response rate for Republicans and a 55% response rate for Democrats. Not a big difference.

Mitofsky joins Blumenthal in dismissing the discrepancy as due to "low response rates." But response rates are neither low nor declining. Since 1994, when VNS began conducting the exit-poll interviews, the response rate has consistently been in the low to mid 50s. Survey response rates in excess of 50% are generally considered very high. Telephone survey rates are now well under 25%, and even in these polls, studies comparing attitudes of respondents with nonrespondents who are subsequently reached through repeated efforts and requests, find minimal nonresponse bias. That is, the attitudes of respondents and nonrespondents are not significantly different.[181]

Unlike most surveys, exit polls can be readily tested for nonresponse bias—that is, whether one group of voters responds less than another. In every election, exit pollsters can compare precinct polling data with the official count in the precinct. If the count is accurate, a parity between the official results and the precinct survey results indicates that respondents are representative of the electorate. After studying such results, political scientists Samuel L. Popkin and Michael P. MacDonald conclude that "exit-poll samples are representative of voters" and that there is minimal nonresponse bias.[182]

The most systematic studies of nonresponse bias in exit polls have been conducted by Mitofsky collaborators Dan Merkle, mentioned above, and Murray Edelman. Comparing response rates based on age, race, and gender in a wide variety of elections, they find minimal differences between groups—a slight propensity for women to respond at higher rates and for the elderly to respond at lower rates. The NEP makes adjustments for both tendencies.[183]

Merkle and Edelman conducted additional tests of nonresponse bias. In particular, they examined the relationship between survey error (all possible forms of error including response bias) and response rates, using data from presidential, congressional, and local elections. They found that neither response rates (high or low) nor miss rates correlate with survey error. All of which suggests that, first, even if response rates had dropped—which they hadn't—it would be unreasonable to attribute an unprecedented exit-poll discrepancy to a small drop in response rates.[184]

Earlier we noted some evidence suggesting that the poor and poorly educated participate in polls at lower rates, but, if anything, this would indicate lower response rates among Democrats. With respect to education, Bush did better among those who never finished college while Kerry did better among both the least and the most educated voters, so neither candidate has a definitive edge. However, Bush's percentage of the vote in the exit polls goes up steadily with income.

The fact is that, in the absence of evidence supporting differential response rates, the 10 percentage-point differential between Republican and Democratic exit-poll response rates that Blumenthal proposes is huge. It's as though you flipped a coin 2,000 times, and rather than 1,000 heads and 1,000 tails, you got 1,100 heads and 900 tails, the likelihood of which is about 1 in 250,000.

DO EXIT POLLS FAVOR DEMOCRATS?

Mitofsky, Blumenthal, and the Gallup's David Moore minimize the importance of the exit-poll discrepancy because of a phenomenon the pollsters refer to as "Democratic overstatement." And it is true that Democrats typically do, on average, 1 or 2 percentage-points better in exit polls than they do in the official count. But let's look a little more closely at how exit polls are affected by vote spoilage.

The most complete set of figures on vote spoilage came from the Harvard University Civil Rights Project's study of the 2000 election.[185] The Civil Rights Project documented that the residual ballot rate, the percentage of ballots cast but not counted, tells a story of race and class. The greater the percentage of poor, African American voters, the higher the percentage of spoiled ballots. The project found that nationwide in the 2000 election, 2% of votes for president (approximately 2 million votes) were "lost" due to a combination of poor equipment and voter error, and that these lost ballots were overwhelmingly concentrated in the poorest—and largely Democratic—counties where 12% or more of the ballots cast could be "spoiled."

A similar study by the House Committee on Government Reform found that voters in low-income, high-minority congressional districts throughout the country were three times more likely to have their votes for president discarded than those in more affluent, low-minority districts.[186]

Given that low-income, high-minority constituents, especially African Americans, vote overwhelmingly Democratic, different spoilage rates suggest that exit polls do gauge voter intent accurately. Exit polls accurately represent the way voters cast their ballots, including both those that are eventually counted and those that may be disallowed from the official count as "spoiled" or "lost."

The 1 to 2 percentage-point discrepancy in exit polls that is attributable to this institutional bias against poor voters and African Americans goes a long way toward explaining what the pollsters wrongly call Democratic overstatement. In their determination to treat official numbers as inviolate, pollsters, like politicians, academics, political scientists, and the media, have systemically failed to put two and two together by not connecting the spoilage and lost-vote rate among the poorest counties with the 1 to 2–percentage-point discrepancy that typically separates the exit-poll results and the official count.

The 1 to 2 percentage-point discrepancy in exit polls that is attributable to Democratic undercount—what the pollsters call "Democratic overstatement"—does not, however, explain the larger discrepancy between the exit polls and the official count of the 2004 U.S. presidential election.

EXIT-POLL "FAILURES"

In explaining the exit-poll discrepancy, Blumenthal and the NEP pollsters also point to the fact that Democratic candidates have at times done much better in the exit polls than in the official count. In particular, they point to a wide exit-poll discrepancy in the 1992 presidential race between Bill Clinton and George H. W. Bush as evidence that exit polls are not reliable.

Richard Morin, the *Washington Post* columnist and director of polling, also expressed doubt that an exit-poll victory translates into a victory at the polls. Pointing to the 1988 election, he wrote:

> I learned early in my *Washington Post* career that exit polls were useful but imperfect mirrors of the electorate. On election night in 1988, we relied on the ABC News exit poll to characterize how demographic subgroups and political constituencies had voted. One problem: The exit poll found the race to be a dead heat, even though Democrat Michael Dukakis lost the popular vote by seven percentage points to Dubya's father.[187]

In his 1992 re-election bid, the official count awarded Bush Senior 5.3 million more votes than exit polls indicated. As in 2004, the discrepancy—a 5-percentage-point difference—was far beyond the polling margin of error. That is to say, Bush Sr. did 5 percentage-points better relative to Bill Clinton in the official count than voter respondents indicated he had done.[188]

In addition to the 1988, 1992, and 2004 presidential elections and the 2000 vote for president in Florida, the only other significant unexplained U.S. exit-poll discrepancies on record are the Republican presidential primaries in New Hampshire in 1992 and Arizona in 1996.[189] In each of these six incidents of an exit-poll discrepancy, the official count benefited the mainstream Republican candidate, whether against Democrats in the general election or a thorny insurgent (Pat Buchanan) in a Republican primary. And remarkably, in five out of the six elections, the candidate whose official numbers far exceeded exit-poll results was named George Bush.

Moreover, in each case, the George Bush in question was running for election with the benefit of incumbency. In 1988, Bush Sr. was the incumbent Vice President. In 1992, he was, of course, President, as was Bush Jr. in 2004. In the single instance when a Bush was not an incumbent—in 2000—the exit-poll discrepancy occurred in Florida, where brother Jeb Bush was governor.

CHAPTER 5

The Inauguration Eve Exit-Poll Report

Eleven weeks after the election, on January 19, 2005, the eve of Bush's inauguration, Mitofsky and Lenski released their promised explanation of why the exit polls diverged so greatly from the official count in 2004. However, their report, "Evaluation of Edison/Mitofsky Election System 2004" (hereafter referred to as "Edison/Mitofsky"), failed to provide satisfactory answers.[190]

Immediately, the report generated headlines such as MSNBC's "Exit Polls Prove That Bush Won." But how could the MSNBC reporter and others reach this conclusion so easily? Edison/Mitofsky was a detailed 77-page report that reporters had only a few hours to review before writing their stories—stories published within hours on the Web or the next day in print—that became the public record of what the report said. There was no way that reporters who were not trained in statistics and polling had time to both read and understand the report on its own merits. The "news" in their stories essentially parroted the information contained in the "Executive Summary" section of Edison/Mitofsky.

As for the headline, "Exit Polls Prove That Bush Won," the report does not even attempt any such proof. Rather, it restates the thesis that the pollsters had previously intimated—that the discrepancy was "most likely due to Kerry voters participating in the exit polls at a higher rate than Bush voters."

How do the pollsters back up this claim?

Edison/Mitofsky begins its analysis by making one important point. The discrepancy between the exit polls and the official tallies was not due to "sampling error." In other words, the 1,480 precincts that the pollsters chose to sample were representative of the nation, and therefore the discrepancy between the exit polls and the official count was not the result of the pollsters' having chosen unrepresentative precincts to sample. They write:

> The inaccuracies in the exit-poll estimates were not due to the sample selection of the polling locations at which the exit polls were conducted. We have not discovered any systematic problem in how the exit-poll data were collected and processed.

The pollsters explain that the sample of the 1,480 exit-poll precincts "produced very good estimates of the final vote count when the final [official] vote returns, rather than exit-poll results, were used to make the estimates." In other words, the official count at the 1,480 exit-poll precincts was representative of the official vote count nationally. In saying this, Lenski and Mitofsky validate a key piece of their methodology—the representativeness of their samples.

If, as the pollsters claim, the fault doesn't lie with their sample, the range of possibilities for error is narrowed. They write, "The additional error in the exit polls must be caused by errors that occurred within the precincts from sampling voters." They call such errors "within precinct error" (WPE), that is, the difference between official precinct tallies and the exit-poll samples from those same precincts. We prefer the more neutral term "within precinct disparity" (WPD), since thus far no proof has been put forward to indicate that the cause of the disparity was polling error.

THE MISSING INGREDIENT FOR A THOROUGH INVESTIGATION

The pollsters don't provide the precinct-level data to back up their assertion that the discrepancy was not due to sampling error, so we are taking them at their word when they say this. We don't have access to the necessary data to independently verify that this was the case.

The data needed to properly investigate the integrity of the election has never been made available. Rather, it remains the property of the NEP consortium that commissioned the exit polls—five major broadcasters, ABC, CBS, CNN, Fox, and NBC, and one news service, the Associated Press.

When they issued their report, Mitofsky and Lenski surprised the polling community by simultaneously announcing the release of the exit-poll data. (They previously had said the data would not be available until spring.)

But the data they released was the individual-respondent data, i.e., data that allows researchers to correlate voter characteristics (race, age, sex, etc.) with voting preferences. It was not data that identified specific exit-poll results with the specific precinct where the exit poll was conducted. And it is this precinct-level data that we would want in order to analyze the election results for the possibility of election fraud. For example, if we had the data by precinct, it would be possible to directly compare the size of the exit-poll discrepancy in that precinct with type of voting technology, the levels of precinct partisanship, and the political party that controlled the voting jurisdiction. Such data would also allow us to directly investigate precincts where the discrepancy was suspiciously large.

Not only did the pollsters fail to release the important data, but they claimed that because they released individual respondent data, they could not release precinct and county data, because doing so could compromise respondent confidentiality. That is, in some extreme circumstances we conceivably might be able to figure out how an individual in that precinct voted, which would mean that that individual's votes would no longer be confidential. For example if there was only one black voter in a precinct and he or she participated in the exit poll, we would know how he or she voted if the precinct-level data was made public.

NEP Director Warren Mitofsky, who chooses his words carefully, shies away from saying that there was no fraud in the 2004 election, asserting only that the exit polls can't prove that there was fraud. And that is the regrettable truth, as long as important exit-poll data are hidden safely away in the files of NEP.

Again, if we had precinct-level summary data, we could investigate precincts with high Within-Precinct Disparities (WPDs). And some of these precincts, location unknown, have impossibly high WPDs. If we knew the location of the precinct, we could look at both that precinct and the county it was in. Since elections are administered on the county level, having this information would allow us to statistically examine effects of voting technology and partisan control.

But we don't have that information. We must demand its release, and meanwhile make the best use we can of the information that was released and what it can tell us, which is quite a lot.

On average, in the 1,460 sampled precincts across the country for which NEP was able to obtain official vote results (in twenty precincts they were unable to do so),[191] Bush did 6.5 percentage-points better in the official vote count, relative to Kerry, than exit-poll samples from those same precincts indicate that he did.

Thus, if what Edison/Mitofsky says about the source of error within precincts is true, there can be only two possible explanations for the Within Precinct Disparity (WPD).

1) More Kerry voters than Bush voters—by a large margin—agreed to fill out the questionnaires offered by interviewers; or

2) The official vote count was somehow corrupted.

BLAMING THE INTERVIEWERS

The Conyers Report documented many egregious examples of vote manipulation. Computer-security experts have shown that electronic voting machines are highly susceptible to fraud. Yet Edison/Mitofsky dismisses out of hand the possibility of a corrupted count and takes as an absolute certainty that the count was correct.

Edison/Mitofsky then proceeds to presume that "Kerry voters were more likely to participate in the exit polls than Bush voters."

For Mitofsky and Lenski, the reason for the error in the exit polls is to be found in the people they hired to do the Election Day exit-poll interviews. To bolster their argument, the pollsters devote a great deal of their report to analyzing interviewer characteristics—that is, they sort and evaluate the poll results by examining the characteristics of the poll-takers: completion rates, age, gender, level of education, date of hire, amount of training, and interactions between poll-takers. They find that the WPD is higher:

➤when interviewers are more than 25 feet away from the polling place.

➤among younger interviewers.

➤among interviewers with advanced degrees.

➤among interviewers in large precincts.

Without ruling out the possibility of interviewer effects—indeed, we cannot, since we do not have the data the report uses—we begin by observing that the data the report presents to bolster their argument indicate that WPDs were very high for all interviewer groups, even those with the lowest discrepancies.

For example, Edison/Mitofsky emphasizes that the discrepancy increases with interviewer distance from the polling place (table

5.1). And although it is true that WPD appears higher when the interviewer was farther away, even in precincts where the interviewer was inside the polling place there was a 5.3 percentage-point deviation between how people said they voted and the way those votes were officially recorded.

TABLE 5.1: "EDISON/MITOFSKY" INTERVIEWER EFFECTS:

DISTANCE FROM THE POLLING PLACE

INTERVIEWER AGE	MEAN WPD	MEDIAN WPD	N
INSIDE	5.3	4.2	416
RIGHT OUTSIDE THE ENTRANCE	6.4	7.5	207
10 TO 25 FEET AWAY	5.6	4.2	220
25 TO 50 FEET AWAY	7.6	7.3	150
50 TO 100 FEET AWAY	9.6	10.3	97
MORE THAN 100 FEET AWAY	12.3	12.1	37

Source for the data: Edison/Mitofsky, page 37.

The report also makes much of "interviewer age" in its analysis (table 5.2). Again, even in the "best performing" age groups, 35–44 and over 65, there was a 4-percentage-point deviation between the exit polls and the official count.

TABLE 5.2: "EDISON/MITOFSKY" INTERVIEWER EFFECTS: INTERVIEWER AGE

INTERVIEWER AGE	MEAN WPD	MEDIAN WPD	N
24 AND UNDER	7.4	8.6	430
25–34	8.2	7.2	182
35–44	4.0	3.9	167
45–54	6.3	4.7	191
55–64	7.0	5.8	143
65 AND OVER	3.7	5.4	68

Source for the data: Edison/Mitofsky, page 43.

Another variable that Edison/Mitofsky emphasizes is "interviewer education." In particular, interviewers with postgraduate degrees "had a significantly greater overstatement of Kerry than any other group" (table 5.3). But again, all groups show *at least* a 4-per-centage-point deviation between the poll results and the official count. So even if Edison/Mitofsky is right in attributing polling error to interviewer effects, it's unlikely that such error could explain the bulk of the discrepancy.

But what evidence is there that WPD is, in fact, attributable to any of these factors at all?

A lower WPD is more accurate only if the count is, in fact, correct. But those with the least education had the highest absolute error, meaning that their results showed both big Kerry skews and Bush skews (table 5.3, column 3).[192] Although their mean WPD was relatively low, the higher absolute number indicates that they were the least precise of any age group, and therefore, quite likely, the least accurate.

Interviewers with advanced degrees had the lowest rates of missed voters and the lowest rates of voters who refused to participate (table 5.3, columns 4–6), suggesting that their results are the most accurate—in other words, because the interviewers with the most education were the most successful in getting voters to complete the exit-poll questionnaires, we can maintain that their results are in fact the most accurate representation of the actual vote.

TABLE 5.3: "EDISON/MITOFSKY" INTERVIEWER EFFECTS: INTERVIEWER EDUCATION

INTERVIEWER EDUCATION	MEAN WPD	MEAN ABS (WPD)	COMPLE-TION RATE	REFUSAL RATE	MISS RATE
HIGH SCHOOL OR LESS	3.9	14.7	52%	36%	11%
ONE TO THREE YEARS OF COLLEGE	7.3	14.0	53%	37%	11%
FOUR YEAR COLLEGE DEGREE	6.3	12.8	55%	34%	11%
SOME GRADUATE CREDITS	5.4	11.9	57%	34%	10%
ADVANCED DEGREE SUCH AS MA, MBA OR PHD	7.9	13.1	60%	32%	8%

Source for the data: Edison/Mitofsky, page 43.

In fact, there is no evidence in Edison/Mitofsky of any interviewers causing any of the discrepancy. Correlations do not imply causality. Murder rates rise with ice cream consumption, but does that mean ice cream incites murder? Of course not; they are joint effects of a common cause, namely, hot weather during the summer season.

Consider Edison/Mitofsky's attribution of WPD to polling distance. It is understandable that absolute error rates might be higher when the interviewer was farther away, for all the reasons Edison/Mitofsky provides—greater possibility that an interviewer will miss respondents or, if there are multiple precincts in the same location, that an interviewer will provide a questionnaire to a respondent from the wrong precinct. But if the errors are honest, they should balance out. That is, they should not favor one candidate over the other. So why should mean WPD increase?

On the other hand, one also must ask why an election officer would want to keep observers from being close to the polling place. In Ohio, NEP had to sue to force Ken Blackwell to allow their people anywhere near the polls. Because the suit was decided so late, Blackwell was successful in forcing many interviewers to keep their distance.

Any time you partition categories you will get variation; some groups will have lower or higher numbers. That's probably the case in the age differences. Is there any good reason to expect that WPD should drop in the 35–44 age range, rise over the next two age groups, and then drop again among those over 65?

That's why scientists are expected to conduct theory-driven analyses, not to simply note correlations and then treat them as explanations. Otherwise, you start looking to Washington Redskin victories to predict presidential election outcomes. (As widely reported in the days prior to the election, since 1940—the first presidential year the Redskins performed in Washington—when the Redskins won their final home game before the voting, then the party in power kept the White House; otherwise, the incumbents get the boot.[193]) Of course, look at enough "predictors" and some will, by chance, "predict."

Edison/Mitofsky says that the discrepancy was due to errors by certain groups of interviewers, but the evidence suggests otherwise. WPD for all interviewer groups was heavily skewed toward Bush. The report presumes that this error is attributable to those interviewers with particularly high WPD, but in fact if the official count was corrupted these interviewers may have been the most accurate.

HAND COUNTS VS. MACHINE TABULATION

Edison/Mitofsky dismisses the possibility of a stolen election. The report says, "Exit polls do not support the allegations of fraud due to rigging of voting equipment" because the WPD for "precincts using touch screen and optical scan voting machines" are "similar to the [WPD] for punch card voting equipment, and less than the [WPD] for mechanical voting equipment."

What the pollsters mean is that they found no systematic differences between precincts that used newer electronic-touch-screen and optical-scan voting systems, and those that used the older punch-card and mechanical voting equipment. Yet Edison/Mitofsky acknowledges that WPD "in precincts with any type of automated voting system is higher than the average error in paper ballot precincts." Figure 5A illustrates this distinction. In precincts that used hand-counted paper ballots, the difference between official results and exit-poll survey results fell within the normal sampling margin of error. But, significantly, in precincts that used one of the machine counts, exit-poll survey results deviated from the official results by about 7 percentage points—a deviation large enough in many cases to change the outcome of the election.

FIGURE 5A: MEDIAN DISCREPANCIES FOR DIFFERENT TYPES OF
VOTING TECHNOLOGIES

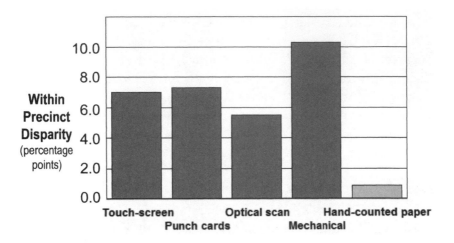

Source for the data: Edison/Mitofsky, p. 40.

But Edison/Mitofsky dismisses these errors as "not necessarily a function of the voting equipment." According to the report, "They appear to be a function of the equipment's location and the voters' responses to the exit poll at precincts that use this equipment." To support this contention, they present figure 5B.

Dividing data into groups, in this case "urban areas" and "rural/small town areas," can almost always sharpen or mute a finding depending on where one creates a partition. For this reason, it is standard scientific practice first to provide a theoretical explanation for any data partition, and second, to provide the data so that others may test alternate partitions or analyses. In this case, we must also wonder about the creation in the report of a group with a sample size of 5 ("Paper Ballot" precincts in "Urban Areas"), a size so small that any such data set is statistically meaningless.

FIGURE 5B: EDISON/MITOFSKY DISMISSAL OF PAPER CORRELATION

Size Of Place	Type of equipment used at polling place	mean WPE	median WPE	mean Abs(WPE)	N
Urban Areas (> 50,000)	Paper Ballot	-6.0	-11.5	15.7	5
	Mechanical Voting Machine	-12.7	-12.5	16.8	92
	Touch Screen	-7.5	-7.6	14.8	272
	Punch Cards	-9.3	-10.0	15.2	108
	Optical Scan	-7.2	-5.8	12.3	350
Rural/Small Town Areas (< 50,000)	Paper Ballot	-1.6	-0.6	10.5	35
	Mechanical Voting Machine	-3.2	-5.4	14.7	26
	Touch Screen	-6.0	-4.8	14.8	88
	Punch Cards	-0.8	-1.7	12.0	50
	Optical Scan	-4.4	-5.0	13.2	223

A meaningless data partition

Rural Area Comparison

Voting Technology	Mean WPE	N
Paper Ballot	-1.6	35
Machine average	-4.4	1117

Source: Edison/Mitofsky, p. 40.

Despite having drawn and presented data so that it dismisses a distinction between hand-counted paper ballots and machine counts, the tables in Edison/Mitofsky reveal the opposite. In the Rural/Small Town category, where we do have a statistically meaningful number of precincts, average WPD for the 1,117 machine-counted precincts is 4.4, almost three times WPD in precincts with paper ballots.

A THESIS UNDERMINED BY ITS OWN SUPPORTING DATA

Not only does Edison/Mitofsky fail to provide data or a theory to substantiate either the thesis of the Reluctant Bush Respondent or that of interviewer bias, the limited data the pollsters do present undermines this rationalization for the discrepancy.

First, consider the logical implications: If Kerry voters were significantly more likely to complete the exit-poll interview than Bush voters, then exit-poll participation rates in precincts where Kerry voters predominated ought to be correspondingly higher than in precincts where Bush voters predominated.

But Edison/Mitofsky presents data that show the exact opposite finding: in precincts where Kerry drew 80% of the vote, the response rate is lower than in those precincts where Bush drew 80% of the vote. In Bush strongholds 56% of voters completed the survey, while in Kerry strongholds only 53% cooperated. These data, presented in figure 5C, undermine the plausibility of the pollsters' central hypothesis and suggest that, if anything, Kerry voters were less likely to participate in the exit polls.

FIGURE 5C: RESPONSE RATES AND PRECINCT PARTISANSHIP

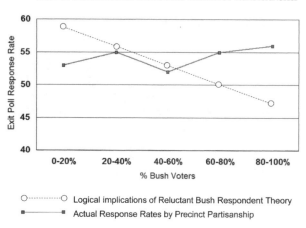

Source for the data: Edison/Mitofsky, p. 37.

This critique of the Edison/Mitofsky Reluctant Bush Respondent Theory was presented in a paper released on March 31, 2005, by U.S. Count Votes, a group of statisticians and research methodologists, including Freeman and academics from eight other research institutions, established to study the exit-poll anomalies.[194]

The U.S. Count Votes report was ignored by the mainstream media. And on his Mystery Pollster Web site, the influential Blumenthal criticized the U.S. Count Votes analysis of the Reluctant Bush Respondent thesis. He wrote that the Edison/Mitofsky hypothesis would hold up "if you assume that Bush voter completion rates tended to be higher where the percentage of Kerry voters in the precincts was lower, or that Kerry voter completion rates tended to be higher where the percentage of Bush voters in the precincts was lower, or both. I am not arguing that this is likely, only that it is possible."[195]

Blumenthal's thesis seems to have a certain psychological plausibility. Perhaps, when in the minority, voters are reluctant to

FIGURE 5D: EXIT-POLL DISCREPANCY RISES WITH % OF BUSH VOTERS

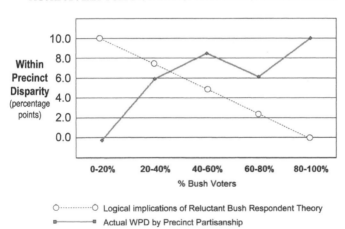

Source for the data: Edison/Mitofsky, p. 36.

express their true opinions (although the questionnaires are confidential; not even the interviewer knows the responses). As it turns out, however, Blumenthal's "reluctant Bush exit-poll participant in predominately Democratic precincts" runs completely counter to the data. The U.S. Count Votes report explains:

If the polls were faulty because Bush voters were shy in the presence of Kerry voters and less likely to cooperate with pollsters, then the polls should be most accurate in those precincts where Bush voters were in the overwhelming majority and where exit-poll participation was also at its maximum.[196]

What we find [as indicated in figure 5D] is just the opposite. The mean exit-poll discrepancy was dramatically higher in Bush strongholds than in Kerry strongholds (10.0 versus -0.3). In precincts with 80–100% Bush voters, where exit-poll participation reached its highest level (56%), there was a full 10% mean difference between official vote tallies and the exit-poll results.

To test whether any pattern of non-response bias might provide a plausible explanation for the discrepancy, U.S. Count Votes researchers mathematically constructed a hypothetical "set of response patterns for Bush and Kerry voters" that used the report's "Response rates based on Precinct Partisanship" (figure 5c) and

FIGURE 5E: PARTICIPATION RATES NEEDED TO SATISFY
"EDISON/MITOFSKY" ASSUMPTIONS

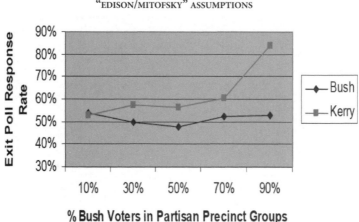

Source: U.S. Count Votes, March 31, 2005.

"WPD [WPE] based on Precinct Partisanship" (figure 5D) and at the same time conformed to the Edison/Mitofsky assertion that 56% of Kerry voters completed exit polls while only 50% of Bush voters did so.

Figure 5E shows the exit-poll completion rates that are required to reconcile the data in the two Edison/Mitofsky charts (the only precinct level data provided).[197]

In order to reconcile the Edison/Mitofsky data two anomalies must occur. First, Kerry voters must respond with their highest rate in Bush strongholds, where they are in the minority, while responding at their lowest rate in Kerry strongholds, where they are among friends. Second, reconciliation requires vastly different response rates of Kerry voters, ranging from a low of 52% to a high of 84%.

The U.S. Count Votes authors conclude:

> The required pattern of exit-poll participation by Kerry and Bush voters to satisfy the "Evaluation of Edison/Mitofsky" exit-poll data defies empirical experience and common sense under any assumed scenario.[198]

Edison/Mitofsky provides other data that raise further questions about the accuracy of the count. The report acknowledges that the discrepancy between the exit polls and the official count was considerably greater in the critical swing states. Precincts in swing states had mean and median WPDs of 7.9 and 8.6 percentage points versus 5.1 and 6.1 percentage points in non-swing states. This is consistent with a hypothesis of fraud—if you are going to steal an election, you go after votes most vigorously where they are most needed, which is in the swing states. Yet Edison/Mitofsky suggests, without providing any data or theory to back up the claim, that the greater discrepancy in swing states "indicates that voters in the swing states (who were exposed to more paid advertising and media coverage than voters in non-swing states) were less likely to respond to the exit poll: but among those who did, they were more likely to be Kerry voters.[199]

Consider also the alternative hypothesis about the data revealed in figure 5D. In light of the charges that the 2000 election was not legitimate, the 2004 Bush-Cheney Campaign clearly wanted to prevail in the popular vote.

If fraud were afoot, it would make sense that the president's people would steal votes in GOP strongholds, where the likelihood of detection was small, where few would be inclined to challenge the result, and where almost nobody would be in a position to do so, since in these strongholds Republicans control the machinery of government.

In those precincts that went at least 80% for Bush, average WPD was a whopping 10.0 percentage points. This means that in those precincts where the president racked up his largest pluralities, the margin of victory was a full 10 percentage-points higher than the exit polls indicated it should have been in those same precincts. For example, in precincts where according to the official count Bush received 90% and Kerry 10%, exit polls indicated that, on average, Bush would get 85% and Kerry 15%. In other words, in Bush strongholds across the country, Kerry, on average, received only about two-thirds of the votes that exit polls predicted. In contrast, in Kerry strongholds, exit polls matched the official count almost exactly, with an average WPD of -0.3 percentage points.

DID THE COUNT MATCH HOW VOTERS SAID THEY CAST THEIR BALLOTS?

Edison/Mitofsky provided several measures of the exit-poll discrepancy. One is what Edison/Mitofsky refers to as the "Composite Estimate," which was based on a composite model that includes the full exit-poll data, excludes the "outlier" precincts (the precincts with the greatest discrepancies), and includes a weighted average of pre-election telephone polls. This was the estimate that the CNN projection was based on.

For use as an Election Day prediction tool, these composite numbers are fine, as are many of the other statistics found in Edison/Mitofsky. After all, NEP provides its clients with projections before they have any official numbers, and must account for absentee-ballot voters, estimates of turnout, etc. But in order to understand the discrepancy between the exit-poll survey results and the official count, the best measure is the simplest rendering of the discrepancy within the precinct itself—that is, WPD, the difference between the way people said they voted and the official count.[200]

Table 5.4 compares exit polls, each state's official vote tally for Bush and Kerry, and their differential (a positive number indicating a victory for the president; a negative number for Kerry). This is the simplest rendering of the data. As such it is different from the more complex analysis that we and others have performed. It is not how Mitofsky and Lensky analyze the data. But in its simplicity, it is revealing and powerful.

TABLE 5.4: WPD AND THE ELECTION OUTCOME BASED ON EXIT-POLL REPORTED VOTING

STATE	(2)Bush Official Count	(3)Kerry Official Count	(4) Official Margin	(5) WPD	(6) Bush Exit Poll	(7) Kerry Exit Poll	(8) Exit Poll Margin	Electoral Votes as per Exit Poll Bush	?	Kerry
ALABAMA	62.5%	36.8%	25.6	11.3	56.8%	42.5%	14.3	9		
ALASKA	61.1%	35.5%	25.5	9.6	56.3%	40.3%	15.9	3		
ARIZONA	54.9%	44.4%	10.5	4.6	52.6%	46.7%	5.9	10		
ARKANSAS	54.3%	44.5%	9.8	0.5	54.1%	44.8%	9.3	6		
CALIFORNIA	44.4%	54.3%	-9.9	10.9	38.9%	59.8%	-20.8			55
*COLORADO	51.7%	47.0%	4.7	6.1	48.6%	50.1%	-1.4		*9	
CONN.	43.9%	54.3%	-10.4	15.7	36.1%	62.2%	-26.1			7
DELAWARE	45.8%	53.3%	-7.6	15.9	37.8%	61.3%	-23.5			3
D.C.	9.3%	89.2%	-79.8	3.4	7.6%	90.9%	-83.2			3
*FLORIDA	52.1%	47.1%	5.0	7.6	48.3%	50.9%	-2.6		*27	
GEORGIA	58.0%	41.4%	16.6	2.2	56.9%	42.5%	14.4	15		
HAWAII	45.3%	54.0%	-8.7	4.7	42.9%	56.4%	-13.4			4
IDAHO	68.4%	30.3%	38.1	1.0	67.9%	30.8%	37.1	4		
ILLINOIS	44.5%	54.8%	-10.3	4.4	42.3%	57.0%	-14.7			21
INDIANA	59.9%	39.3%	20.7	1.5	59.2%	40.0%	19.2	11		
*IOWA	49.9%	49.2%	0.7	3.0	48.4%	50.7%	-2.3		*7	
KANSAS	62.0%	36.6%	25.4	1.7	61.2%	37.5%	23.7	6		
KENTUCKY	59.6%	39.7%	19.9	-0.1	59.6%	39.6%	20.0	8		

STATE	(2) Bush Official Count	(3) Kerry Official Count	(4) Official Margin	(5) WPD	(6) Bush Exit Poll	(7) Kerry Exit Poll	(8) Exit Poll Margin	Electoral Votes as per Exit Poll Bush	?	Kerry
LOUISIANA	56.7%	42.2%	14.5	3.8	54.8%	44.1%	10.7	9		
MAINE	44.6%	53.6%	-9.0	3.8	42.7%	55.5%	-12.8			4
MARYLAND	42.9%	55.9%	-13.0	8.1	38.9%	60.0%	-21.1			10
MASSACHUSETTS	36.8%	61.9%	-25.2	5.8	33.9%	64.8%	-31.0			12
MICHIGAN	47.8%	51.2%	-3.4	6.3	44.7%	54.4%	-9.7			17
MINNESOTA	47.6%	51.1%	-3.5	9.3	43.0%	55.7%	-12.8			10
MISSISSIPPI	59.0%	40.2%	18.9	11.3	53.4%	45.8%	7.6	6		
MISSOURI	53.3%	46.1%	7.2	5.8	50.4%	49.0%	1.4		11	
MONTANA	59.1%	38.6%	20.5	-1.8	60.0%	37.7%	22.3	3		
NEBRASKA	65.9%	32.7%	33.2	8.1	61.8%	36.7%	25.1	5		
**NEVADA	50.5%	47.9%	2.6	10.1	45.4%	52.9%	-7.5			**5
NEW HAMP.	48.9%	50.2%	-1.4	13.6	42.1%	57.0%	-15.0			4
NEW JERSEY	46.2%	52.9%	-6.7	9.7	41.4%	57.8%	-16.4			15
**NEW MEXICO	49.8%	49.0%	0.8	7.8	45.9%	52.9%	-7.0			**5
NEW YORK	40.1%	58.4%	-18.3	11.4	34.4%	64.1%	-29.7			31
N. CAROLINA	56.0%	43.6%	12.4	11.3	50.4%	49.2%	1.1		15	
N. DAKOTA.	62.9%	35.5%	27.4	-5.2	65.5%	32.9%	32.6	3		
**OHIO	50.8%	48.7%	2.1	10.9	45.4%	54.2%	-8.8			**20
OKLAHOMA	65.6%	34.4%	31.1	-1.9	66.5%	33.5%	33.0	7		
OREGON	47.2%	51.3%	-4.2	NA						7
PENNSYLVANIA	48.4%	50.9%	-2.5	8.8	44.0%	55.3%	-11.3			21
RHODE ISLAND	38.7%	59.4%	-20.8	4.7	36.3%	61.8%	-25.5			4
S. CAROLINA	58.0%	40.9%	17.1	10.0	53.0%	45.9%	7.1	8		
S. DAKOTA	59.9%	38.4%	21.5	-4.2	62.0%	36.3%	25.7	3		
TENNESSEE	56.8%	42.5%	14.3	0.5	56.5%	42.8%	13.8	11		
TEXAS	61.1%	38.2%	22.9	4.8	58.7%	40.6%	18.1	34		
UTAH	71.5%	26.0%	45.5	6.4	68.3%	29.2%	39.1	5		
VERMONT	38.8%	58.9%	-20.1	15.0	31.3%	66.4%	-35.1			3
VIRGINIA	53.7%	45.5%	8.2	7.9	49.7%	49.4%	0.3		13	
WASHINGTON	45.6%	52.8%	-7.2	8.4	41.4%	57.0%	-15.6			11
W. VIRGINIA	56.1%	43.2%	12.9	-5.8	59.0%	40.3%	18.7	5		
WISCONSIN	49.3%	49.7%	-0.4	4.7	47.0%	52.0%	-5.1			10
WYOMING	68.9%	29.1%	39.8	4.3	66.7%	31.2%	35.5	3		
TOTAL U.S.	50.7%	48.3%	2.5	7.1	47.2%	51.8%	4.6	174	82	282

Bold = states won by Bush in which exit polls projected an advantage to Kerry. One asterisk = a Kerry margin of victory within the polling margin of error; two asterisks = a Kerry margin of victory beyond the polling margin of error, i.e., a likelihood of at least 97.5% that Kerry would have won. WPD (within precinct disparity, column 5) is the difference between the exit polls and the official count (data from Edison/Mikofsky, pp. 32–33). A positive WPD is a disparity in which Bush did better in the official count than in the exit poll; a negative WPD is a disparity in which Bush did worse in the official count than in the exit poll. "Exit-Poll Margin" (8) is calculated by subtracting WPD (5) from the official margin (4). For both "Exit-Poll Margin" and "Official Margin," a positive number indicates a Bush victory margin; a negative number, a Kerry victory margin. The three right hand columns show the resultant electoral vote. States within the polling margin of error are in the middle column labeled "?".

We calculated the exit-poll respondents' reported vote for Bush (6) and Kerry (7). Edison/Mitofsky never provides these numbers directly, but they are easily calculable. Column 4 indicates the official margin of victory; WPD (column 5) is the difference between how people said they voted in exit-poll surveys throughout the state and the official count in those same precincts. By combining these two numbers, we could calculate what the exit polls would have indicated as the margin of victory (column 8) had the data not been adjusted to conform with the count.

Based on the exit polls, Kerry won three states that he would lose in the official count: Ohio (by 8.8 percentage points), Nevada (7.5 points), New Mexico (7.0 points); had a lead within the polling margin of error in three more: Florida (2.6 points), Iowa (2.3 points), and Colorado (1.4 points); and was trailing within the margin of error in three others: Virginia (0.3 points), North Carolina (1.1 points), and Missouri (1.4 points). The net result is an electoral victory for Kerry of 282–174, with 82 electoral votes too close to call.

There is nothing controversial about how these figures were calculated. They emerge directly from the very definition of WPD.

Based on their entire sample of 114,559 voters,[201] Edison/Mitofsky calculated an average WPD of 6.5 for the election. This is to say that in all surveyed precincts across that nation, Bush did on average 6.5 percentage-points better in the official tally than his surveyed results in those very same precincts.[202]

Was the disparity due to some form of polling bias, as Mitofsky, Lenski and Blumenthal insist it must be, or might it have been due to a corrupted count?

POLLING VARIABLES

Edison/Mitofsky provides, along with WPD figures, statewide participation rates. This gives us a different test of the Reluctant Bush Respondent Theory. If Bush voters were less likely to participate in the polls, we would expect higher participation rates in states with a lower percentage of Bush voters, and low participation rates in states with a higher percentage of Bush voters.

Figure 5F compares participation rates with Bush support.[203] Each dot on the scatterplot represents a state, identified by its two-letter postal code. Participation rates are indicated by position on the vertical axis. States with high participation rates such as Tennessee (0.667 survey completion rate) appear high on the plot, and states with low participation rates such as Indiana (0.386 survey completion rate) appear at the bottom. Bush's percentage of the vote is indicated by position on the horizontal axis. Utah, where Bush received 71.5% of the vote, appears on the far right of the plot; Massachusetts, Vermont, and Rhode Island, where Bush received, respectively, 36.8%, 38.8% and 38.7% appear at the left.

The line in figure 5F represents an average of all the points. If there were no underlying relationship between Bush support and participation in the polls, the line and the ellipse in figure 5F would be horizontal. That is, there would be an equal chance of high or low participation regardless of the percentage of Bush voters. If, in fact, Bush voters were truly less likely to participate in the exit polls, as per Reluctant Bush Respondent Theory, states with more Bush voters would have lower participation rates and vice versa, in which case the ellipse and fitted line would trend downward from left to right.

But figure 5F indicates precisely the opposite. States such as Utah, Wyoming, Idaho, and Nebraska that produced Bush's largest pluralities, also had very high participation rates. Just as Bush precincts show higher rather than lower response rates, so do Bush states. Not only is the Reluctant Bush Respondent thesis unsubstantiated, but once again, the data indicates that, if anything, Bush voters were overrepresented in the exit polls.

FIGURE 5F: PARTICIPATION RATE BY BUSH % OF STATE VOTE

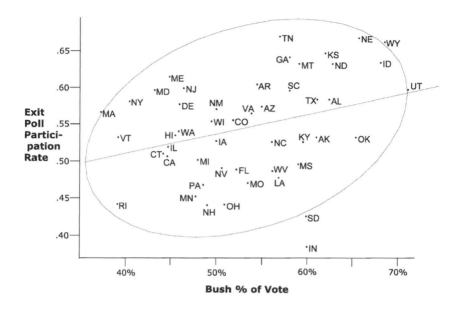

Source for the data: Participation Rates: Edison/Mitofsky, pp. 54–55.

ACCEPTED IMPROBABILITIES AND NEGLECTED CORRELATIONS

Statistics is a study of probabilities and correlations. Absolute certainty is rare in the real world, but at a certain point we can say with confidence that something is true. And at a certain point of improbability, we can say with confidence that something is not true. Given the data that Edison/Mitofsky provides, we can say with confidence that the report's conclusion, that Kerry voters were far more likely to participate in the exit polls than Bush voters, cannot be true. Indeed, Edison/Mitofsky provides an abundance of data that undermine any conclusion that the vote count was accurate.

Here are some other correlations that were not explored in the report. Although the 2004 Bush-Cheney Campaign openly sought a popular-vote victory, the foremost priority was, of course, to retain the presidency. Thus, it would make sense that votes would be most vigorously pursued in the swing states, where Electoral College votes were up for grabs. Sure enough, Edison/Mitofsky reported higher WPD in the precincts from swing states than in precincts throughout the rest of the nation. In other words, in swing state precincts there was a greater discrepancy between how people said they voted and what the official count indicated than in non-swing states. The report implies that the exit-poll discrepancy in the swing states was a function of exposure to greater advertising and media coverage, a barrage that might leave voters less willing to respond to an exit poll.[204] But the pollsters provided no evidence that would support such a connection, while turning a blind eye to the more obvious hypothesis—if you were going to steal the election, these were the places where you had to do it.

If election fraud were to be committed, then it would be committed where vote-switching or other forms of electoral manipulation would impact the election's outcome. It other words, if fraud were part of the 2004 Bush-Cheney Campaign arsenal, it would be more aggressively used in the battleground states, and most aggressively of all in the critical swing states of Florida, Ohio, and Pennsylvania. Drawing from the data provided in table 5.4, we see that, consistent with a hypothesis of election fraud, the average WPD in the eleven battleground states is significantly higher than in noncompetitive states.

	NO. OF STATES	MEAN WPD	MEDIAN WPD
NONCOMPETITIVE STATES	39	5.4	4.7
BATTLEGROUND STATES	11	8.0	7.8

Throughout the eleven battleground states, average WPD—the difference between how people said they voted and the way those votes were officially recorded—was 8 percentage points. In other words, confidential, anonymous reports from voters leaving the polling place indicated that, on average, Bush did 4 percentage-points worse in each battleground state, and Kerry did 4 percentage-points better than the official count indicated—enough to tip every one of those states into the Kerry column. And in Ohio, Florida, and Pennsylvania, average WPD was higher yet—more than 9 percentage points.

	NO. OF STATES	MEAN WPD	MEDIAN WPD
NONCRITICAL BATTLEGROUND STATES	8	7.6	7.6
CRITICAL BATTLEGROUND STATES	3	9.1	8.8

WHOSE QUESTIONNAIRES—OR VOTES— ARE NOT BEING COUNTED?

Correlations between voter demographics and WPD could be consistent with either polling error or miscount, depending on the underlying cause. Because NEP did not allow the release of the precinct- or county-level data, we use the state-level data to examine the relationship between demographic variables and WPD.

If votes of African Americans, who are disenfranchised in so many other ways, were improperly recorded, then we would expect to see a positive correlation between the proportion of African Americans in a state and that state's WPD. If the count is off, we would expect higher WPD among states with large numbers of disadvantaged minorities, especially African Americans.

As the percentage of minorities in a state increases, so too does the exit-poll discrepancy. WPD is, in fact, positively correlated with minority and urban demographic groups, including the proportion of African Americans and households in which a second language is spoken. Figure 5G illustrates graphically that states with higher percentages of African Americans trend toward higher WPDs. Many states with the highest percentages of African Americans—Mississippi, North and South Carolina, Maryland,

FIGURE 5G: AFRICAN AMERICAN PERCENTAGE OF STATE POPULATION BY WPD

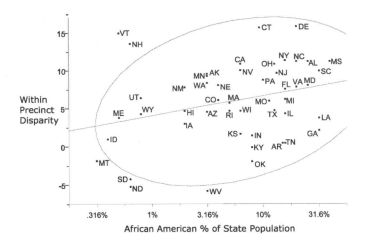

Source for demographic data: U.S. Census Bureau.

Alabama, Virginia, Delaware, and New York—also had among the highest WPDs. Statistical analyses reveal that these numbers are unlikely to be a coincidence. That being the case, there are two explanations: either African Americans disproportionately participated in the exit polls, thus indicating more support for their preferred candidate (Kerry) than their voting numbers justified, or their votes were not counted as they reported them cast. If African Americans did in fact, participate in the exit polls at higher rates, we would expect to see a correlation between the percentage of African Americans in a state and participation rates, but no such correlations are observed.

WHO'S IN THE GOVERNOR'S MANSION?

The exit-poll discrepancy also comes into relief when we compare the WPD among states with a Republican governor on November

2, 2004, and states with a Democratic governor. We illustrate this discrepancy with a histogram in figure 5H. Fully half of the twenty-eight states with a Republican governor have extreme WPDs of 8.0 or higher. Ten—Alabama, California, Connecticut, Mississippi, Ohio, Nevada, New Hampshire, New York, South Carolina, and Vermont—had WPDs of 10.0 or higher. Most of the 21 states with Democratic governors have relatively moderate WPDs of 5.0 or less.

FIGURE 5H: WPD AND GUBERNATORIAL CONTROL

WPD	Democratic Gov.	Republican Gov.	WPD
Over 10			Over 10
5-9.9		Median 7.85	5-9.9
0-4.9	Median 4.6		0-4.9
<0 (Kerry)			<0

COMPLAINTS AS DATA

Complaints of voting irregularities or obstruction were documented on Election Day, and they can be studied as possible indicators of count corruption.

On Election Day 2004, MSNBC, with the collaboration of the University of Pennsylvania's Fels Institute of Government, two electoral reform groups (one Democratic and one Republican), and VoterLink Data Systems, produced an Election Incident Monitor. Voters called a well-publicized toll-free telephone number to redress voting problems.[205] The system recorded their complaints and reported the number of calls by state. Figure 5I shows the number of Election Day calls per million residents.

The types of complaints they received included problems with voting machinery, long registration lines, and so on. It turns out that Election Day complaints are significantly correlated to WPD. Figure 5I illustrates that states with the highest per capita number of complaints had far larger than average discrepancies between exit-poll results and the official count. Eleven states had significantly more than their share of complaints—Delaware, Florida, Maryland, Michigan, Nevada, New Jersey, New York, Ohio, Pennsylvania, Rhode Island, South Carolina. These eleven averaged 344 calls per million residents as compared to 88 for the rest of the nation, and an average WPD of 8.4 as compared to 5.0.

FIGURE 51: ELECTION DAY CALLS BY WPD

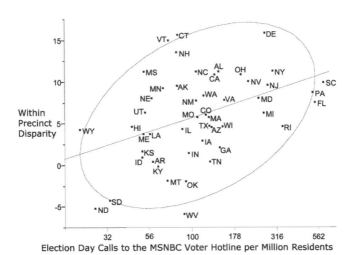

Election Day Calls to the MSNBC Voter Hotline per Million Residents

WHAT IT ALL ADDS UP TO

Correlations are the beginning, rather than the end, of any search for causality. But the lack of correlation between polling variables— response rates, miss rates, interviewer characteristics—and WPD do indicate a lack of causality. The available data do not substantiate the official explanation of the reluctant Bush responder. They do suggest that the official count overstated the president's actual voting support.

Whereas no polling or demographic variables indicate any evidence that either polling bias or nonresponse bias underestimated support for Bush, demographic, political, and voting-process variables—racial makeup of a state, partisan control of governorships, whether a state is a swing state, and precincts where paper ballots were not used—all correlate positively with WPD. Any one of these correlations is grounds for further investigation of all available data. That all of them could be manifested without there being an underlying relationship would be extraordinarily unlikely. Unless some compelling explanation comes forth, we must conclude that there is a causal link.

For Edison/Mitofsky the only conceivable explanation for the discrepancy is that Kerry voters completed more exit-poll questionnaires than Bush voters. "The average completion rate for all exit-poll precincts was 53 percent," the pollsters write, raising an argument similar to Blumenthal's. "While we cannot measure the completion rate by Democratic and Republican voters, hypothetical completion rates of 56% among Kerry voters and 50% among Bush voters overall would account for the entire within-precinct error that we observed in 2004."

In other words, nonresponse by Bush voters must be what happened, because the only other explanation for the exit-poll discrepancy is election fraud—and that is unthinkable, even though such a hypothesis is supported by all the numerical evidence.

The Edison/Mitofsky thesis that Bush voters must have disproportionately failed to participate in the exit polls, and the headlines that it generated, are curiously detached from the data presented in the report itself. Apparently, Lenski and Mitofsky found it more expedient to provide an explanation unsupported by theory, data, or precedent than to impugn the machinery of American democracy as practiced in the 2004 presidential election. And their media clients likewise found it preferable to accept a nonconfrontational thesis, however implausible, than to suggest the possibility of foul play.

In their report Mitofsky and Lenski implicitly admit that their position is based on faith that the official count is right, rather than evidence, when they write, "It is difficult to pinpoint precisely the reasons that, in general, Kerry voters were more likely to participate in the exit polls than Bush voters."[206]

WORTHY OF INVESTIGATION

Our investigation and analysis of the exit polls and the official count of the November 2, 2004, presidential election suggests that the official vote count deviated dramatically from how votes were actually cast. The deviation was large enough to have swung the election, both in Ohio and nationwide.

Taken together, the long experience of the pollsters, the absence of any particular reasons to doubt the integrity of NEP procedures, and the magnitude and pervasiveness of the exit-poll discrepancy all cry out for further scrutiny.

Had we an open, accessible, transparent national exit poll, it would be possible to verify or refute the implications of the discrepancy through direct inspection of the data and processes. The same is true for the nation's voting systems. Had we open, accessible, transparent national voting processes, we could directly inspect and test machines and software, examine ballots, and ascertain conclusively whether or not we had a fair count in the 2004 U.S. presidential election. But without either the polling data or the access to voting-machine technology, we are left in doubt and uncertainty. The media consortium will not release precinct-level data. The voting-machine technology is proprietary and not open to inspection.

Neither of these obstacles is unavoidable or unassailable. In both cases, the information exists and could be accessed. Laws could be passed to require transparency on the part of pollsters and the voting-machine industry. The precinct-level exit-poll data could be subpoenaed.

The very idea that a U.S. presidential election could be stolen—

or that the vote count could be corrupted enough to change the outcome—is difficult for most Americans to consider. Russ Baker, a reporter who has been outspoken in defense of the integrity of the 2004 election, has written, "Half-baked conspiracy theories are damaging to the public confidence in democracy."[207] Perhaps, but honest inquiry into the integrity of our national elections neither divides the country nor damages democracy. On the contrary, the way to restore people's already damaged confidence in our democracy is to pose these questions, to investigate them with all available resources, and then begin a public debate, since what is at stake is not only the outcome of the last presidential election, but also our future as a democracy and our identity as a people.

CHAPTER 6

How Did America Really Vote?

When a company cooks the books or when a scientist fudges figures, a contradiction is created. It may not be easy to find and, even then, it may be complicated to explain, but the beauty of numbers is an integrity in the entirety. The presence of a persistent and irreconcilable contradiction is a sure sign that something is amiss. Such a contradiction exists between the national exit polls and the official count in both the 2000 and 2004 presidential elections.

It was interesting to read the Gallup Poll's blog in the run-up to the 2004 election. Mari from Georgia predicted a Bush landslide because she doesn't know anyone who is voting for Kerry. Tim from San Francisco responded that he doesn't know anyone who is voting for Bush. Pattie in Texas found Gallup's numbers hard to believe because even deep in the heart of Bush-country so few of her neighbors support him. Unfortunately, one cannot readily extrapolate from personal observations the consensus of even a small town, let alone a nation of nearly 300 million people. So no individual observer in the electoral process is in a position to detect the miscounting or theft of even a large number of votes. If electoral counts are corrupted, we have very few alternate ways of ascertaining voter intent.

One technique that social scientists and research analysts use to estimate unknown values is a process called "anchor and adjust."

The idea is to anchor estimates on a known value and make adjustments based on observable changes. In the case of the 2004 election, we would begin by anchoring our estimates based on the known results from 2000 and then consider changes that might have occurred between the two elections.

The 2000 count was not clean. We know that Democrats suffered disproportionate losses among the 2 million spoiled votes (2% of the national vote total) and that the official vote count in Florida was considerably off and may have been even worse than anything reported. But at least in the 2000 election, electronic voting was not widespread, and the WPD in the national exit polls was skewed by only 2 percentage points. (As in 2004 and every other presidential election, Republicans did better than the exit polls suggested they would.) So the 2000 election seems a reasonable anchor for estimating the 2004 vote. Since the 2000 election likely overstates Bush's percentage of the overall vote, if anything, we're crediting the Republicans with a larger 2000 election base relative to the Democrats than a true count would warrant.

In 2000, despite losses due to vote spoilage and other factors, Gore won the popular vote by more than half a million votes. But in the 2004 election, which was essentially a supercharged rerun, Bush beat Kerry by 3 million votes. In the 2004 campaign, Bush and Kerry each had four potential sources of votes: their own base, their opponent's base, those who previously voted for Ralph Nader, and new voters. What changed between 2000 and 2004?

Figure 6A reveals how the different groups voted in 2004. This chart, based on NEP data, analyzes the 2004 vote based on how (and whether) voters had voted in the 2000 presidential election. (The 12,219[208] voters filling out this national survey were a subset of the 114,559 voters who filled out NEP exit-poll surveys on Election Day 2004.)

FIGURE 6A: PRESIDENTIAL VOTE IN 2004 BASED ON 2000 PRESIDENTIAL VOTE
(ELECTION NIGHT, NOVEMBER 2, 2004)

PRESIDENTIAL VOTE IN 2000	BUSH		KERRY	NADER
TOTAL	2004	2000	2004	2004
Did Not Vote (17%)	41%	n/a	57%	2%
Gore (39%)	8%	n/a	91%	1%
Bush (41%)	90%	n/a	10%	0%
Other (4%)	17%	n/a	64%	14%

Source: CNN screen shot, November 2, 2004.

The election night national exit-poll respondents confirmed consensus wisdom that the bases remained largely constant. In contrast, third-party votes were down from 4% of the total votes cast in the 2000 presidential election to less than 1% in 2004. Most of those lost votes came from Ralph Nader's 2000 base; Nader attracted 2.5 million fewer voters in 2004, and not surprisingly, most of these ex-Nader votes went to Kerry.

Note that the numbers strongly suggest that Republicans and Bush voters were overrepresented in the 2000 exit polls. Given that Gore won the popular vote in 2000, if all segments of the population were equally represented in the exit polls, there would be slightly more Gore voters than Bush 2000 voters. Instead, the numbers in parentheses in the first column of figure 6A indicate that 41% of the 2004 electorate voted for Bush in 2000 and only 39%— 2% less—of the 2004 electorate voted for Gore in 2000.

But rather than adjusting their numbers so as to account for this apparent overrepresentation of Bush support, NEP adjusted the numbers in the other direction. Figure 6B is the CNN screen shot taken the following morning.[209]

FIGURE 6B: PRESIDENTIAL VOTE IN 2004 BASED ON 2000 PRESIDENTIAL VOTE

(NOVEMBER 3, 2004)

PRESIDENTIAL VOTE IN 2000	BUSH		KERRY	NADER
TOTAL	2004	2000	2004	2004
Did Not Vote (17%)	45%	n/a	54%	1%
Gore (37%)	10%	n/a	90%	0%
Bush (43%)	91%	n/a	9%	0%
Other (3%)	21%	n/a	71%	3%

Source: CNN screen shot, November 3, 2004

A WONDERLAND OF NUMBERS

In an attempt to match their survey results to the official count, NEP made two sets of adjustments. First, they weighted Bush supporters in each category more heavily so that they now report that 45%, rather than 41% of 2000 election nonvoters, supported Bush. They also weighted particular respondent categories more heavily. And despite evidence indicating otherwise, NEP assigned greater weight to Bush 2000 voters, such that they assume the actual electorate in 2004 consisted of 43% Bush 2000 voters and only 37% Gore 2000 voters.

By these calculations, the 2004 electorate comprised 45.2 million Gore 2000 voters and a remarkable 52.6 million Bush 2000 voters—remarkable because in 2000 Bush received only 50.5 million votes. If we are to believe the NEP figures, this is indeed the greatest miracle of all in the 2004 election: One in nine Gore voters, through death, disability, or divine intervention, disappeared from the electorate; but no such fate befell a single Bush 2000 voter. Indeed, another two million miraculously appeared.

Aside from 52.6 million Bush 2000 voters, NEP's finagling of the numbers resulted in another mathematical impossibility. In the bottom row of figures 6A and 6B, we see that overnight the 2004 votes of those who supported third-party candidates in 2000 went from

17% Bush, 64% Kerry, and 14% Nader (figure 6A) to 21% Bush, 71% Kerry, and only 3% Nader (figure 6B). With nonresponse rates under 50%, it is simply not mathematically possible that Nader voters could have been overrepresented in the polls by 367%.

Comparing changes in the CNN exit-poll data between November 2 and November 3, 2004 reveals that in order to bring the exit-poll numbers into closer conformity with the actual result, NEP increased the proportion of Bush supporters among every single demographic group. So now we are presuming not only that Republicans disproportionately refused to participate in the exit polls, but also that among Asian Americans, young people, old people, union members, gun owners, churchgoers, high income, low income, and so on, Bush supporters disproportionately refused to participate.

We could hardly have a surer sign of a corrupted count. NEP adjustments resulted in not just statistical unlikelihoods, but mathematical impossibilities. And even then, after making these implausible and impossible adjustments, the adjusted exit polls still deviate from the count by a margin well beyond the margin of polling error.[210]

THE 10 MILLION-VOTE DISCREPANCY

The intense get-out-the-vote efforts by both camps seem to have been successful, leading to 17 million more votes in 2004 than in 2000. In table 6.1, we calculate and add up the numbers. According to CNN exit-poll data represented in figure 6A, 83% of the 2004 electorate had voted in 2000 and 17% had not. The 83% represents 101.5 million repeat voters, and the 17% represents 21 million new voters. The 101.5 million repeat voters represent 96% of the total 2000 electorate, which, apportioned out, represents 48.5 million Bush 2000 voters, 49 million Gore voters, and 4 million who voted for other candidates in 2000 (3 million of whom voted for Nader).[211]

TABLE 6.1: EXPECTED PRESIDENTIAL VOTES BASED ON CHANGES

FROM THE 2000 ELECTION (ALL VOTE FIGURES IN MILLIONS)

	BUSH	GORE/KERRY	OTHER	TOTAL
2000 OFFICIAL RESULTS	50.5 (48%)	51.0 (48%)	4.0 (4%)	105.5
2004 OFFICIAL RESULTS	62.0 (51%)	59.0 (48%)	1.0 (1%)	122.5
2004 EXPECTED RESULTS				
Base from 2000 Election	48.5 (48%)	49.0 (48%)	4.0 (4%)	101.5
(1) Bush 2000 Redistributed	43.5 (90%)	5.0 (10%)		48.5
(2) Gore Redistributed	4.0 (8%)	44.5 (91%)	0.5 (1%)	49.0
(3) Third party Redistributed	0.5 (17%)	2.5 (64%)	0.5 (19%)	4.0
(4) New Voters Distributed	8.5 (41%)	12.0 (57%)	0.5 (2%)	21.0
Expected Total	56.5 (46%)	64.0 (52%)	1.5 (1%)	122.5
Discrepancy Between Expected and Official Results	-5.5 million	5.0 million		

* All vote counts and projections are rounded to the nearest 500,000. Rows do not always total exactly due to rounding.

Line 1 denotes the votes of Bush's 2000 base. Bush held 43.5 million votes (90%), while Kerry captured 5 million votes (10%). A strong performance for Bush.

Line 2, however, shows the vote totals from Kerry's even stronger performance among Gore voters. Kerry held 44.5 million (91%), while Bush captured only 4 million Gore votes (8%).

Line 3 denotes the redistribution of third-party votes: 500,000 to Bush, 2,500,000 to Kerry, with well under 1 million voting again for a third-party candidate. Not surprisingly, Kerry amassed the lion's share of the mostly ex-Nader 2000 third-party votes, 64% compared to 17% captured by Bush.

Line 4 denotes the distribution of those who did not vote in 2000. Bush's 41% share of this number represents 8.5 million votes; Kerry's 57% share is 12 million votes. Bush did well to attract as many new voters as he did. But among new voters and others who did not vote in 2000, Democrats, as is generally the case, won by a healthy margin, 57% to 41%.

Added together, this amounts to a discrepancy on the order of 10 million votes. The numbers indicate that Bush received 56.5 million votes, 6 million more than he received in 2000—a good showing, but far fewer than the 11.5 million vote increase certified in the official state counts. Kerry's totals from the four vote sources aggregate to 64 million votes, 5 million more votes than the official totals credit.

WHAT CHANGED? ENDORSEMENTS, NEW VOTERS, AND TURNOUT

One could say that we employ circular reasoning in using the figures from the national exit poll to show 2004 votes based on voter choices in 2000, when the accuracy of the exit polls is itself at issue. But it's not just exit polls; these numbers are consistent with everything else we know about the campaign and the election. Moreover, they illustrate the basic arithmetic of the election: Kerry begins with a slightly larger base and more new voters to draw on. So how could Bush emerge with a 3 million-vote margin of victory?

Both sides played to the party faithful. Throughout the 2004 campaign and well before, most observers were struck by how firmly divided the country was, with the bases staying quite constant; indeed, they seemed polarized and petrified. To the degree that those on the margins broke off from the core, however, it would seem that Bush lost more supporters than attracted converts.

One of the only measurable indicators of total change in political sentiment other than polls is newspaper endorsements. On this count, *Editor & Publisher* magazine reported a final count of 213 for Kerry to 205 for Bush. Editor Greg Mitchell wrote:

> Looking back at various E&P surveys in past decades, we can see this was a rare occasion with the Democratic candidate for president getting more editorial nods than the Republican. . . . We have also been tabulating the circulation

of papers supporting each candidate—and double- and triple-checking our math. In our final total, Kerry won that race handily, 20,882,889 to 15,743,799.[212]

Mitchell observed that "more than 60 papers that backed Bush in 2000 switched to Kerry or endorsed neither candidate. Fewer than 10 switched the other way after backing Al Gore in 2000."[213]

Even if the Republicans held their entire base, they could not have won this election without attracting votes from whose who voted Democratic in 2000—but there is no indication that Bush did attract a significant number of such voters. Indeed, as many observers noted during the Democratic convention, Bush was, for the Democrats, unintentionally and unexpectedly true to his 2000 campaign promise to be "a uniter, not a divider." The disparate elements within the Democratic Party faithful have rarely, if ever, been so united as in their desire to defeat a specific candidate. Kerry may not have been popular in all elements of the party, but he was going to get their votes; even groups such as "Kerry Haters for Kerry" were surprisingly active in the campaign.

Regarding third-party votes, it's hard to imagine what could motivate large numbers of Nader 2000 voters to support Bush in 2004. Indeed, Bush did well to capture 600,000 third-party 2000 votes. For the Democratic Party, however, recapturing the bulk of Nader's 2.9 million votes from the 2000 election was an important goal in 2004. Democrats devoted significant resources to keeping Nader off the ballot in many states and were often successful. In those states where they were not, top Nader 2000 supporters argued that there was a difference between Bush and Kerry, and that a vote for Nader would thus be "wasted." To the degree this was persuasive, and judging by Nader's vote decline it was, ex–Nader supporters would naturally vote for Kerry.

The biggest effort on both sides, of course, went into attracting new voters. In September 2004, the *New York Times* reported that one

Democratic Party group, America Votes, says its constituents—labor unions, trial lawyers, environmental groups, community organizations—will spend $300 million on registration and turnout in swing states."[214] This is twice as much as the $150 million in public financing shared between the two candidates for the entire fall campaign. The linchpin of the Bush campaign was attracting new conservative voters, especially getting evangelicals to the polls. Bush strategist Karl Rove put it this way:

> If you look at the model of the electorate, and you look at the model of who voted, the big discrepancy is among self-identified, white, evangelical Protestants, Pentecostals, and fundamentalists. . . . [In 2000], there should have been 19 million of them, and instead there were 15 million of them. Just over four million of them failed to turn out and vote.[215]

This was restated continually as a winning campaign strategy, and in the aftermath of the election, Bush's victory was widely attributed to the success of this effort.[216] Some analysts have challenged the existence of these 4 million Republican fundamentalists as a ruse, but even were they to exist and had the GOP reined in every last one of them, the numbers still do not add up.[217]

Republicans may well have been successful at attracting new evangelical voters and other conservative voters, but evidence suggests that new Democratic registrations far outnumbered new Republican registrations. Such data is not easy to come by. We were able to obtain new registrations by party for only two states, Kentucky and Maryland. Both of these states—one of which has been solidly Republican in presidential elections, the other equivalently Democratic—show more new Democratic registrations than Republican throughout 2004, in Maryland by a 2:1 margin.

In other states, determining new registrations takes some fieldwork and/or calculations. But in the two most important states of the election, the critical swing states of Ohio and Florida, the evidence indicates that Democratic voter registration campaigns far exceeded the efforts of Republicans. The *New York Times* reported:

> County-by-county data shows that in Democratic areas of Ohio—primarily low-income and minority neighborhoods—new registrations since January have risen 250 percent over the same period in 2000. In comparison, new registrations have increased just 25 percent in Republican areas. A similar pattern is apparent in Florida: in the strongest Democratic areas, the pace of new registration is 60 percent higher than in 2000, while it has risen just 12 percent in the heaviest Republican areas.[218]

Even if Rove were correct that 4 million potential Bush voters failed to turn out in 2000, the fact is that there were many millions more potential Gore voters who did not vote in 2000 (or voted for Nader). The poor, the less educated, and the young—all Democratic constituencies in 2004—traditionally produce among the lowest election turnout, and 2000 was no exception. In 2004, the Democrats ran an unusually well-organized and unusually well-funded get-out-the-vote drive (whereas Republicans are usually well organized and funded), and they simply had many more potential voters to draw upon.

It may well be that the Republicans were able to attract 6 million new voters to the polls—a good showing—but that still leaves the official count off by 10 million votes. Even under the rosiest scenarios, a Bush popular-vote victory without attracting significant numbers of Gore 2000 votes was not possible.

THE DEMOCRATS INVESTIGATE

The Democratic Party has tried to make sense of its defeat in the presidential election. In December 2004 the Democratic National Committee (DNC) announced that it was going to investigate what happened in Ohio. But the DNC's subsequent report, *Democracy at Risk: The 2004 Election in Ohio*, released in June 2005, failed to address either the question of the exit-poll discrepancy or the possibility of wide-scale fraud. The report's authors list the following as one of five key questions:[219]

> Were there anomalies in the reported voting results compared, for example, with exit polls or with a county's voting history, that cannot be explained by factors other than machine malfunction, misreporting and/or mistabulation?

Yet in the 204-page report they never mention exit polls again, let alone document the discrepancy or investigate it.

The report presents, instead, damning evidence of vote suppression and Election Day voting problems.

In Ohio, 52% of blacks experienced problems voting, including waits up to eight hours, often in a driving rain; demands for identification above and beyond that required by law; machines malfunctioning; and so on. All told, the report's authors conclude that voting numbers were suppressed by 2% to 3%, primarily in heavily Democratic areas. And that percentage doesn't include all those whose registration forms were discarded or otherwise went unprocessed. In addition, the report found that spoilage rates were high in Democratic precincts, with many precincts having lost-ballot rates in excess of 10%. Provisional ballot rates were high in the state (much higher in Ohio than elsewhere in the country), and particularly high in Democratic counties. Of these provisional ballots, only 78% were counted, and that number was lower in

Democratic counties—66% in Cleveland's Cuyahoga County, for example. DRE electronic voting machines, aside from their vulnerability to fraud, were a major source of lost votes and other problems. All told, 56% of all voters using touch-screen machines experienced problems.

And yet, the DNC investigators downplay the significance of these findings, noting that in each instance the lost votes were not enough to change the election result. Nor do they seem to consider the overall impact of the numerous individual irregularities. Rather, they conclude that the statistical study of precinct-level data does not suggest the occurrence of widespread fraud that systematically misallocated votes for Kerry to Bush. The principal evidence they provide is:

> ➤The pattern of voting for Kerry is similar to the pattern of voting for the Democratic candidate for governor in 2002.

> ➤Kerry's support across precincts also increased with the support for Eric Fingerhut, the Democratic candidate for U.S. Senate, decreased with support for Issue 1 (the ballot initiative opposing same-sex marriage), and increased with the proportion of African American votes.

These findings, while noteworthy, do not begin to support an assertion that widespread fraud did not occur.

Regardless of whether or not there was widespread fraud, the pattern of voting for Kerry would likely be similar to the pattern of voting for the Democratic candidate for governor in 2002 and for the Democratic nominee for U.S. Senate. And support for Kerry would increase with the proportion of African American votes and decrease with the support for Issue 1 (the ballot initiative opposing same-sex marriage).

No type of fraud would produce completely arbitrary, fabricated numbers. Rather, widespread fraud, if it occurred, would have been accomplished by switching, adding, or subtracting some percentage of votes in many precincts throughout the state and possibly to a greater degree some precincts. Nothing in the DNC report is inconsistent with such fraud. Indeed, the authors repeatedly qualify their findings. For example, they note, "A larger increase in registration is associated with a higher proportion of votes for Kerry everywhere except among the optical scan precincts."[220] But what does this mean, especially in conjunction with the documented fraud in Clermont County? Given the testimony on stickers covering the Kerry/Edwards ovals in optical scan machines of Clermont County, it would be reasonable to conclude that this statistical anomaly is due to a fraudulent count.

In their precinct-level analysis of the proportion of Kerry votes in relation to the proportion of Fingerhut votes, of votes on Issue 1 and of the voting population that is African American, the DNC investigators find many anomalous precincts, particularly in Cuyahoga County, where, in every case, Bush is beneficiary of the discrepancy. But they fail to draw the conclusions suggested by their own findings of vote-switching due to ballot-order differences in Cuyahoga County.

The report's authors do, however, raise two serious contentions:

> ➤Whereas increases in registration were associated with a higher proportion of votes for Kerry (leading one to believe that, in fact, new registrants might have swung the state for Kerry), increases in turnout were not. The authors found a flat (or slightly negative) relationship between turnout increases and proportion of votes counted for Kerry. This leads them to conclude that whereas Democrats may have won the registration battle, Republicans may have prevailed in the effort to get new voters to the polls.

➤Turnout in 2004 increases with the proportion of Yes votes for Issue 1. These results support the claim that Issue 1 mobilized some people to vote who may not have done so otherwise.

These observations about turnout do suggest the possibility that, by placing Issue 1 on the November ballot, Republicans did increase turnout.

But what does this say about fraud? Issue 1 proponents such as Secretary of State Blackwell may well have been successful in increasing turnout for supporters and suppressing turnout among opponents. However the exit polls, which the DNC report never examines, take an equal measure of all those who cast a ballot and they indicated a decisive 8.5 percentage-point victory for Kerry in Ohio on November, 2, 2004.

Given this fact and the reference made in the introduction of *Democracy At Risk* to the exit-poll discrepancy as one of five key questions to answer, the natural next step would have been for the DNC investigators to have analyzed the exit-poll results together with other indications that the 2004 presidential election may have been stolen. This they stopped short of doing.

The DNC report never seriously considered the question of fraud.

WHERE THE POLLING ERRORS REALLY ARE

Rather than examine the exit-poll discrepancy, much was made in the media about how the pre-election telephone polls got it right.[221]

Table 6.2 lists the results of the fourteen national telephone polls taken the week before the election. They projected an average edge for Bush of 1.5 percentage points, which was fairly close to the official vote count.

TABLE 6.2: FINAL 2004 NATIONAL PRE-ELECTION POLLS

Days before the election	Pollsters	Dates conducted	Bush	Kerry	Nader	Edge	Unallocated
1 day	Marist	1-Nov	49%	50%	0%	Kerry +1	1%
2 days	GW/Battleground	10/31–11/1	50%	46%	0%	Bush +4	4%
3 days	TIPP	10/30–11/1	50.1%	48.0%	1.1%	Bush +2.1	.8%
	FOX News	10/30–10/31	46%	48%	1%	Kerry +2	5%
4 days	CBS News	10/29–11/1	49%	47%	1%	Bush +2	3%
	Harris	10/29–11/1	49%	48%	2%	Bush +1	1%
	Reuters/Zogby	10/29–10/31	48%	47%	1%	Bush +1	4%
	CNN/USA/Gallup	10/29–10/31	49%	49%	1%	TIE	1%
	NBC/WSJ	10/29–10/31	48%	47%	1%	Bush +1	4%
5 days	ABC/Wash Post	10/28–10/31	49%	48%	0%	Bush +1	3%
	ARG	10/28–10/30	48%	48%	1%	TIE	3%
	CBS/NY Times	10/28–10/30	49%	46%	1%	Bush +3	4%
6 days	Pew Research	10/27–10/30	51%	48%	1%	Bush +3	-
	Newsweek	10/27–10/29	50%	44%	1%	Bush +6	5%
	Averages		**48.9%**	**47.4%**	**.9%**	**Bush +1.5**	**2.8%**

Source for the data: RealClearPolitics poll average. www.realclearpolitics.com/ bush_vs_kerry.html

These numbers, however, warrant a closer look.

These results would seem to confirm the official count, but telephone polls give far less cause for confidence than exit polls. Not only do telephone polls suffer from nonresponse rates far in excess of exit polls, pre-election telephone polls have three important additional sources of error that do not affect exit polls. One, respondents may change whom they decide to vote for prior to the election. Two, telephone polls suffer from coverage bias—in particular, they miss those voters who do not own or often use landline telephones, and those who are unlikely to answer the phone during the hours that pollsters call. Three, not everyone who says they will vote actually will. Some respondents are more likely to vote than others. Evidence also suggests that the voting preferences of likely voters differ from the preferences of those unlikely to vote. So pollsters must make some estimate of the probability that any respondent will, in fact, vote.

In past U.S. presidential elections involving incumbents, the changes that occur between telephone polling and voting follow a pattern. Undecided voters, along with some previously decided voters, break heavily for challengers. There have been four incumbent presidential elections (1980, 1984, 1992, and 1996) in the past quarter century. On average, the incumbent comes in half a point below his final telephone-poll result; challengers exceed their final poll result by an average of four points. Pollster and political analyst Guy Molyneux explains:

> This happens because elections are fundamentally a referendum on the incumbent. The first step in voters' decision-making process is to answer the question "does he deserve re-election?" Undecided voters have basically answered that question in the negative, and their undecided status reflects the fact that they don't know enough about the challenger (yet) to feel comfortable stating a public preference. . . . In addition, some who support the incumbent in pre-election polls are low-information voters basing their answer simply on name recognition, but who defect to the challenger at the last moment. . . . In any case, the net effect is crystal clear: We can expect George W. Bush to receive about the same share of the vote—or a bit less—on November 2 as he receives in the final public polls.[222]

Historically, presidential-performance rating has been a better predictor of results than stated preference. In the days before the election, pollster John Zogby asked voters in ten battleground states, "Overall, how would you rate President Bush's performance on the job?"[223] Table 6.3 reveals that in every battleground state Bush had approval rates below 50%. In all but one state, Nevada, the number of voters disapproving of his performance exceeded the number of approvers by at least 6 percentage points.

TABLE **6.3**: ELECTION DAY PRESIDENTIAL APPROVAL RATINGS

DATES CONDUCTED	STATE	BUSH APPROVAL	BUSH DISAPPROVAL
10/31/04 thru 11/2/04	Colorado	46%	54%
11/1/04 thru 11/2/04	Florida	46%	53%
11/1/04 thru 11/2/04	Iowa	45%	55%
10/31/04 thru 11/2/04	Michigan	46%	54%
11/1/04 thru 11/2/04	Minnesota	43%	56%
10/31/04 thru 11/2/04	Nevada	49%	51%
10/31/04 thru 11/2/04	New Mexico	47%	53%
11/1/04 thru 11/2/04	Ohio	43%	49%
11/1/04 thru 11/2/04	Pennsylvania	44%	55%
11/1/04 thru 11/2/04	Wisconsin	45%	55%

Source for the data: Zogby International.

Consistent with the observations of Molyneux and Gallup, table 6.4 reveals that as we got closer to the election, Kerry's numbers went up. The one poll entirely conducted the day before the election, the Marist poll, shows Kerry up by 1 percentage point. Based on his same-day polling, Zogby called the election for Kerry 311 to 213 electoral votes (with 14 electoral votes too close to call) and gave Bush a narrow edge in the popular vote. The polls are combined based on the date initiated and then averaged in table 6.4.

TABLE **6.4**: PRE-ELECTION POLLS AND ELECTION PROXIMITY

# polls	Date Initiated	Bush	Kerry	Edge
2	October 27	50.5%	46.0%	Bush 4.5%
3	October 28	48.7%	47.3%	Bush 1.3%
5	October 29	48.6%	47.6%	Bush 1.0%
4	October 30 or later	48.8%	48.0%	Bush 0.8%

Gallup likewise calculates that in every election with an incumbent president since telephone polling was developed—eight elections in all—88% of the final undecided vote went to the challenger.[224]

For the 2004 election, Gallup decided to allocate 74% of the undecided voters to Kerry and 26% to Bush. Unlike Gallup, most pollsters did not allocate undecided voters. On average, among all fourteen telephone polls conducted within the six days before the election, 2.8% of likely voters were undecided and unallocated. This is considerably more than the 1.5-percentage-point average Bush edge in the polls. If these voters were allocated in a historically consistent manner, most polls, even if they were to make no other adjustments, would have shown Kerry dead even or slightly ahead.

CELL-PHONE USERS DON'T COUNT

Unlike Election Day exit polls, telephone polls suffer from what is known as "coverage bias," that is, error that is not random but rather due to how those being polled are chosen. Rather than having an equal chance of reaching all voters, as exit polls do, the likelihood that a person will be chosen for participation in a telephone poll is a function of the likelihood that that person will answer an incoming call on a home landline phone during survey hours. Because of this, telephone polls select out the young, the mobile, those who do not own or use landline phones, and non–English speakers, all of whom vote disproportionately Democratic. According to the 2004 election exit polls, 9% of the American electorate did not even own a landline phone, 2% of voters reported owning no phone, and 7% reported using cell phones exclusively, numbers that are corroborated by a Harris Interactive survey.[225] Among the remaining 91% of the electorate, telephone-answering practices vary dramatically. Many people do not answer phones at all without positively identifying the caller. Mobile, active people will be far less likely to answer their telephones than the homebound and sedentary. Those who work in lower-wage retail sectors are less likely to be home during prime polling hours than those who work traditional higher-wage jobs. In short, not only do we know that telephone polls have a selection bias, but we also have good reasons to suspect significant differences in voting preferences between those more likely to be reached by telephone polls and those who are less likely to be reached.

To avoid the shortcomings of telephone polling, some pollsters have been developing online interactive polls. Harris Interactive, the most advanced company in this new field, was the only polling firm to publish a national pre-election poll. According to the National Council on Public Polls' "Evaluation of the Performance of 2000 Presidential Polls," Harris Interactive predicted the final results of the 2000 presidential election more closely than any telephone poll. Harris Poll's online survey of likely voters for the 2004 presidential election, conducted between October 29 and November 1, 2004, obtained results that deviated as sharply from the official count as the exit polls, and in the critical state of Florida, far more sharply still.

TABLE 6.5: PRE-ELECTION HARRIS ONLINE INTERACTIVE POLL, 2004

	Sample size	Bush pred.	Kerry pred.	Pred. winner	Bush official	Kerry official	Official winner	Official vs. pred.
FLORIDA	1,433	47%	51%	Kerry 4%	52.1%	47.1%	Bush 5.0	Bush 9.0
OHIO	1,218	47%	51%	Kerry 4%	50.8%	48.7%	Bush 2.1	Bush 6.1
PENN.	1,204	48%	50%	Kerry 2%	48.4%	50.9%	Kerry 2.5	Kerry 0.5
NATION	5,508	47%	50%	Kerry 3%	48.3%	50.8%	Bush 2.5	Bush 5.5

Source for the data: Harris Interactive, "Final Pre-election Harris Polls: Still Too Close to Call but Kerry Makes Modest Gains," The Harris Poll #87, November 2, 2004.

In fact, on Election Day, NEP discovered that non–telephone owners do differ politically from those who own telephones, and that therefore this coverage bias would have also led to an overstatement of the president's support in the pre-election telephone polls. The

Pew Center for Research on People and the Press, using NEP's adjusted data, reports that the 7% of 2004 voters who have cell phones but no landline telephone favored Kerry by 7 percentage-points more than did the population that does own a landline phone. The 2% of voters with no telephone at all favored Kerry by 12 percentage points more than did the population that does own a landline phone.[226]

TABLE 6.6: ARE VOTERS WITHOUT LANDLINE TELEPHONES DIFFERENT?

	% OF TOTAL	BUSH	KERRY	MARGIN
LANDLINE PHONE	91%	52	47	Bush 5
CELL PHONE ONLY	7%	45	54	Kerry 9
NO TELEPHONE	2%	39	58	Kerry 19

Source for the data: Pew Center for Research on People and the Press, data from "corrected" exit polls.

The total effect of this coverage bias was to increase the president's apparent share of the vote by 1 percentage point and correspondingly decrease Kerry's apparent share by 1 point, thereby skewing the difference between them by 2 points or, again, considerably more than the 1.5 percentage-point average Bush edge. So, it seems likely that had it not been for coverage bias, most polls, even if they were to make no other adjustments, would have shown Kerry dead even or slightly ahead.

CHOOSING WHOSE OPINIONS COUNT

You would think that reporting telephone-polling results would be a straightforward procedure, but in fact there is play in the system that allows the pollsters to shape the results. The models that pollsters use to predict voting behavior do not match what we know about how people vote in real life. In other words, a discrepancy exists between voters' real-life voting behavior and the models the pollsters create—models created to conform to the official count.

Not everyone eligible to vote does vote. Therefore, predicting election results depends not only on which candidate respondents say they will vote for, but also on which respondents are more likely to vote. This uncertainty creates a potential source of major error, and nearly all pollsters compensate for this uncertainty by using highly flawed likely voter "cutoff" procedures that lead them to overestimate Republican voting intent by a several percentage points.

To illustrate this flaw and its consequences, we use as an example the methods of the Gallup Organization, the world's oldest, best-known, and probably most-copied telephone-polling company.[227] Gallup asks respondents a series of questions about their past voting behavior and political awareness to create a likely-voter scale. Gallup's 2004 questionnaire to determine likely voters, which was posted by *USA Today* on its Web site, asks the following:

1) How much have you thought about the upcoming elections for president, quite a lot or only a little? (Quite a lot = 1 point)

2) Do you happen to know where people who live in your neighborhood go to vote? (Yes = 1 point)

3) Have you ever voted in your precinct or election district? (Yes = 1 point)

4) How often would you say you vote, always, nearly always, part of the time or seldom? (Always or nearly always = 1 point)

5) Do you plan to vote in the presidential election this November? (Yes = 1 point)

6) In the last presidential election, did you vote for Al Gore or George Bush, or did things come up to keep you from voting? (Voted = 1 point)

7) If "1" represents someone who will definitely not vote and "10" represents someone who definitely will vote,

where on this scale would you place yourself? (Currently, 7–10 = 1 point)[228]

Republicans tend to answer these questions in the affirmative more often than Democrats and are therefore more often categorized as "likely voters." As a result, polls of "likely voters" yield projections that are much more Republican than polls of all registered voters. For example, table 6.7 shows that in the 2000 election, polls of registered voters projected, on average, a Gore victory of 3%, whereas polls of likely voters projected, on average, a Bush victory by 2%, a 5-percentage-point differential.

TABLE 6.7: REGISTERED VS. LIKELY VOTERS IN THE FINAL

2000 PRE-ELECTION POLLS

REGISTERED VOTERS	BUSH/ CHENEY	GORE/ LIEBERMAN	OTHER & UNDECIDED	MARGIN
Newsweek (10/31–11/2/00)	41%	44%	5%	Gore +3
Pew (11/2–11/5/00)	41%	45%	5%	Gore +4
Gallup (11/4–11/5/00)	44%	46%	5%	Gore +2
AVERAGE REGISTERED VOTERS	42%	45%	5%	Gore +3
"LIKELY VOTERS"				
Newsweek (10/31–11/2/00)	45%	43%	12%	Bush +2
Pew (11/2–11/5/00)	45%	43%	12%	Bush +2
Gallup (11/4–11/5/00)	47%	45%	8%	Bush +2
AVERAGE "LIKELY VOTERS"	46%	44%	11%	Bush +2

Source for the data: mysterypollster.com.

The big problem arises not in estimating the likelihood that a given respondent will, in fact, vote, but in the cutoff models employed by Gallup and almost every other national polling firm. Gallup, for example, counts those who score a perfect seven out of seven as likely voters; if this is less than the estimated turnout, Gallup weights down those who scored six to make the weighted value of the likely voters equal to the projected turnout. Anyone scoring five or less is selected out entirely—their responses simply do not count.

This procedure of ignoring voters who score five or less, however, constitutes a severe methodological flaw because it pretends contrary to reason and fact that those who score five or less play no role in the vote. Even if we assume that the Gallup questionnaire does, in fact, predict which voters are most likely to vote, it is most assuredly not the case that all the respondents who score seven will vote, that only one-fifth of those who score six will, and that none of those who score five or lower will. The most conscientious citizen may intend to vote, but fall ill or be unavoidably detained. A politically active citizen who has never missed an election but who has recently moved cannot score seven and is unlikely to even score six. And, a very unlikely voter may very well vote if her neighbor registers her and then offers to take her to the polls. This flaw, as it turns out, can make a big difference.

The Center for Political Studies at the University of Michigan actually checked registration records to validate voting rates of likely and unlikely voters. Reproduced in table 6.8 are data from a report on the results of that validation study.[229] The estimations of likely voting had been made by CBS-TV based on respondent reports of past voting and interest in the campaign, a system comparable to that employed by Gallup. The right column reveals the percentage of each group of respondents that actually voted in the 1980 election for president.

TABLE 6.8: VERIFIED LIKELIHOOD OF LIKELY AND UNLIKELY VOTERS' VOTING

Estimation of Voting Likelihood	Proportion of Voting Age Population	Validated Voting Rate
Max Registered—Past Voter—High Interest	51.0%	74.6%
Registered—Past Voter—Low Interest	10.3%	61.9%
Registered—Nonvoter—High Interest	9.0%	58.2%
Registered—Nonvoter—Low Interest	3.7%	27.6%
Not registered	26.0%	10.0%

Source for the data: Traugott and Tucker (1984) report of the 1980 National Election Study conducted by the Center for Political Studies at the University of Michigan

If Republicans score higher than Democrats on the likely voter test, then likely voter models will overestimate actual Republican election day vote. The overestimate can be substantial, and this is true regardless of whether or not Republicans are, in fact, more likely to vote.

If, for example, half of Gallup's sample answered affirmatively all seven questions[230] and they preferred Bush 55% to 45%; and the other half who answer six or fewer questions affirmatively preferred Kerry 60% to 40%, Gallup's poll would project a 54% to 46% Bush victory, but based on the actual validated University of Michigan findings of "likely voters" actual propensity to vote, Kerry would actually prevail at the polls by 52% to 48%—a 12 percentage-point swing.[231]

EMPIRICAL EVIDENCE THAT LIKELY VOTER CUTOFF MODELS ARE FLAWED

We are not the first to note this methodological flaw. Steve Soto at leftcoaster.com, suspicious about a September 15, 2004, Gallup poll showing Bush with a huge 55% to 42% lead, obtained the company's "breakdowns by party identification for their likely voter samples" and found out that the Gallup model assumed that 40% of those turning out to vote in November would be Republicans and only 33% would be Democrats.[232] Two weeks later, the party breakdown had turned even more Republican so as to assume an electorate that was 43% Republican and only 31% Democratic—a full 12-percentage-point differential—despite no indication that Republican registrations or self-identification even equaled that of the Democratic Party.

Ruy Teixeira, a senior fellow at the Center for American Progress, examined a Gallup poll and found its likely voter sample to be very unrepresentative of the electorate, with implausibly low representation among key Kerry constituencies.[233] According to Gallup's model voting sample, African Americans make up 7.5% of the electorate, minorities in general represent 14.5% of the electorate, and young people, those age 18 to 29, compose only 11% of the electorate.

The unadjusted Election Day 2004 exit-poll figures[234] bear Teixeira and Soto out. According to the NEP numbers, African Americans comprised 11% of voters, supporting Kerry over Bush 90% to 10%; minorities, in general, represented 23% of voters, supporting Kerry over Bush 72% to 26%; and young people, those age 18 to 29, represented 17% of voters, supporting Kerry over Bush 56% to 42%. These demographic distortions, in themselves, fully account for the discrepancy between the pre-election telephone-poll projections and the Election Day exit polls.

FIGURE 6C: DISTORTIONS IN THE GALLUP LIKELY VOTER SURVEY SAMPLE

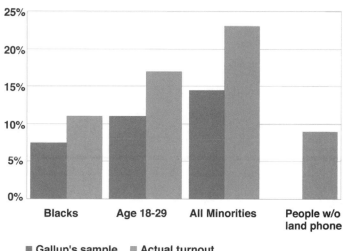

■ Gallup's sample ■ Actual turnout

Gallup is not the only polling firm to use these flawed likely-voter cutoff models. Shortly before the 2004 election, Blumenthal conducted a survey of twenty-two national pollsters and found that all but one of them use a cutoff procedure to define likely voters.[235]

Newsweek's sample of registered voters, for example, in a post–G.O.P. convention, early September 2004 poll consisted of 38% Republicans, 31% Democrats, and 31% Independent voters. Pollster John Zogby took issue with *Newsweek*'s findings that Bush had an 11-percentage-point lead over Kerry. His polls at the time showed Bush with a 2 percentage-point lead. "There is no evidence anywhere to suggest the Democrats will only represent 31% of the total vote this year," he said.[236] Zogby also pointed out that in both the 1996 and 2000 elections his polling came closest to the official results.

These concerns about polling methodology are not trivial. As summarized in table 6.9, flawed methodologies produce a large swing. The results of eight presidential elections—all the experience we have with measuring public opinion—suggest that nearly all the undecided votes ought to be allocated to the challenger. If in 2004 we allocate them only 2:1 Kerry, that produces a 1% swing. An adjustment for those with no landline telephone—nearly one-tenth of the population with significantly different attributes, attitudes, and preferences—produces a swing of more than 2 percentage points. Most important is an adjustment for flawed likely-voter models. No careful methodologist would even consider using a cutoff model, as given what we know about these models and the samples they produce, it's probably conservative to estimate that they systematically produce a 4 percentage-point swing. Add them together, as in table 6.9, and you have a swing of about 7 percentage points in the 2004 U.S. presidential election.

TABLE 6.9: ADJUSTMENT TO TELEPHONE POLLS FOR METHODOLOGICAL FLAWS

	BUSH	KERRY	MARGIN
TELEPHONE POLLS (REPORTED)	49%	47%	Bush +1.5%
a. Adjustment for undecideds	1%	2%	
b. Adjustment for those with no landline phone	-1%	1%	
c. Adjustment for flawed likely voter models	-2%	2%	
ADJUSTED TELEPHONE POLL ESTIMATES	47%	52%	Kerry +5%

How could polling organizations make such a mistake? Pollsters are, after all, smart people in a highly competitive business, one that's dependent on good results. But good results are defined as those that matched the official count.

Every election cycle, both exit pollsters and telephone pollsters adjust their models—and the assumptions behind their models—to come up with a new model that would have accurately predicted the count of the past election. They thereby create an iterative loop that is based less on sound methodology and more on official election results—results that pollsters assume as a matter of course to be correct. If in previous elections votes have gone uncounted or fraud had been committed, for the next election pollsters would create models that have unwittingly incorporated such miscount or fraud, regardless of how methodologically flawed those new models might be. For this reason it is important to examine the merits of exit pollsters' research methods independently of any assumption that the official count was correct. With their models adapted to match the count, if fraud or systematic variance from voter intent were to gradually enter into the system, pollsters would be unable to detect the continued or marginally incremented distortions created by the fraud.

SO HOW DID AMERICA VOTE?

Our inquiries that began with an investigation of the exit-poll discrepancy, by force expanded to address larger questions about how our democracy works and about polling methodology. In the absence of a verifiable count we have considered every other means at our disposal for estimating how America really voted.

One estimate is the election-night exit polls, which projected a 3 percentage-point Kerry victory. A second, also based on the exit polls, relies on WPD. (Even the "unadjusted" election-night exit polls were compromised by averaging with telephone polls.)

These numbers extrapolated out to a 4.6 percentage-point Kerry victory.

A different estimate is derived from using the 2000 election as an anchor and making adjustments on the basis of measurable changes. This analysis extrapolated out to a 5 percentage-point Kerry victory.

Finally, we analyzed polling data, not so as to track the count as the pollsters do, but rather to attempt to accurately assess actual voting behavior. Our analysis showed that on average pre-election polls would have swung estimates by about 7 percentage points in this election. Therefore, rather than a 1.5 to 2 percentage-point Bush edge, polling data probably reflected what should have been a 5 percentage-point Kerry victory.

So how did America really vote? Every independent measure points to a Kerry victory of about 5 percentage points in the popular vote nationwide, a swing of 8 to 10 million votes from the official count. And, if anything, the exit-poll numbers understated Kerry's share of the vote. All indications are that—contrary to Edison/Mitofsky—Bush voters participated in the exit polls at a slightly higher rate than Kerry voters. Higher response rates in Bush precincts, Bush states, and among Bush 2000 voters all suggest that Kerry's share of the vote should have been higher than the exit-poll numbers indicated.

Moreover, as we have previously pointed out, WPD does not account for all the sources of fraud and disenfranchisement. All our calculations up until now have not even taken into account Americans who tried and failed to register or tried and failed to vote. Nor do they account for any fraud associated with absentee ballots and early voting.

All these additional sources of miscount almost certainly helped Bush and hurt Kerry. In Ohio, there is little doubt that many tens of thousands of mostly Democratic voters were denied the opportunity to register and that Democrats were disproportionately dissuaded or prevented from casting a ballot owing to broken or unallocated voting machines. Our estimate that Kerry won nationally by 5 percentage points does not even take into account these lost votes, which were heavily for Kerry. In Florida, there is little doubt that widespread loss and disqualification of absentee ballots in Democratic Broward and Palm Beach counties cost thousands of net Kerry votes. Yet we did not attempt to quantify or figure in this factor either.

Table 5.4 revealed the outcome in each state based on how exit-poll respondents reported casting their votes. These exit-poll reports indicate that Kerry should have prevailed in Ohio by about 8.8 percentage points, in Nevada by about 7.5 points, and in New Mexico by about 7.0 points. These large margins leave very little room for doubt. Victory in these three states (or even only in Ohio) would have given Kerry the presidency.

Kerry likely also won at least two of the other states in which exit polls indicated he had an edge (albeit within the polling margin of error): Florida (2.9 percentage points), Iowa (2.3 points), and Colorado (1.4 points). He may well have also received a plurality of votes in one or more of the three states in which he trailed, but by less than the polling margin of error: Virginia (0.3 points), North Carolina (1.1 points), and Missouri (1.4 points).

In short, every calculation of how America voted indicates that, rather than giving Bush a 3-million-vote plurality, American voters gave Kerry a plurality of at least 5 to 7 million votes. And had ballots been counted as cast, Kerry would have received between 282 and 364 electoral votes, more than the 270 required to win.

CHAPTER 7

Responsible Journalism Versus Conspiracy Theory

In November 2004, concern about a possible fraudulent election based on an exit-poll discrepancy made headlines across America. However, it was not that month's U.S. presidential election that generated interest, but rather an election in a former Soviet republic halfway around the globe where the exit polls indicated election fraud was afoot. Yet the U.S. media never questioned why a comparable discrepancy here meant nothing, despite the fact that the U.S. exit poll suffered from none of the shortcomings observed in Ukraine.

Indeed, the mainstream media showered their scorn on the very idea that the U.S. exit-poll discrepancy was a possible indication of election fraud before even investigating the allegation. Given what had happened in 2000 and, for that matter, 2002, one might have expected an imperative to look at election issues closely. But the trend since 2000, when the Republicans took the White House through a judicial ruling, has not been toward greater vigilance, but toward no vigilance.

In the days following the presidential election, media coverage of the exit-poll discrepancy was strikingly limited. The brouhaha reported in the mainstream media was not the discrepancy between the exit polls and the count, but the fact that so-called "uncorrected" data had been released to the public.[237]

The six media outlets that established the NEP provided virtually no analysis of why this had happened. The *New York Times* reported that it obtained a report by pollsters that "debunked the possibility that the exit polls are right and the vote count is wrong,"[238] but the *Times* did not explain how the report "debunked" the discrepancy. In fact, no one in the media presented any evidence of skewed survey data or of any other problem with the polls other than the fact that they did not match the count.

Following Election Day 2004, the Internet was abuzz with prominent bloggers, journalists on network news sites, and political activists raising questions about whether the election was stolen. Some were sincere yet uninformed speculations, but others were sober statistical studies of the election results that raised legitimate questions.

In the days following the election, two different analyses of the election results were published on the Web, both raising questions about the integrity of the official 2004 vote count.

Steven Freeman, one of the authors of this book, examined the unexplained discrepancy between the exit polls and the official count, which we outline in Chapter 4.[239] And Michael Hout, a sociologist at the University of California, Berkeley, examined correlations between voting-machine technology and anomalies in the official count in Florida, which we discuss in Chapter 3.

A month later, in December 2004, a group of statisticians, mathematicians, and survey methodologists formed an ad hoc group, U.S. Count Votes. (We examined their work in Chapter 5.) The group posted studies examining the exit-poll discrepancy and 2004 electoral anomalies. And, fostering a spirit of academic inquiry, they also published (or provided links to) critiques of their work by fellow academics, and then responded to that criticism.

Unfortunately, this level of analysis and subsequent debate has been confined to the Web. It has failed to find its way into either print or broadcast media. And when these issues were covered, it was done badly. The reasons for this, if understandable, are unacceptable.

One of the problems is that the mainstream media showered their scorn on the very idea of a stolen election before having done any investigation. This could not have been more unlike what happened in 2000.

Dan Thanh Dang of the *Baltimore Sun* put it this way: "John F. Kerry barely had time to concede the presidential race before the conspiracy theory began circulating." The headline for that story: "Election Paranoia Surfaces; Conspiracy Theorists Call Results Rigged."[240]

The *Washington Post*'s Manuel Roig-Franzia and Dan Keating, in an article titled "Latest Conspiracy Theory—Kerry Won—Hits the Ether," wrote, "The bloggers and the mortally wounded party loyalists and the spreadsheet-wielding conspiracy theorists are filling the Internet with head-turning allegations."[241]

By treating allegations of election fraud as the domain of the unhinged, these and other stories in the mainstream press established an official story about the official count. The story of Election Day vote fraud became one that journalists pursued at their peril. For a journalist to publicly raise questions about the integrity of the election, that is, question conventional wisdom, was to invite ridicule.

This was particularly true because the "facts" of the story, as presented by the media, make it appear that the case against election fraud was rock solid. Alexander Cockburn in the December 6 *Nation* dismissed any speculation about the integrity of the election: "As usual, the conspiracy nuts think plans of inconceivable complexity worked at 100% efficiency." His sentiments were echoed on the *Nightline* report "Conspiracy Theory: Did George W. Bush Steal the Election?" ABC News' Cokie Roberts explained, "This notion . . . [t]hat there's just this vast conspiracy flies in the face of human experience. We've never known a conspiracy to work that well."[242] Or at least not since 2000, when the Republican Party shifted into conspiratorial overdrive to prevent a recount in Florida. Besides, Roberts presents a tautology. Other conspiracies have been attempted and subsequently exposed—Watergate and the Iran-contra scandal, to name two. The conspiracies that work are, by definition, not widely known.

Daniel Tokaji, an assistant professor of law at Ohio State University, echoed Cockburn's and Roberts's sentiments on his Web site:

> How in the world do [the statisticians at U.S. Vote Counts] hypothesize that hundreds of thousands of votes were switched on election night, in the 13,000 or so different local jurisdictions that are responsible for administering elections, using different types of voting equipment manufactured by several different companies? Were all of these folks in on some grand conspiracy? ... The decentralization of our election system has many disadvantages, but one of its advantages is that it makes it practically impossible to pull off the sort of grand conspiracy that USCV hypothesizes. You may be able to bribe one election official or even a dozen. But how do you bribe thousands without being detected?[243]

To the average intelligent person, it would appear that Cockburn, Roberts, and Tokaji have a good point. However, electronic voting machines are vulnerable to fraud precisely because corrupting them does not require "plans of inconceivable complexity."

Unlike financial institutions, where computer-security firewalls ensure against electronic theft, few safeguards are in place to protect voting equipment from outside interference. (See Chapter 3.) O'Dell, of U.S. Count Votes, responded to this complexity argument:

> Modern voting systems are geographically distributed computing systems, and computer security professionals regard all such systems as inherently vulnerable. Regardless of the nature and type of pre-release testing and certification, the process of replicating software to the hundreds or thousands

of devices to be deployed in the field is *inherently* vulnerable to systematic manipulation. It would only take a few malicious insiders to corrupt the master copies of voting software, thereby undetectably altering the behavior of thousands of voting machines. Worse yet, rogue insiders have first-hand, detailed knowledge of any internal security mechanisms and are thus ideally equipped to subvert them. Since just three companies tally upwards of 80% of the U.S. vote, the potential risk of systematic nationwide manipulation of vote counting equipment by a small group of rogue insiders cannot be dismissed out-of-hand.... These considerations are so obvious to computer professionals that an overwhelming majority of 95% of the computer scientists and software engineers polled by the Association for Computing Machinery in 2004 opposed deployment of unauditable electronic voting systems. The vendors of electronic voting systems and their advocates in academia and industry are out-of-step with the mainstream. Computer security professionals know that human ingenuity knows no bounds when the prize is sufficiently large.[244]

The *New York Times* has provided the most extensive mainstream coverage of the exit-poll discrepancies and allegations that fraud tainted the 2004 election. Yet the *Times*'s coverage was always based on the premise that there is nothing to such allegations, and that the problem lay with the pollsters and their faulty exit polls. Indeed, the *Times* requested that NEP provide a partial refund. Catherine Mathis, the paper's spokeswoman, explained that Executive Editor Bill Keller had written NEP "expressing our sense that we were ill-served."[245]

The way the *Times* handled the story is significant. As the "newspaper of record," the *Times* provides what is considered the factually accurate account of events. And in this role it sets the tone and defines the limits of public debate.

On November 12, in the wake of Freeman posting his analysis on the Web and the considerable attention it generated, the *New York Times*'s Tom Zeller began his front-page story, "Vote Fraud Theories, Spread by Blogs, Are Quickly Buried," with language that dismissed the possibility of fraud:

> The e-mail messages and Web postings had all the twitchy cloak-and-dagger thrust of a Hollywood blockbuster. . . . In the space of seven days, an online market of dark ideas surrounding last week's presidential election took root and multiplied.

To back up this assertion, Zeller told his readers of "ground zero in the online rumor mill"—a misinformed analysis of the Florida election results that was posted by Kathy Dopp on ustogether.org. Dopp wrote that in many Florida counties Bush got more votes than the number of registered Republicans—and she provided the data to back it up. What she said was true, and her observation swirled around the Internet. But, as Zeller noted, political scientists soon pointed out that "many of those Democratic counties in Florida have a long tradition of voting Republican in presidential elections." Zeller wasn't alone; reporters at the *Washington Post* and *The Nation*'s David Corn similarly pointed to Dopp's failure to understand Dixiecrat politics and dismissed the allegations of fraud.

Zeller next turned to the Election Day exit polls. He wrote:

> The early Election Day polls, conducted for a consortium of television networks and The Associated Press, which proved largely inaccurate in showing Mr. Kerry leading in Florida and Ohio, continued to be offered as evidence that the Bush team somehow cheated. . . . A preliminary study produced by the Voting Technology Project, a cooperative effort between the California Institute of Technology and

the Massachusetts Institute of Technology . . . found "no particular patterns" relating to voting systems and the final results of the election. "The 'facts' that are being circulated on the Internet," the study concluded, "appear to be selectively chosen to make the point."

Zeller was right. The MIT-CalTech Voting Technology Project, the only research center established to examine voting technologies, issued a report on November 9, 2004, refuting allegations of vote fraud.[246] Voting Technology Project analysts concluded that exit-poll data were consistent with official state tallies and that there was no correlation between the exit-poll discrepancies and the voting technology used—systems using electronic, hand-counted, or punch-card ballots, for example.

Yet it turned out the Voting Technology Project validated their claim by relying on exit-poll data that were adjusted—or "corrected," as the pollsters put it—by NEP to conform to the official count. In other words, they used data that was formulated based on the official count (which was presumed to be correct) to prove that the count is correct. On December 5, 2004, the MIT-Caltech Voting Technology Project corrected its miscalculation and issued an addendum to the report that acknowledged both their mistake and the fact that the exit-poll discrepancy was real:

> Early polls released [and cited by the Voting Technology Project in its report "Voting Machines and the Underestimate of the Bush Vote"] were "corrected" to more closely correspond with officially reported election results, and therefore did not accurately represent the large inaccuracies in exit-poll data.[247]

No corresponding correction was ever issued in the *New York Times* or the *Washington Post*, both of which also cited the Voting

Technology Project report. The public record was thus not corrected where it mattered most.

Given that members of the media had been provided with misinformation by research institutions as august as MIT and CalTech—misinformation that explicitly discounted the relevance of the exit-poll discrepancy—the paralysis was partly understandable. Nonetheless, the absence of major investigations by major news organizations on so important a story remains a mystery.

John Allen Paulos, a professor of mathematics at Temple University, has written one of the few articles examining the exit-poll discrepancy to be published in the mainstream press. Paulos is the author of "Who's Counting," a monthly column for ABC News' Web site[248] and was the 2003 winner of the American Association for the Advancement of Science award for the promotion of public understanding of science. In an op-ed article for the *Philadelphia Inquirer*, he reported on Freeman's Web-published research, writing, "If the people sampled in the exit polls were a random sample of voters, Freeman's standard statistical techniques show that these large discrepancies are way, way beyond the margins of error."

Paulos doesn't understand why his colleagues don't take a greater interest in the exit-poll discrepancy. "What I find more interesting than media indifference is academic indifference," says Paulos. "The country is full of mathematicians, scientists and others who know enough statistics and have enough common sense to understand the importance of the issue."[249]

A culture of open inquiry has not been fostered in the media. ABC's *Nightline* devoted its inauguration-eve broadcast to a segment titled, "Conspiracy Theory: Did George W. Bush Steal the Election?" *Nightline* discussed the exit polls, but only to dismiss them.

Warren Mitofsky, who that day had released Edison/Mitofsky, appeared on camera and reiterated his core assumption: "Our analysis of the exit polls suggests that we had slightly better cooperation from the Kerry voters than from the Bush voters. In other words, the nonresponse was not even. There was some unevenness to it. And it favored Kerry."

The *Nightline* voice-over then says, "Even Democratic pollsters such as Mark Blumenthal are satisfied with that." Rather than invite serious comment from a prominent pollster such as John Zogby or one of the academics who had written about the exit polls, such as ABC's own columnist, John Allen Paulos, *Nightline* offered Mystery Pollster Mark Blumenthal, who duly parroted Mitofsky's rationale.

> There is a bit of a statistical food fight here if you go on the Internet, between those who really want to find that the exit polls are evidence of some fraud, and some of us who are more skeptical. And what I've said before is I think it's a lot of sound and fury signifying not very much. Because, at the end of the day, Warren Mitofsky agrees, I agree, everyone agrees that there was a small and probably insignificant error across the whole country.

At which point, Blumenthal says it's time to move on and the *Nightline* voice-over says: "But even tonight, as the capital sky lights up to celebrate tomorrow's inauguration, a certain segment of the electorate, disappointed and frustrated, cannot seem to let go of the election that their man lost. So, in Web sites and e-mails and corner taverns, the argument will go on, while the history books record that George W. Bush won the 2004 presidential election by a margin of 3,000,169." Case closed.

Against this backdrop of indifference in the media in an open-minded inquiry, the Chicago Tribune Company turned to censorship. The company's syndication branch, Tribune Media Services (TMS), killed one of the three columns on the subject written by Robert Koehler.

In April 2005, Koehler, who is both a regular columnist and an editor at the service, attended the National Election Reform Conference, sponsored by a broad coalition and held in Nashville. Subsequently, he wrote two columns that were distributed by TMS: "The Silent Scream of Numbers—The 2004 Election Was Stolen—Will Someone Please Tell the Media?" and "Democracy's Abu Ghraib—If They Can Disable an Election What's Coming Next?"

And while the *Chicago Tribune* itself did not run Koehler's column, the paper's "Public Editor," Don Wycliffe, did write a column, "Winning Isn't Everything," in which he tried to rebut Koehler's first column, by invoking the example of Richard Nixon, not the Watergate Nixon but the one who in 1960 gracefully accepted defeat rather than charge electoral fraud. In response, Koehler devoted his next column to a rebuttal of Wycliffe. This was the column that TMS promptly killed.

Koehler had opened that ill-fated third column with a quotation from Lord Thomas Babington Macaulay, the nineteenth-century Scottish historian, whose words are enshrined on the lobby of the neo-Gothic *Chicago Tribune* building: "Where there is a free press the governors must live in constant awe of the opinions of the governed."

He continued, writing in part:

> Wycliffe was speaking only for himself, not "the media," but because his column was one of the few pieces to appear in a major publication even acknowledging that a huge number of Americans are distraught at mounting evidence of large-scale disenfranchisement in 2004 (and no guarantee that 2006 and 2008 will be any different), his words, by default, have special resonance. They stand in for the prejudices of the media as a whole. . . . Could it be we can't have election reform without media reform?

Some outlets in the independent media also gave discussion of 2004 election irregularities short shrift. The online journal tompaine.com initially ran a story by Greg Palast that cast doubt on the election results, but then turned to freelance journalist Russ Baker to continue its post-election coverage.

Baker wrote an article that belittled the idea that the exit-poll discrepancy was in any way an indication of fraud. "We listen to their conspiracy theories because—frightened by the direction our country has taken—we want to believe them." To support this contention, Baker cited an unnamed source who told him, "You're talking about a bunch of naïve people that had [only] the first course in statistics."

Tompaine.com allowed Freeman to respond in a letter to the editor. Freeman wrote, in part:

> One can understand why incumbent politicians would try to dismiss threatening thought as "conspiracy theory," but a serious journalist would not use pejorative labels so as to avoid engaging in the merits of a discussion. Scrutiny of an election with many unanswered questions does not damage public confidence in the democracy; absence of scrutiny does. Baker proudly claims to be an "old fashioned investigative reporter," which makes this article all the more disappointing. Investigative reporting is exactly what the country needs.[250]

Baker answered Freeman with a rebuttal. He criticized Freeman both for his exit-poll analysis and for his citation of the investigation by Rep. John Conyers (D.-Mich.) and his Democratic House Judiciary Committee staff. Baker writes:

> He credits a "commission" headed by Rep. John Conyers. But that "commission" didn't extensively investigate first hand.

Mostly it just took statements from voters and activists, statements that were not fully vetted for their accuracy or for the likelihood that specific cases could be broadly extrapolated.

Conyers then entered the debate. On the subject of the exit-poll discrepancy, he wrote:

> Baker is correct when he says that aberrant results in exit polls are not proof of election irregularities. They are one indicia or warning that something may have gone wrong, either with the polling or with the election, and that the election results bear greater scrutiny. In this election, the exit polls were divergent from official results to a degree that was unprecedented and I concluded more examination of the official results was needed. After such examination and a lack of any plausible explanation for the exit-poll discrepancies, I have reached the conclusions described ... in my report.

Conyers defended his Judiciary Committee investigation this way:

> Baker makes a number of assertions about my work and the work of my staff that I believe are unfounded and inaccurate. Among other things, he says that I and my staff did not "extensively investigate first hand" allegations of voter disenfranchisement. In fact, my staff reviewed thousands of pages of primary source materials, including copies of actual ballots, voter registration data bases, and poll books and met with several individuals having first hand knowledge of irregularities.

Baker's widely read articles on Tompaine.com were significant, because they served to squelch further inquiry by establishing a "conventional wisdom" in the independent press. It became a story very few news outlets wanted to touch.

A November 14, 2004, *New York Times* editorial at least recognized the scope and nature of the problem posed by easily corruptible voting systems. The editorial put it this way:

> There is no evidence of vote theft or errors on a large scale.... There is also no way to be sure that the nightmare scenario of electronic voting critics did not occur: votes surreptitiously shifted from one candidate to another inside the machines, by secret software.

However, the editorial failed to consider the one chain of evidence that indicates vote theft or errors did occur on a large scale: the exit-poll discrepancy.

Given that august research institutions—specifically the MIT-CalTech Voting Technology Project—had two days earlier provided members of the media, including the *Times*'s Zeller, with misinformation that explicitly but mistakenly denied the existence of the exit-poll discrepancy, the *New York Times*'s editorial oversight is partly understandable. The Voting Technology Project posted their correction, but when the issue refused to go away (first because of mostly anecdotal complaints and then the release of the Conyers and DNC reports) the *Times* should have undertaken further investigation. That it never did so is inexcusable.

Whether the subject is highly suspicious election results or concocted intelligence reports, since Election Day 2000, the 2000 Bush-Cheney Campaign and then the Bush administration have had unprecedented success in shaping and guiding the nation's political discourse. In that same period, the nation's premier newspapers and network news shows have increasingly refused to challenge the Bush administration, whether on election fraud, the rationale for war, or, as most recently, the brazen reinterpretation of the Constitution in order to grant the president greater power at the expense of Congress.

In a January 16, 2006, speech, Al Gore directly confronted Bush's presidential power grab:

> An Executive who abrogates to himself the power to ignore the legitimate legislative directives of the Congress or to act free of the check of the judiciary becomes the central threat that the Founders sought to nullify in the Constitution—an all-powerful Executive too reminiscent of the King from whom they had broken free. . . . As the Executive acts outside its constitutionally prescribed role and is able to control access to information that would expose its actions, it becomes increasingly difficult for the other branches to police it. Once that ability is lost, democracy itself is threatened and we become a government of men and not laws.

Yet by not raising an alarm, the media has passively enabled a power grab on the part of this president. Instead of using their vast power to inform public opinion, they have, in large part, refused to step outside their "objective" bubble to challenge the Bush administration. Journalist Robert Parry, who as a *Newsweek* reporter in the 1980s helped expose the Iran-contra scandal, has put it bluntly:

> George W. Bush has gutted the U.S. Constitution, the Bill of Rights, the Geneva Conventions and the United Nations Charter—yet this extraordinary story does not lead the nation's newspapers and the evening news every day. Nor does the press corps tie Bush's remarkable abrogation of both U.S. and international law together in any coherent way for the American people. At best, disparate elements of

Bush's authoritarian powers are dealt with individually as if they are not part of some larger, more frightening whole.[251]

Part of that "frightening whole" is the extent to which the Bush administration and its political campaign operations have successfully corrupted the last two presidential elections. As we have laid out in this book, the results of the 2000 and 2004 elections are far more suggestive of a stolen election than an honest election. We have found almost no substantiation of the official results by which Bush was reelected–and multiple factors confirming that Kerry won in 2004 with a 5% plurality. Yet the national press corps has thus far refused even to seriously investigate the possibility that the 2004 election was stolen.

So why the silence on the part of the press?

That a journalistic examination of the exit-poll discrepancy is deemed "not fit to print" by both the corporate and the independent media indicates how far our standards have devolved. It seems undeniable to us that the very same set of facts applied to a foreign election anywhere in the world would have garnered front-page coverage in every American newspaper and would have been the lead story on every American news program. If election fraud in Ukraine or in Haiti is news, why isn't election fraud in the United States?

CHAPTER 8

There Can Be No Moving On

This book asks questions about the health of the American electoral system in light of the irregularities that plagued the 2004 presidential election. Over and over we have attempted to bring the facts to bear in our search for answers as those fact become available.

Our investigations were never fruitless. The longer and harder we looked, the more we read as new information became available, the clearer the picture became. There was the Conyers Report, released on January 6, 2005, the Evaluation of Edison/Mitofsky, released on January 19, 2005, the Democratic National Committee report, released June 22, 2005, and the GAO's Report to Congressional Requesters, released on September 21, 2005. Although none of these documents pretended to have all the answers, they all contained vital information. Far from relying only on the exit-poll data, we read widely and had countless soul-searching conversations with each other and with our colleagues.

We devote entire chapters to important related issues—the dilemma of new electronic voting franchises and their impact on elections, the legacy of Florida 2000 and its impact on our present electoral reality, and most importantly, the wealth of information exit polls can provide when they are analyzed in an informed way.

The story of exit-poll discrepancy is decidedly nonpartisan. We cannot let *Firing Line*–style partisan politics turn this into a partisan issue. Exit polls are a vital tool to ensure election integrity. The best use of the exit polls is not to oppose or replace the official count, but rather to serve as an alarm system to ensure democratic process. It may turn out to be the case that the most accurate count in the 2004 presidential election was the exit-poll result. But the point isn't to have to choose now between the exit-poll result and the official count. In a working democracy, other checks and balances step in to carry the investigation to its proper conclusion. When exit polls contradict rather than confirm the official count, other parts of the machinery of democracy need to be activated, including the free press, which has the skills and the responsibility to investigate, and nonpartisan government bodies, which, through an entirely different array of methods, also have the skills and a civic mandate to investigate. The exit polls are a vital and most useful trigger. They can be and have been the primary basis to overturn a national election, but in a working democracy they must also serve as catalysts to spur greater public involvement until the truth is found out and acted upon. The concerns raised by the exit polls in this election should have been enough to set into motion an array of investigations and regulations and dissent.

THE FACTS SPEAK LOUDLY AND WITH STARTLING CONSISTENCY

Our investigations lead us to conclude that we have little reason to trust the official results in the 2004 U.S. presidential election. Few jurisdictions provided compelling verification that votes were counted as cast. Sixty-four percent of Americans voted on DRE voting machines or optical-scan systems, both of which are, to different degrees, vulnerable to interference through hacking or programming fraud. In most cases we are being asked in effect to place our absolute trust in voting-machine corporations that have failed to meet minimal expectations of impartiality, honesty, freedom from conflict of interest, and transparency.

Why haven't the companies that produce electronic voting machines made them so that they provide an audit trail (which is easily achieved through paper records)? And why haven't they allowed government regulators to inspect their software? The answer to both these questions is that no one has effectively demanded that they do so. The American people do need to insist.

But even where paper records exist, few jurisdictions provided compelling verification that votes were counted as cast. We devoted a chapter to the ills of electronic voting, but a critical lesson from the 2004 election is that not only DREs, but all kinds of voting machine systems are suspect. Edison/Mitofsky data showed that while hand counted ballots accurately reflected exit-poll survey results, counts from all the major categories of voting machines did not. The only fundamental difference between DREs and many other voting systems is a paper record, but a paper record ensures a fair count only if it is properly used.

Where audit trails exist, financial hurdles, statutory prohibitions, and extralegal mechanisms prevent manual recounts. Even when audits or "recounts" are conducted, lax procedures regarding machine and ballot custody cast doubt upon inspections performed weeks later.

As is the case in any system where there are incentives to cheat, random audits must be conducted to keep voting machine companies and office holders honest. In Ohio, the Green Party paid for a recount of Ohio's ballots, but rather than acting in accord with Ohio law that counties choose a random sample of 3% of the total votes cast, Blackwell interpreted "random" to mean a sample of the county's choosing. As American Statistical Association President Fritz Scheuren put it, this is "analogous to IRS agents allowing taxpayers to choose for themselves the items on their tax returns to be audited."

Highly partisan election officials have, in 2000 and 2004, bent and broken rules with impunity. Widespread malfeasance and many thousands individual acts of vote suppression, some legal, others not, have been documented. Representative Conyers's report is a damning document, but too few voices in Congress are taking up the case.

Unless new facts surface to lend credibility to the official outcome of the 2004 election, a large segment of the American population will always believe that had the votes been counted as cast Bush would have been decisively defeated. A democracy cannot long withstand this level of doubt in its own most fundamental integrity.

National exit polls indicate that Bush suffered a defeat in the popular vote by approximately 7 million votes, a margin of about 5 percentage points. On the other hand, the official story of Bush's 3 million vote victory is simply not substantiated by the data. The only conclusion consistent with the data is that the 2004 U.S. presidential election was stolen.

None of the explanations given thus far for why the official count differed so dramatically from the exit-poll results explains the disparity. They must be investigated impartially and by institutions that can be trusted to conduct such investigations. Why have neither the national press nor our national government conducted any of the investigations that would disabuse us of our doubt in the election result? Why isn't the election industry, especially the electronic-voting-system industry, heavily regulated? Why is it not at least as heavily regulated as the slot-machine industry?

PROOF AND DISPROOF

We looked closely at evidence that might disprove the possibility of a stolen election. Many considered New Hampshire to be such evidence, as Ralph Nader's organization paid for a manual recount in that state to explain the large exit-poll discrepancy there and the recount appeared to validate the official count.

Yet in New Hampshire, a small battleground state with a comparatively open recount law, anyone intending to steal the election would have proceeded cautiously so as not to be detected. And because it is fairly easy for a candidate to request a recount in this state, it was foreseeable that there would be one.

Nothing about the count or recount in New Hampshire—one of the states, by the way, that Kerry won in both the exit polls and the official count—in any way changes the near–statistical impossibility of the nationwide prevalence of discrepancies that favored Bush in the official count. One anecdotal piece of evidence does not disprove an analysis based on an overwhelming preponderance of data. That there would be a few states beyond the polling margin of error is not surprising or even suspicious; what is suspicious is that in 44 out of 50 states, Bush's official numbers were better than respondents reported in confidential exit-poll surveys. We would expect this number to be within a range of 14 to 36, not 44 (see Appendix B). Even more astounding, in 26 of these 44 states, the disparity is beyond the polling margin of error. We would expect no more than 1 or 2 such anomalies.

New Hampshire may well deserve further scrutiny in any event. We learned on pages 32 and 33 of Edison/Mitofsky that, until 2004, only four state WPDs of 10.0 or higher had ever been recorded in a presidential election. Two of the four were in New Hampshire. In 1992, Bush Sr.'s official count was 10.1 percentage points better, relative to Clinton, than voters reported. In 1996, Dole's official count was 12.2 percentage points better, relative to Clinton, than voters reported.

CURES WORSE THAN THE DISEASE

In the aftermath of Florida 2000, the media and academics roundly ridiculed punch-card voting systems. But rather than investigate, report, and prosecute criminal actions, Congress both blamed and put faith in technology. And so the United States rushed headlong into a brave new world of electronic voting, trading the imprecision of counting chads for blind trust in Diebold, ES&S, and Sequoia. The result: HAVA, the 2002 and 2004 general elections, and our present precipitous position. Unfortunately, in response to the chaos of November 2004 and the scramble to meet the new election systems requirements of the 2002 HAVA legislation, history may be repeating itself. Rather than address the root problems of fraud and verifiability with courage and honesty, election officials have embarked on another set of cures that may prove worse than the disease.

Agencies overseeing U.S. elections—the National Association of State Election Directors, the Federal Elections Commission, and the United States Election Assistance Commission (established to oversee and aid HAVA spending)—have politely listened to testimony about the importance of voting verification, but have done little to ensure it. On the other hand, they have been moving forward with a variety of measures designed to increase early voting, voting by mail and absentee voting. Although these measures are proposed as important conveniences, such voting systems present both new invitations for fraud and extreme hurdles for verifiability. Absentee, early, and mail voting all raise chain-of-custody issues. In an honest voting system, all ballots would be kept secure from the time they are cast until the time they are counted. It's hard enough to ensure that with Election Day voting. Given current levels of election administration disorganization, it is not plausible that verifiable chains-of-custody can be secured for a week or more of early voting.

Absentee, early, and mail voting also obviate independent verification through an exit poll. If large numbers of voters cast their vote through alternative systems, we will no longer have a representative sample of voters showing up at the polls, from which accurate exit-poll surveys can be conducted.

Worst of all, we may never have another meaningful exit poll. A backlash against exit polling began when the official result sharply diverged from projections in the Florida 2000 presidential election. Computer malfunctions reportedly prevented the release of exit-poll data on Election Day 2002, and voting preference results were never released, although other public opinion data from the polls were. Speaking to the National Press Club in the aftermath of the 2004 election, Republican National Committee Chairman Ed Gillespie said, "I would encourage the media to abandon exit surveys on Election Day. . . . I've been through this before. In 2000 the exit data was wrong on Election Day. In 2002, the exit returns were wrong on Election Day. And in 2004, the exit data were wrong on Election Day—all three times, by the way, in a way that skewed against Republicans and had a dispiriting effect on Republican voters across the country."[252]

Even if exit polls are to be conducted, we may never again know the unadjusted results. We were only able to uncover the exit-poll discrepancy in 2004 because a technological glitch prevented NEP from doing "timely" update of adjusted data. In discussion of "improvements" for future elections, NEP pollster Warren Mitofsky emphasizes that no early unadjusted data will be released even to their clients.[253]

MOVING FORWARD

But there is still hope. In statehouses across the country, new legislation has been proposed and important lawsuits and legal actions are under way.

As of this writing, the most significant proposed national legislation is Representative Rush Holt's (D.-N.J.) Voter Confidence and Increased Accessibility Act, Bill HR 550, which would require the use of the voter-verified paper record in audits and recounts and make the paper ballot the ballot of record in the case of inconsistencies with elec-

tronic totals. HR 550 would also prohibit the use of undisclosed software and wireless communication devices in voting systems.

The bill, which needs to get through the Committee on House
Administration before it can be taken to a floor vote, has the support of Common Cause, Electronic Frontier Foundation,
VerifiedVoting.org, VotersUnite.org, VoteTrustUSA, and Working
Assets among others, although some voting rights activists are concerned that federal regulation of voting processes could have unin-
tended consequences.[254]

Because elections are administered at the state rather than the
federal level, most of the other significant developments are at the
state level, with closely watched reforms proposed in California,
New Mexico and critical swing states such as Ohio, Pennsylvania, and
Florida.

In Ohio, the League of Women Voters has brought a lawsuit
claiming that an inadequate statewide elections system has failed
to protect the fundamental rights of eligible Ohio voters to cast a
meaningful ballot, as required by the Equal Protection and Due
Process Clauses of the Fourteenth Amendment to the United States
Constitution. While the League of Women Voters' lawsuit does not
challenge the 2004 election results, it claims that the system treats
voters differently based on where they vote. Evidence in the claim
dates back as far as 1971.

In Pennsylvania, concerns in many counties over new machine
purchases have led to a proposed bipartisan bill, HB 2000, that
would give anyone who votes on an electronic machine the right to
inspect the paper record of the vote and correct mistakes before
leaving the polling place. The bill would also provide routine audits
of 5% of the votes in each county. According to VoteTrustUSA, over
half the states have already established requirements for voter verified paper records of every vote, and legislation has been introduced in a dozen others.

Finally, DRE machines themselves continue to be scrutinized, even as one of the major vendors, Diebold, faces a securities lawsuit and rumors that it may discontinue its voting-machine division. In Leon County, Florida, the supervisor of elections, Ion Sancho, authorized a "test" of his Diebold voting system to see if election results could be altered using only a memory card. Harri Hursti a computer programmer from Finland, who has been working with Black Box Voting, facilitated the test in which voters vote on an unnetworked touch-screen machine and also recorded their votes separately. By using a doctored memory card in the machine, Hursti was able to produce results completely different from what the test voters intended. When Diebold and other vendors then refused to sell new voting machines to Leon County, voting rights groups across the country wrote to Florida officials in support of Sancho.

And in California, a national citizens' group, VoterAction, has filed suit to nullify the California secretary of state's conditional certification of Diebold DREs scheduled to be used in 18 of the state's 52 counties in 2006. VoterAction led the successful recent litigation in New Mexico to stop the purchase and use of the most error prone voting machines there, leading Governor Richardson to advocate paper ballots for the state.

Although many of these initiatives would indicate a growing awareness of and a willingness to grapple with the problems, many state officials and elections commissioners—most but not all of them Republican, and many with close party ties—are actively resisting proposed reforms. These officials appear quite comfortable with and protective of the system as it is, and the HAVA-triggered move toward electronic voting.

LINGERING QUESTIONS AND THE TONE OF THE DEBATE

To many of the readers of this book one outstanding question is what happened to the Democrats. Had Kerry and the Democrats demanded an investigation and delayed their acceptance of defeat, would their speaking out then have acted as the spark to kick-start the safeguards of our democracy in the national press and in the federal government? Clearly some Americans believe they have been betrayed not just by the winners of the 2004 election, but also by the losers. It is one thing to steal an election, another to let it be stolen.

The tone of a debate and its quality are inextricably intertwined. In the absence of in-depth investigations, the few who questioned the election results—U.S. Representative John Conyers, the journalist Christopher Hitchens, the writer Mark Crispin Miller, blogger Keith Olbermann, investigative journalist Greg Palast, and others—were disparaged or ignored altogether.

In response to the release and spread of Freeman's initial report, "Unexplained Exit-Poll Discrepancy," Ken Mayer, a University of Wisconsin political science professor, told the *Capital Times* of Madison, Wisconsin, "We also have an obligation not to stoke the fires of conspiracy theories in the absence of real evidence." Although we wonder what Mayer would accept as "real evidence," his view is highly representative. Many in positions of responsibility are disinclined to raise questions or challenge the official count.

Are we at a crossroads in our history? Is this a time when we must confront a vast discrepancy of a different kind—between who we say we are as a people, and who we really are? Kurt Vonnegut, an American writer of German descent, once asked the German writer Günter Grass what the flaw was in the German character. Grass replied, "Obedience." If we have become a nation of "Good Germans," this is a change that would surprise most of us.

SKEPTICISM, INQUIRY, AND DEMOCRACY

You shouldn't have to *presume* a fair count. The mainstream media has, to all effects and purposes, established (to borrow the phrase of another great American novelist, Joseph Heller) a Catch-22 for election investigation. No investigation without proof—but then, what proof can be had without investigation?

The American public has a right to be skeptical about whether there was a fair count in the last presidential election, and to have their skepticism proven wrong by overwhelming evidence. In any functioning democracy, this test would consistently be met without stirring controversy. We shouldn't have to presume that the count is fair. Rather, given any of the many transgressions and statistical improbabilities in the 2004 presidential election, we have an obligation to question it. And those responsible have an obligation to investigate. Inquiry does not destroy a democracy, but rather strengthens it.

Elections are often likened to sporting contests. The thinking goes that Bush and the Republican Party fought hard for reelection, just as Kerry and the Democrats fought hard to defeat them, and once it's over it's time to accept the result and stand united as one nation. If we have any hope at all for civil relations after a hard-fought fight, we shake hands and congratulate our opponent. But elections are not sporting contests. And unless we can know without a shadow of a doubt that our elections are legitimate, we no longer have a functioning democracy.

Whether or not we have a functioning democracy is precisely what's at issue. Absence of scrutiny does not make a democracy function; democratic processes do. And among these processes is scrutiny by an independent national press. In the case of the 2004 presidential election, the absence of reporting on the election controversy has left the public highly suspicious. A Zogby Interactive online poll one month after the election revealed that 28.5% of respondents thought that questions about the accuracy of the official count in the election were "very valid", and another 14% thought that concerns were "somewhat valid." In other words, 42% of all Americans had immediate concerns about what had happened on November 2.[255] Even if our election processes were absolutely honest, the fact that so many doubt that they are undermines the credibility of our government. Our shockingly low turnout, among the lowest in all modern democracies, is in part a result of this lack of confidence in the results. So long as the suspicions are left to fester, the role of elections to confer legitimacy on elected officials has already been lost.

An insightful commentary on elections and their purposes comes from Jim Schiller, a Southeast Asian scholar who wrote: "Elections allow winners to say to losers: 'You have had your say, but we have won. Now you must follow the rules and let us go ahead with our policies.'"[256] But those who lost the election will accept the victors as legitimate only if they believe that they, in fact, had a fair shot, and that even though they may have lost this time, they have a fair chance to prevail in subsequent elections.

Honest inquiry into the integrity of the election does not divide the country. To the contrary, the only way to ever restore faith in our democracy is to ensure that reasonable questions receive thorough answers.

The cavalier attitude that seems to have taken hold thus far with regard to investigating the 2004 election, spanning academia, the media, and governmental and nongovernmental oversight bodies, is puzzling. What could be more important? This is not a Democratic or Republican issue. It concerns everyone, and it concerns everyone equally.

During his recent confirmation hearings, Supreme Court Chief Justice Designate John Roberts was forced to acknowledge, of the right to vote, that it "is preservative of all other rights." Without the power to elect our representatives, and especially, to vote out of office those who misuse power—ultimately we have no rights at all.

WHAT THE FUTURE HOLDS

We fear greatly for our country.

In *Battle for Florida*, deHaven-Smith, the professor of public policy at Florida State University, writes, "As an expert on Florida government and policy, I had been . . . aware that Florida's election laws were being undermined and subverted by the very people who were responsible for assuring their proper execution."[257] However, deHaven-Smith says that initially he was not too upset by this because he expected the dispute over the Florida 2000 election to lead to reforms in the electoral processes similar to those that arose from flawed presidential elections in 1800 and 1876.[258] But, that did not happen. He writes:

> What alarmed me was not the malfeasance and misfeasance of high officials but rather the inability of both the public and the media . . . to conduct a postmortem of the election fiasco, determine who was responsible for the electoral breakdown, hold officials accountable for any crimes, and enact constitutional and statutory reforms as necessary to root out corruption and to correct flaws in the system.

Lance deHaven-Smith, a scholar of the political history of Western Civilization, notes that the United States in undermining democracy is following a path of ancient Athens and Rome. Referring to the two great democracies of antiquity, he writes:

> . . . the first step of degeneration was a subversion of law in the name of higher values, such as stability and national security; and the decline into tyranny went unchecked by institutionalized oversight bodies, which we now refer to as the courts, because these bodies themselves became involved in the rivalry fueling the downward spiral.[259]

The courts and the media are widely recognized as the bulwarks of democracy. But the Supreme Court in *Bush v. Gore* inserted partisan politics into the judicial process and derailed the democratic process, while the U.S. media has, since that ruling, systematically avoided any reporting of serious election dysfunction. The U.S. exit-poll discrepancy went unreported here while an exit-poll discrepancy halfway around the world in the Ukraine generated front-page headlines here that very same month. The exit polls in Ukraine were sufficient evidence to overturn the elections there, but a far more reliable exit poll here in the United States was insufficient to even make the news.

In a way we are too complacent when we place the blame only on the media and our national oversight bodies. A nation depends also on its professional and educated elite to protect, or at least speak out about, abuse of power. But so few of the professionals and academics, who sit comfortably atop the status quo, have been willing to take responsibility as individual citizens. And in the end the question does rest with the citizenry, all the citizenry. How far are we going to let things go? How hard are we willing to fight for our democratic principles and processes?

If meaningful change is to come, it will be because something changed in us all, bringing a new wave of skepticism, of hope, of honest inquiry, of anger, and of common purpose.

German Exit Polls

In Germany, as soon as the polls close, polling agencies release prognoses that have proven highly reliable. In the three most recent national elections there, poll percentages diverged from official counts by an average of only 0.26% (table A1). They have been almost as accurate for the German vote in the European Parliament Elections (table A2), averaging 0.44% differential from tallied results over the past three elections.

TABLE A1: EXIT-POLL PREDICTIONS VS. OFFICIAL COUNTS IN

GERMAN NATIONAL ELECTIONS[260]

PARTIES	2002 PRED.	2002 TALLIED	2002 DIFF	1998 PRED.	1998 TALLIED	1998 DIFF	1994 PRED.	1994 TALLIED	1994 DIFF	AVG. DIFF
SPD	38.0%	38.5%	0.5%	41.0%	40.9%	0.1%	36.5%	36.4%	0.1%	
CDU/CSU	38.0%	38.5%	0.5%	35.0%	35.2%	0.2%	42.0%	41.4%	0.6%	
GREEN	9.0%	8.6%	0.4%	6.5%	6.7%	0.2%	7.0%	7.3%	0.3%	
FDP	7.5%	7.4%	0.1%	6.5%	6.2%	0.3%	7.0%	6.9%	0.1%	
PDS	4.0%	4.0%	0.0%	5.0%	5.1%	0.1%	4.0%	4.4%	0.4%	
REST	9.0%	8.6%		6.0%	5.9%		3.5%	3.6%		
AVERAGE DIFFERENTIAL			0.30%			0.18%			0.30%	0.26%

TABLE A2: EXIT-POLL PREDICTIONS VS. COUNTS IN EUROPEAN
PARLIAMENT ELECTIONS (GERMAN PART)

PARTIES	2004 PRED.	2004 TALLIED	2004 DIFF	1999 PRED.	1999 TALLIED	1999 DIFF	1998 PRED.	1998 TALLIED	1998 DIFF	AVG. DIFF
SPD	22.0%	21.5%	0.5%	31.0%	30.7%	0.3%	33.0%	32.2%	0.8%	
CDU/CSU	45.5%	44.5%	1.0%	48.0%	48.7%	0.7%	40.5%	38.8%	1.7%	
GREEN	11.5%	11.9%	0.4%	7.0%	6.4%	0.6%	10.0%	10.1%	0.1%	
FDP	6.0%	6.1%	0.1%	3.0%	3.0%	0.0%	4.0%	4.1%	0.1%	
PDS	6.0%	6.1%	0.1%	6.0%	5.8%	0.2%	4.5%	4.7%	0.2%	
REP							3.5%	3.9%	0.4	
REST	9.0%	9.8%		5.0%	5.4%		4.5%	6.2%		
AVERAGE DIFFERENTIAL		0.42%			0.36%				0.55%	0.44%

To make the numbers more comparable to the U.S. presidential election, I have grouped the parties into their coalitions in table A3.[261] The results are very accurate, in all cases predict correctly the winner, and show no systematic skew.

TABLE A3: EXIT-POLL PREDICTIONS VS. COUNTS FOR COALITIONS IN
GERMAN NATIONAL ELECTIONS

Coalition Election	SPD/ Green pred.	CDU/CSU FDP pred.	Pred. diff.	SPD/ Green tallied	CU/ FDP tallied	Tallied diff.	Tall. vs. pred.
2004 EUROPEAN PARLIAMENT	33.5%	51.5%	CF 18.0	33.4%	50.6%	CF 17.2	SG 0.8
2002 NATIONAL ELECTION	47.0%	45.5%	SG 1.5	47.1%	45.9%	SG 1.2	CF 0.3
1999 EUROPEAN PARLIAMENT	38.0%	51.0%	CF 13.0	37.1%	51.7%	CF 14.6	CF 1.6
1998 NATIONAL ELECTION	47.5%	41.5%	SG 6.0	47.6%	41.4%	SG 6.2	SG 0.2
1994 EUROPEAN PARLIAMENT	43.0%	44.5%	CF 1.5	42.3%	42.9%	CF 0.6	SG 0.9
1994 NATIONAL ELECTION	43.5%	49.0%	CF 5.5	43.7%	48.3%	CF 4.6	SG 0.9

How Small Samples Can Accurately Portray Large Populations

The statistical part of our thesis has not been questioned. In fact, the sampling theory on which we rely is just the same as what Mitofsky, Lensky, and other pollsters routinely use to report margins of error in public opinion surveys, and our contention that the 2004 exit poll results cannot be explained by chance is echoed in the report by NEP, and by others who have written about the subject.

Nevertheless, many people are skeptical about statistical claims that they don't understand, and for good reason. Readers who have never studied probability may wonder how we can learn something definite about millions of people by questioning just a few thousand of them, and for you we have included this appendix.

A key part of a pollster's job is to try to select polling subjects *at random*. This is really the difficult part. It may be that people who vote for Tom tend to live in the Western part of the state, while people in the East were more liable to vote for Harry. Or it may be that people who vote for Harry tend to vote early in the day, while those who vote for Tom come late to the polls. Choosing a selection of voters to question that is truly random is the pollster's art, and all of the discussion about the validity of the 2004 exit polls rightly focused on this question. What is not questioned is the logical consequence of assuming that they have done their job well, so that for all practical purposes, the sample is random.

If the pollsters succeeded in polling voters at random, then each person polled had the same probability of being a Harry-voter as the proportion of Harry-voters in the population. Let's say that half of all voters in a state cast their ballot for Harry, and the other half cast their ballot for Tom; then the probability of any one questionnaire saying "Harry" should be just 50%, like a coin toss. If 2,000 voters are chosen at random, then the probabilities associated with various possibilities for the composition of those 2,000 questionnaires is taken right from the mathematics of counting "heads" when you toss a coin 2,000 times.

We get the probabilities for various outcomes from the familiar bell-shaped curve. If we sample just a few voters, the bell-shaped curve is broad and chunky. For ten voters, it looks like this:

FIGURE B1: LIKELIHOOD OF THE NUMBERS OF HEADS IN TEN FAIR COIN TOSSES

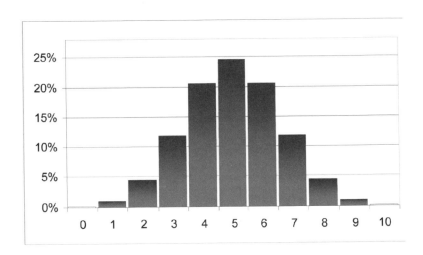

But as the number of coin tosses increases, the relative width of the bell curve narrows, and the probabilities in the wings go way down. Here is a version of the same curve for 50 coin tosses:

FIGURE B2: LIKELIHOOD OF THE NUMBERS OF HEADS IN FIFTY FAIR COIN TOSSES

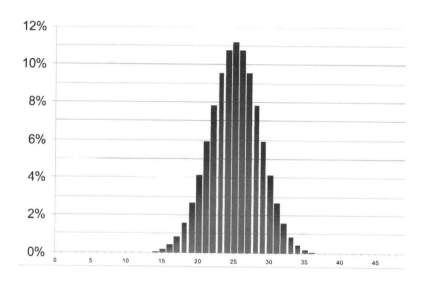

Notice that the entire bell extends between 14 and 36. There really are bars outside of these limits, but they're too small to show up in a diagram of this size. This means that if you toss a coin 50 times, you'll never get less than 14 heads. Not literally "never," but so infrequently that you can forget about it. There is only about 1 chance in 1,000 that with 50 coin tosses, one would obtain 14 or fewer heads, and the odds drop sharply as you go to 13 or 12. There is only about 1 chance in 100,000 that with 50 coin tosses, one would obtain 10 or fewer heads.

Here's an application right out of the 2004 election: There were 50 state exit polls (none for Oregon, but one for D.C.), and if chance were the only factor, we'd expect that about 25 of them would err in favor of Bush and 25 would err in favor of Kerry, that is the "error" of the exit polls—the direction of the difference between the exit poll prediction and the official counts—should be evenly distributed between Bush and Kerry, like a coin toss.

But, in fact, Bush's count outperformed his polling numbers in 44 states, and Kerry's count outperformed his polling numbers in only 6 states. The odds against this occurring by chance are tens of millions to one. The probability is tiny because 6 is so far outside the 14 to 36 range where all the probability is located.

Election polls, like other public opinion polls, are typically designed to survey about 800–2,000 respondents. The bell-shaped curve for 2,000 "coin flips" is much narrower and smoother than the one for 50 coin flips that we just examined. The range in which substantially all the probability is located is centered, of course, at 1,000 heads, and it extends from about 930 to 1,070. Any result outside this range is effectively ruled out by the laws of probability.

So what happens if in an election there are more Harry-supporters than Tom supporters? If the ratio is close to 50-50, then everything we said above still applies.

The width of the band that contains all the probability is just about the same. The only change is that the center shifts over, so that the most likely result tracks the actual number of Harry voters. For example, if Harry got 51% of the vote, then the center of the range would be at 51% of 2,000, or 1,020 instead of 1,000. The range would go from 950 to 1,090.

In figure 4D, the bell curve of Kerry's Ohio results, we illustrated the probabilities based on the CNN election night data. We were to learn later from Edison/Mitofsky that the actual exit poll numbers were far more extreme. In most states, the disparity between official tallies and the tallies of how voters said they voted in the exit polls in those same precincts was larger than the CNN election-night numbers indicated, often much larger—in Ohio, for example, this disparity was 10.9 percentage points. We also learned that the total number

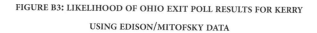

FIGURE B3: LIKELIHOOD OF OHIO EXIT POLL RESULTS FOR KERRY

USING EDISON/MITOFSKY DATA

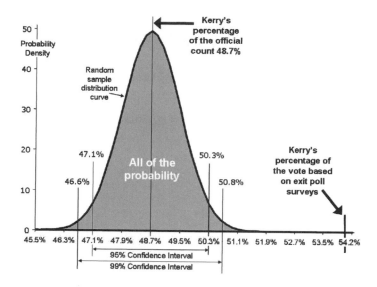

of respondents was considerably larger than the reported CNN totals—about 3,845 in Ohio—thereby narrowing the confidence interval. Edison/Mitofsky doesn't report the number of respondents statewide, but based on the national totals (114,559 respondents in 1,460 precincts), we can calculate the average number of respondents per precinct (78.5), which would mean about 3,845 total respondents for Ohio's 49 precincts. Readers will notice the curve in figure B3 is much steeper and narrower than in figure 4D. First, because the 54.2% figure is so far outside the curve, we had to condense the horizontal scale to be able to fit everything onto the same graph. Second, the greater number of respondents directly narrows and steepens the curve. And because we are able to compare exit poll results with the official counts in those same precincts, contingencies used in the calculations for 4D for possible clustering effects are no longer necessary.[262]

In the final 2004 Ohio election tally Kerry was credited with 48.7% of the vote. The 10.9 percentage point disparity between the official count and the exit poll results in those same precincts indicates that Bush's exit poll results was 5.45 percentage points lower than his official numbers and that Kerry's exit poll result was 5.45 percentage points higher, or 54.2% (see Chapter 5).

A layman's intuition may tell you that the difference between 48.7% and 54.2% is not large and you might be tempted to write it off "to chance." But the bell curve mathematics tells us that the expected range, the polling margin of error, should have been within 47.1% to 50.3%.[263] This can be seen in figure B3, in which 95% of the area under the distribution curve is within this range. And 99% of the time the result would fall between 46.6% and 50.8%.

If, in fact, 48.7% of the voters in the surveyed Ohio precincts had cast their ballots for Kerry, there should be an even probability (0.5) of his receiving 48.7% or less in the exit poll survey. The mark at 54.2% represents the exit poll result. You can see that it is well outside the area where all the probability is located. There is virtually no chance that such a survey would produce a result higher than around 51.9%. The odds against the result that was reported in Ohio are well over a hundred million to one.

And this is just one state. All told, 26 states had similar anomalous results. The odds are astronomical that the exit poll results could have been so far off in the same direction in so many states.

We reiterate that this does not prove that the official vote count was fraudulent. What it does say is that the discrepancy between the official count and the exit polls can't be just a statistical fluke, but it commands some kind of systematic explanation: Either the exit poll was deeply flawed or else the vote count was corrupted.

Notes

PREFACE

1. Thom Hartmann, "The Ultimate Felony against Democracy," commondreams.org, November 4, 2004.

2. Nick Anderson and Faye Fiore, "Early Data for Kerry Proved Misleading; Some Treated the Raw Numbers, Used Mainly to Predict Trends, Like Full-Scale Surveys," *Los Angeles Times*, November 4, 2004.

3. Jim Rutenberg, "Report Says Problems Led to Skewed Surveying Data," *New York Times*, November 5, 2004. The *Times* also ran a series in which Richard J. Meislin, the *Times* editor of news surveys and election analysis, answered questions on exit polls and election results. In that series, he deflected many questions such as the ones that are raised in this book with the equally uninformative announcement that the people "who did them acknowledged yesterday that there had been more problems than were initially revealed to their news media customers. See Jim Rutenberg's excellent article today."

4. Richard Morin, "New Woes Surface in Use of Estimates," *Washington Post*, November 4, 2004.

5. See http://www.democraticunderground.com/discuss/duboard.php?az=view_all&address=203x36314.

6. See Manuel Roig-Franzia and Dan Keating, "Latest Conspiracy Theory—Kerry Won—Hits the Ether," *Washington Post*, November 11, 2004; Tom Zeller Jr., "Vote Fraud Theories, Spread by Blogs, Are Quickly Buried," *New York Times*, November 12, 2004; John Schwartz, "Mostly Good Reviews for Electronic Voting," *New York Times*, November 12, 2004; Farhad Manjoo, "Was the Election Stolen? The System Is Clearly Broken. But There Is No Evidence that Bush Won Because of Voter Fraud," salon.com, November 10, 2004.

7. Fritz Scheuren, "Prominent Statistician Calls for Fair and Meaningful Recount of Ohio's Election Results," unpublished manuscript. Scheuren actively participated in on-the-ground efforts in Ohio to ensure a fair election before, during, and after November 2.

8. Paulos's article, "The Final Tallies Minus Exit Polls = A Statistical Mystery!" was published as an op-ed in the *Philadelphia Inquirer*, November 24, 2004. This was the last that *Philadelphia Inquirer* had to do with the subject. When Steve Freeman tried to publish an op-ed prior to the inauguration, the editor declined because "the nation has moved on."

9. See http://www.cnn.com/2004/ALLPOLITICS/11/03/ohio.blackwell/.

10. For example, in response to my initial report, Ken Mayer, a University of Wisconsin political science professor and chair of the elections division of the American Political Science Association, told the *Capital Times* of Madison, Wisconsin, that he felt there was "an obligation not to stoke the fires of conspiracy theories in the absence of real evidence." (Rob Zaleski, "Prof. says vote numbers don't add up," *Capital Times*, December 8, 2004.) Putting aside the question of what constitutes real evidence, Mayer's view is widespread: questioning the integrity of the election, since it could undermine our confidence in the legitimacy of our government, constitutes a threat to our democracy.

CHAPTER 1: DATELINE NOVEMBER 2, 2004

11. High turnout is widely considered good news for the Democratic Party, as the increase comes disproportionately from voters in socioeconomic groups that traditionally vote Democratic. See Jack Citrin, Eric Schickler, and John Sides, "What If Everyone Voted? Simulating the Impact of Increased Turnout in Senate Elections," *American Journal of Political Science* 47, no. 1 (2003): 75–90.

12. John Zogby, "Election 2004 Zogby Battleground State Polls," http://www.zogby.com/state.html. The President's job-approval rating by state was as follows (approval/disapproval): Colorado 46%/54%, Florida 46%/53%, Iowa 45%/55%, Michigan 46%/54%, Minnesota 43%/56%, New Mexico 47%/53%, Nevada 49%/51%, Ohio 43%/49%, Pennsylvania 44%/55%, and Wisconsin 45%/55%.

13. There have been four incumbent presidential elections in the past quarter-century. On average, the incumbent comes in half a point below his final poll result; challengers exceed their final poll result by an average of 4 points. (See Guy Molyneux, "The Big Five-Oh," The American Prospect Online, October 1, 2004.)

14. Robert Parry, consortiumnews.com, November 6, 2004. Parry writes, "During the day, even Bush's aides informed the president that he was losing the election by about three percentage points, according to a source with access to information inside the White House. But Bush's political adviser Karl Rove reportedly voiced confidence that the vote would turn around. By evening, Bush was displaying a cool confidence that he would prevail." And conversation with Bob Parry. The official story is that the phone-in interviews were canceled because thuderstorms interfered with the satellite communications system on Air Force One. Bush's tantrums have been referenced to *New York Daily News* and *Capital Hill Blue* by Doug Thompson.

15. Although the media rejected the polled presidential voting results, they did rely heavily on those same exit polls to report that the Democrats had lost because they were out of touch with the heartland on moral values. This is ironic because whereas the question asking whom the respondent voted for is unambiguous, the questions asking why are problematic. First, we presume that voters know and can express why they voted as they did, which is often not the case. Second, it is highly dependent on how the questionnaire is framed or what options the respondent is given. Had "terrorism" and "Iraq" not been separated, for example, then their combined 34% would have trumped the 22% attributed to "moral values." Likewise, if, say, "family values" and "abortion" were broken out,

then each would have received well under 22%. Third, these numbers are themselves based on "corrected" exit-poll data. As Dick Meyer of CBS news wrote, "We're building a worldview out of a small, odd vista." http://www.cbsnews.com/stories/2004/11/05/opinion/meyer/main653931.shtml

16. Jimmy Carter, "Still Seeking a Fair Florida Vote," *Washington Post*, Monday, September 27, 2004.

17. See http://www.house.gov/judiciary_democrats/issues/issues/election.html

18. Kenneth Blackwell, as quoted on WTOL.com, a CBS affiliate in Toledo, Ohio. See http://www.gay.com/news/article.html?2004/10/21/3.

19. Mark Niquette, "Critics Drop Lawsuits Challenging Election of Bush: Activists Still Will Investigate Voting Problems," *Columbus Dispatch*, January 12, 2005, Home Final Edition, News Section.

20. "Throwing the voters out," *National Review*, March 10, 1997 v49 n4 p12 (3).

21. Letter from John Conyers, Jr., Jerrold Nadler, Tammy Baldwin, Melvin L. Watt, Linda Sanchez, Robert Wexler, Maxine Waters, Sheila Jackson Lee, Martin Meehan, Zoe Lofgren, and Anthony Weiner to the Honorable J. Kenneth Blackwell, Ohio Secretary of State (Dec. 2, 2004) (on file with the House Judiciary Committee Democratic Staff and at http://www.house.gov/judiciary_democrats/ohblackwellltr12204.pdf).

22. Democratic National Committee's Voting Rights Institute, *Democracy at Risk: The 2004 Election in Ohio*, Executive Summary. http://www.democrats.org/a/2005/06/ democracy_at_ri.php; http://www.house.gov/judiciary_democrats/issues/ issues/election.html.

23. Catherine Candisky, "Blackwell Ends Paper Chase: Some Could Be Unable to Vote Because of Flap Over Registration Forms," *Columbus Dispatch*, September 29, 2004.

24. For details of Franklin County, see: Bob Fitrakis, "How the Ohio Election Was Rigged for Bush," *The Free Press*, November 22, 2004; Bob Fitrakis, "Document Reveals Columbus, Ohio Voters Waited Hours as Election Officials Held Back Machines," *The Free Press*, November 16, 2004; US House Judiciary Hearing transcript at 65, 68 (Dec. 8, 2004); Michael Powell and Peter Slevin, "Several Factors Contributed to 'Lost' Voters in Ohio," *Washington Post*, December 15, 2004; and James Dao et al., "Voting Problems in Ohio Spur Call for Overhaul," *New York Times*, December 24, 2004, A1.

25. Conyers' letter, op cit. http://www.house.gov/judiciary_democrats/ ohblackwellltr12204.pdf.

26. Secretary of State Web site of Ohio, http://www.sos.state.oh.us/.

27. James Q. Jacobs, "How Kerry Votes Were Switched to Bush Votes." http://www.jqjacobs.net/bush/xls/ohio.htm.

28. Although it's true that Ohio election boards consist of both Republicans and Democrats, both serve ultimately, at the pleasure of Ken Blackwell, the secretary of state and 2004 Bush-Cheney campaign manager, who nominates and can dismiss any county election board members. Political scientist Bob Fitrakis has shown how this leads repeatedly to "Blackwell Democrats" serving the interests of Blackwell, as opposed to ensuring honest election counts and investigations.

29. See http://www.house.gov/judiciary_democrats/issues/issues/election.html.

30. Election Protection Coalition, "Shattering the Myth: An Initial Snapshot of Voter Disenfranchisement in the 2004 Elections," December 1, 2004, http://www.pfaw.org/pfaw/dfiles/file_477.pdf.

31. Andrew Welsh-Huggins, "Independent Party Candidates Begin Recount Requests," Associated Press, December 8, 2004.

32. Official Ohio election results from the Ohio Secretary of State Office: http://www.sos.state.oh.us/sos/ElectionsVoter/Results2004.aspx and http://www.sos.state.oh.us/sos/ElectionsVoter/Results2000.aspx. Source of data for comparison of state visits: Eric M. Appleman, Democracy in Action Web site: http://www.gwu.edu/~action/2004/about.html.

33. Affidavits filed by Stephen M. Spraley, Jeannine Tater, and Carolyn Betts on file with the House Judiciary Committee's Democratic members. See http://www.house.gov/judiciary_democrats/issues/issues/election.html.

34. Affidavit from Sherole Eaton, deputy director of elections, http://www.house.gov/judiciary_democrats/issues/issues/election.html.

35. See http://www.opensecrets.org.

36. Sherole Eaton affidavit on file at the House Judiciary Committee.

37. John Conyers to Brett A. Rapp and Michael Barbian Jr., December 22, 2004.

38. Douglas W. Jones affidavit on file at the House Judiciary Committee.

39. John Conyers to the editor of tompaine.com, unpublished letter, February 1, 2005.

40. John Conyers to Kevin R. Brock (Special Agent in Charge, FBI Cincinnati), December 15, 2005.

41. Jon Craig, "'04 Election in Hocking County; Worker Who Questioned Recounts Is Asked to Quit" Columbus Dispatch, June 1, 2005, Wednesday, Home Final Edition; "Prosecutor Putting Investigator onto Elections Complaint; Hocking County Still in Turmoil with Charges," Columbus Dispatch, July 15, 2005, Friday, Home Final Edition.

42. Harvey Wasserman, "Ohio's Secretary of State Blackwell Slanders Election Protection Attorney at Junket Sponsored by Voting Machine Vendors," The Free Press, January 27, 2005.

43. Mark Niquette and Jon Craig, "Presidential Election Challenge; Those Behind Election Lawsuit Should Be Punished, Petro Says," Columbus Dispatch, January 19, 2005.

44. Paul M. Weyrich, "Ken Blackwell: An Extraordinary Individual," February 8, 2005, http://www.freecongress.org./commentaries/2005/050208.asp.

45. See http://www.electionprotection2004.org/coalition.htm.

46. Ritt Goldstein, "US Election: Democracy in Question," Inter Press Service, November 18, 2004, http://www.ips.org, http://www.commondreams.org/headlines04/1118-11.htm.

47. See http://www.salon.com/news/feature/2004/10-25/contra/index_np.html.

CHAPTER 2: FLORIDA SETS THE STAGE IN 2000

48. Christopher Uggen and Jeff Manza, "Democratic Contraction? Political Consequences of Felon Disenfranchisement in the United States American" Sociological Review 67 (December 2002): 797.

49. Jamie Fellner and Marc Mauer, "Losing the Vote: The Impact of Felony Disenfranchisement Laws in the United States" (Washington, D.C.: Human Rights Watch and The Sentencing Project, 1998).

50. Angela Behrens, Christopher Uggen, and Jeff Manza, "Ballot Manipulation and the 'Menace of Negro Domination': Racial Threat and Felon Disenfranchisement in the United States, 1850–2002," AJS 109, no. 3 (November 2003): 559–605. Florida's law was adopted in 1868 (see p. 566). Examples provided here are drawn from this journal article.

51. "Journal of the Proceedings of the Constitutional Convention of the State of Alabama" (Montgomery, Ala.: Brown Printing Co., 1901), 12. Cited in Behrens, Uggen, and Manza, "Ballot Manipulation," 571.

52. *Ratliff v. Beale*, 74 Miss. 266–67, Supreme Court of Mississippi, 1896. Cited in Behrens, Uggen, and Manza, "Ballot Manipulation," 569.

53. Fellner and Mauer, "Losing the Vote," p. 8. Others are Alabama, Delaware, Iowa, Kentucky, Mississippi, Nevada, New Mexico, Virginia, and Wyoming. Arizona and Maryland disenfranchise permanently those convicted of a second felony; Tennessee and Washington disenfranchise permanently those convicted prior to 1986 and 1984, respectively. In addition, in Texas a convicted felon's right to vote is not restored until two years after discharge from prison, probation, or parole.

54. Fellner and Mauer, "Losing the Vote," p. 4.

55. Uggen and Manza, "Democratic Contraction?" *Americans Behind Bars: U.S. and International Use of Incarceration, 1995* (Washington, D.C.: Sentencing Project; U.S. Department of Justice, 2002); *Prison and Jail Inmates at Mid-year 2001* (Washington, D.C.: U.S. Government Printing Office; and Roy Walmsley, 2002), *World Prison Population List*, No. 116, *Research Findings*, 3d ed. (London, England: Home Office Research, Development and Statistics Directorate).

56. Uggen and Manza estimate that 68.9% of this group would have voted for Gore in 2000 (interestingly 85.4% would have supported Clinton in 1996). They estimate turnout of this group would have been 29.7%, compared to 56% for the general voting-eligible electorate (these groups were much more likely to turn out for Clinton—39% in 1992 and 36.1% in 1996).

57. Greg Palast, *The Best Democracy Money Can Buy* (New York: Plume, 2004), 44–47. DBT was subsequently merged into ChoicePoint Corporation.

58. Ibid., 45. The industry norm is $0.27 per record.

59. Palast was subsequently able to obtain a copy of the contract between the State of Florida and Database Technologies Inc., including one sheet—the sheet that contains this quotation—marked "DBT Confidential and Trade Secret" (a copy appears in Palast, *Best Democracy*, 50).

60. Greg Palast, "What Really Happened in Florida?" BBC Broadcast, February 16, 2001.

61. Palast, *Best Democracy*, 54.

62. John Nichols, *Jews for Buchanan* (New York: The New Press, 2001), 38.

63. Palast, *Best Democracy*, 33.

64. Ibid., 46.

65. Robert E. Pierre, "Botched Name Purge Denied Some the Right to Vote," *Washington Post*, Thursday, May 31, 2001.

66. "NAACP Files Florida Voting Rights Lawsuit," November 28, 2000, Florida Voting Irregularities Transcript Given to Justice Department, November 16, 2000, "Florida Voters Testify About Voting Irregularities," November 11, 2000. United States Commission on Civil Rights, "Voting Irregularities in Florida During the 2000 Presidential Election," Appendix (Washington, D.C.: U.S. Government Printing Office, 2001).

67. United States Commission on Civil Rights (USCCR), *Voting Irregularities in Florida During the 2000 Presidential Election* (Washington, D.C.: U.S. Government Printing Office, 2001).

68. Nichols, *Jews for Buchanan*, 46-49.

69. USCCR.

70. Nichols, p 51.

71. Ibid.

72. Alicia Montgomery, "Powerless at the Polls: Black Voters Complain about their Treatment at Florida Polls," salon.com, November 11, 2000, http://dir.salon.com/story/politics/feature/2000/11/11/naacp/index.xml.

73. "To set the record straight, there are 16,695 voters in Palm Beach County who registered as a member of the Independent Party, the Reform Party, or the American Reform Party, which were the labels borne this year by the reform effort in Florida. This in an increase of 110% over the registration totals for the same party in 1996." Karl Rove at a Bush campaign press conference, November 9, 2000. See http://www.presidency.ucsb.edu/showflorida2000.php?fileid=pressbush11-09.

74. Bill O'Reilly as quoted in Nichols, p, 61.

75. Ann Coulter, "Just Go!" *Jewish World Review*, November 9, 2000.

76. Don A. Dillman as quoted in Karin Meadows, "Punch-ballots Confuse Some Voters in Florida," *Associated Press*, November 9, 2000. (Cited in Nichols, p. 62.)

77. Nichols, p. 87.

78. Florida Statute 101.5614(5) states that "no vote shall be declared invalid or void if there is a clear indication of the intent of the voter." A century of Florida Supreme Court decisions affirmed that "courts should not frustrate the will of voters if that will can be determined." (*Beckstrom v. Volusia County Canvassing Board*, 1998). In 1988 the court ruled that voter disenfranchisement is improper where the intent of voter can be ascertained (*State ex rel. Chappell v. Martinez*), and in *Boardman v. Esteva* (1975), they ruled, "The right to vote is . . . the right to be heard. . . . By refusing to recognize an otherwise valid exercise of the right of a citizen to vote for the sake of sacred, unyielding adherence to statutory scripture, we would in effect nullify that right." Material drawn from *The Battle for Florida: An Annotated Compendium of Materials from the 2000 Presidential Election* by Lance deHaven-Smith (Gainesville: University Press of Florida, 2005), judicial precedent: 37, 115–116; Florida Statutes: 37, 48–54.

79. "Dade Undervotes Support Bush Win: Review of Ballots by Herald Suggests Gore Recount Effort Would Have Failed," *Miami Herald*, February 26, 2001. *USA Today* "Study: Gore would not have won on recount."

80. DeHaven-Smith, from table 2.2, p. 39.

81. Michael Isikoff, "The Final Word? New documents raise questions about news media's findings on the 2000 presidential election," *Newsweek*, November 19, 2001. Source: http://www.msnbc.com/news/660124.asp. See also Robert Parry, "So Bush Did Steal the White House," consortiumnews.com, November 22, 2001.

82. Ford Fessenden and John M. Broder, "Study of Disputed Florida Ballots Finds Justices Did Not Cast the Deciding Vote," *New York Times*, November 12, 2001. The audit was completed on September 10, 2001, although the newspapers did not report on it until two months later.

83. U.S. Commission on Civil Rights, Voting Irregularities in Florida, June 2001. See http://www.usccr.gov/pubs/vote2000/report/main.htm.

84. Jeffrey Toobin, *Too Close to Call: The Thirty-Six-Day Battle to Decide the 2000 Election*, (New York: Random House, 2001), p. 174.

85. Evan Shapiro, feedmag.com, November 8, 2000, http://web.archive.org/web/20010604002528/www.feedmag.com/templates/daily_master.php3?a_id=1389.

86. Warren J. Mitofsky, "Fool Me Twice: An Election Nightmare," *Public Perspective*, May/June 2001, 37.

87. Toobin, p. 281.

88. Statement by Bush campaign official James A. Baker, November 11, 2000, http://www.issues2000.org: "The vote in Florida has been counted and then recounted. Governor Bush was the winner of the vote. He was also the winner of the recount. Based on these results, we urged the Gore campaign to accept the finality of the election, subject only to the counting of the overseas absentee ballots in accordance with law. We will . . . vigorously oppose the Gore campaign's efforts to keep recounting until it likes the result."

89. Toobin, *Too Close to Call*. See also interview by Carolyn Kay of makethemaccountable.com at http://www.makethemaccountable.com/caro/audio/Interview_Toobin_Jeffrey_011108.ram http://www.makethemaccountable.com/caro/Interview_Toobin_Jeffrey_011108_Transcript.htm:

    "[I]n terms of shocking new facts, the one that struck me most in *Too Close To Call* relates to Katherine Harris. Because if there's one thing we heard over and over again during the recount was James Baker and others saying that the votes had been counted and recounted. But I learned that in the so-called automatic recount, during the first two days after the election, not all the votes were recounted. In fact, a quarter of the votes, 16 counties, 1.25 million votes, have never been recounted to this day. Because Katherine Harris's office didn't want to take the chance that those votes, having been recounted, would put Gore into the lead."

90. Ibid.

91. Joan Konner, "The Case for Caution: This System Is Dangerously Flawed," *Public Opinion Quarterly* 67 (2003): 5–18.

92. Linda Mason, CBS News; Kathleen Frankovic, CBS News; and Kathleen Hall Jamieson, The Annenberg School for Communication, University of Pennsylvania, "CBS News Coverage of Election Night 2000: Investigation, Analysis, Recommendations," report prepared for CBS News, January 2001, p. 20, 26, 33.

93. Bev Harris, *Black Box Voting: Ballot Tampering in the 21st Century* (Renton, Wash.: Talion Publishing, 2003), chapter 11.

94. Letter from Senator Richard Lugar, emailed to Marc Bogonovich on December 10, 2004, 16:32:10 -0500<Senator_Lugar@lugar.senate.gov>.

95. Nichols, 151.

96. Ibid., 153–54.

97. Toobin, 156.

98. Nichols, 154-55.

99. Toobin, 49–50.

100. Conflict of interest goes well beyond appointment: Scalia's son was working for the law firm of the lawyer representing Bush; Clarence Thomas's wife had been recruiting staff for the (as yet) unelected Bush administration; Rehnquist and O'Connor had made clear their desire to retire under a Republican administration; and O'Connor's wild "disdain was well known. Toobin, in *Too Close to Call*, 248, reports:

    "On . . . the day of the Supreme Court's first opinion on the election, O'Connor and her husband had attended a party for about thirty people at the home of a wealthy couple named Lee and Julie Folger. When the subject of the election controversy came up, Justice O'Connor was livid. "You just don't know what those Gore people have been doing," she said. "They went into a nursing home and registered people that they shouldn't have. It was outrageous." It was unclear where the justice had picked up this unproved accusation, which had circulated only in the more eccentric right-wing outlets, but O'Connor recounted the story with fervor."

    Writing for the *Georgetown Journal of Legal Ethics*, Richard K. Neumann Jr. concluded that, based on widespread press reports, Justices O'Connor and Scalia both "violated the federal judicial conflict-of-interest statute and the Constitutional due process clause by participating in Bush v. Gore." From, "Examining the data and the statues, Conflicts of interest in Bush v. Gore: Did Some Justices Vote Illegally? [Spring 2003]. (Press reports are equivocal on whether facts existed that would have created a conflict of interest for Rehnquist.)

101. Toobin, 267.

102. Jamin B. Raskin, "Bandits in Black Robes: Why You Should Still Be Angry about Bush v. Gore," *Washington Monthly*, March 2001. The Dred Scott decision (1857), often listed as the worst case in U.S. Supreme Court history, found that African Americans could not be "citizens" within the meaning of the diversity jurisdiction clause of the Constitution.

103. Gary Kamiya, "Supreme Court to Democracy: Drop Dead," salon.com, December 14, 2000.

CHAPTER 3: ELECTRONIC VOTING:
AN INVITATION FOR FRAUD

104. David Legard, "Paperless E-Voting Gets Thumbs Down from ACM," IDG News Service, September 28, 2004.

105. Material on voting machine industry concentration; criminal violations by Diebold managers, software developers and designers; and conflict of interest drawn from the following sources:

    Bev Harris, *Black Box Voting: Ballot Tampering in the 21st Century* (Renton, Wash.: Talion Publishing, 2003), especially chapter 8, "Company Information (What you won't find on the company Web sites)," and chapter 3, "Why We Need Disclosure of Owners."

    Bob Fitrakas and Harvey Wasserman, "Diebold's Political Machine," *Mother Jones*, March 5, 2004, http://www.motherjones.com/commentary/columns/2004/03/03_200.html.

    "Con Job at Diebold Subsidary," Associated Press, December 17, 2003, from *Wired* (www.wired.com/news/evote/0,2645,61640,00.html).

    Alexander Bolton, "Hagel's Ethics Filings Pose Disclosure Issue," *The Hill*, January 29, 2003. See http://www.hillnews.com/news/012903/hagel.aspx.

106. Bob Fitrakas and Harvey Wasserman, "Diebold's Political Machine," *Mother Jones*, March 5, 2004, http://www.motherjones.com/commentary/columns/2004/03/03_200.html.

107. "Con Job at Diebold Subsidary," Associated Press, December 17, 2003, from *Wired*, www.wired.com/news/evote/0,2645,61640,00.html.

108. According to the findings of fact in case no. 89-1-04034-1 (Washington State, King County District Court): "Defendant's thefts occurred over a 2 1/2 year period of time, there were multiple incidents, more than the standard range can account for, the actual monetary loss was substantially greater than typical for the offense, the crimes and their cover-up involved a high degree of sophistication and planning in the use and alteration of records in the computerized accounting system that defendant maintained for the victim, and the defendant used his position of trust and fiduciary responsibility as a computer systems and accounting consultant for the victim to facilitate the commission of the offenses."

109. "The Maverick on Bush's Short List," *Business Week*, July 10, 2000.

110. *The Hill*, Page 9.

111. Kim Zetter, "How E-Voting Threatens Democracy," *Wired*, March 29, 2004, http://www.wired.com/news/evote/0,2645,62790,00.htm.

112. *Business Week* described Hagel's victory as a "landslide upset."

113. Adam Cohen, "The Results Are in and the Winner Is . . . or Maybe Not," *New York Times*, February 29, 2004.

114. *The Baton Rouge Advocate*, February 1, 2001.

115. Rebecca Mercuri, "A Better Ballot Box?: New Electronic Voting Systems Pose Risks as Well as Solutions" October 2, 2002, IEEE Spectrum Online.

116. Aviel D. Rubin, "An Election Day Clouded in Doubt," *Baltimore Sun*, October 27, 2004.

117. Tadayoshi Kohno, Adam Stubblefield, Aviel D. Rubin, and Dan S. Wallach, "Analysis of an Electronic Voting System," Johns Hopkins University Information Security Institute, technical report TR-2003-19, July 23, 2003.

118. Ted Selker, "Fixing the Vote: Electronic Voting Machines Promise to Make Elections More Accurate than Ever Before, But Only If Certain Problems—with the Machines and the Wider Electoral Process—Are Rectified" *Scientific American*, October 2004, 90–97.

119. John Fund, "No Doctored DRE: Democrats Use Computer Hysteria to Get Out the Vote," *Wall Street Journal*, July 27, 2004.

120. Palast, *Best Democracy*, 31, 46.

121. U.S. Commission on Civil Rights, *Voting Irregularities in Florida During the 2000 Presidential Election*, June 2001, http://www.usccr.gov/pubs/vote2000/report/main.htm.

    African American voters were placed on purge lists more often and more erroneously than Hispanic or white voters. For instance, in the state's largest county, Miami-Dade, more than 65% of the names on the purge list were African Americans, who represented only 20.4% of the population. Hispanics were 57.4% of the population, but only 16.6% of the purge list; whites were 77.6% of the population but 17.6% of those purged.

122. Jim Ash, "Bush Taps LePore and Newell for Task Force," *Palm Beach Post* (Florida), November 25, 2002. And Greg Palast, "Madame Butterfly Flies Off with Ballots: Florida Fixed Again? Absentee Ballots Go Absent," commondreams.org, August 31, 2004.

123. Wyatt Olson, "Out of Touch—You Press the Screen. The Machine Tells You that Your Vote Has Been Counted. But How Can You Be for Sure?" *New Times Broward-Palm Beach* (Florida), April 24, 2003.

124. George Bennett, "Voting by Touch Will Require Faith in Technology," *Palm Beach Post* (Florida), May 20, 2001.

125. Ibid.

126. Andrew Gumble, "Something Rotten in the State of Florida," *The Independent*, September 29, 2004.

127. Wyatt Olson, "Out of Touch."

128. Steve Bousquet, "2004's First Election Stirs Ghosts of Past," *St. Petersburg Times*, January 9, 2004.

129. Erika Blostad, Gary Fineout, and Amy Sherman, "Missing Ballots to be Remailed," *Miami Herald*, October 28, 2004. Also BBC News, "Florida ballot papers go missing: Tens of thousands of postal ballots have gone missing in the state of Florida, sparking fresh fears of irregularities in the U.S. poll campaign," October 28, 2004.

130. Greg Palast, "Madame Butterfly Flies Off with Ballots."

131. Associated Press State & Local Wire, "Congressman Sues, Wants Voting Machines to Create Paper Printouts," January 17, 2004, Boca Raton, Florida.

132. Andrew Gumbel, "Something Rotten in the State of Florida," *The Independent*, September 29, 2004, 2.

133. Henry Norr, "Florida Vote Suspicious, Says UC Group's Study," *Berkeley Daily Planet*, November 19, 2004.

134. Michael P. McDonald, "A Critique of the Berkeley Voting Study," http://elections.gmu.edu/Berkeley.html. Andrew Gelman and Bruce Shaw of Columbia University posted a graphical analysis online at http://www.stat.columbia.edu/~cook/movabletype/archives/2004/11/vote_swings_in.html.

135. Paul R. Lehto and Jeffrey Hoffman, "Evidence of Election Irregularities in Snohomish County, Washington General Election, 2004," http://www.votersunite.org/info/SnohomishElectionFraudInvestigation.pdf.

136. Election Data Services, 2002. "Election Data Services Inc. Unveils 2002 Voting Equipment Study." Press release, October 9, 2002.

137. Denis Wright, "Meet Cathy Diebold," May 23, 2004 http://www.countthevote.org/cathy_diebold.htm.

138. Adam Cohen, "The Results Are in and the Winner Is . . . or Maybe Not," *New York Times*, February 29, 2004.

139. Douglas Waller, with reporting by Matthew Cooper, John F. Dickerson, and Karen Tumulty, "How Jeffords Got Away," *Inside Politics*, CNN, May 28, 2001.

140. In the fifth race, South Dakota, Democratic Tim Johnson edged Republican John Thune by less than 1% (the polls accurately projected the race even). Republicans also won one close race that was not projected to be that tight. Republican Jim Talent edged Jean Carnahan by 1% in the Missouri Senate race, despite leading in polls by from 4% to 7%. Republicans have regularly complained of Democratic vote fraud in St. Louis, and recently across the river in East St. Louis, five Democrats were convicted of vote fraud. Michael Shaw. "Defendants Guilty of Vote Fraud" *St. Louis Post-Dispatch*, June 28, 2005.

141. John Zogby, "All the President's Votes?" *The Independent*, October 14, 2003.

142. Mary Wiltenburg, "A Better Ballot?" *Christian Science Monitor*, November 3, 2003.

143. Aviel D. Rubin, Testimony, U.S. Election Assistance Commission, May 5, 2004.

CHAPTER 4: BIASED POLLS OR BIASED COUNT?

144. Michael Barone, "The Second Bush Term," *U.S. News & World Report*, November 3, 2004.

145. David Corn, "A Stolen Election," *The Nation*, November 29, 2004.

146. Jim Ruttenberg, "Survey Experts Cite Problems with Data and Interpretation," *New York Times*, November 4, 2004.

147. Michael Barone, "The 51% Nation," *U.S. News & World Report*, November 15, 2004.

148. Michael Barone, "Exit polls in Venezuela," *U.S. News & World Report*, August 20, 2004.

149. Richard Morin, "New Woes Surface in Use of Estimates," *Washington Post*, November 4, 2004.

150. Herbert Asher, *Polling and the Public: What Every Citizen Should Know*, 4th ed. (Washington, D.C.: Congressional Quarterly Press, 2004: 125). Older voters are slightly less likely to respond, but pollsters can compensate for this by weighting more heavily older voters who do respond.

151. A methodological description can be found with the National Election Pool General Election Exit Polls, 2004 Computer file, ICPSR version. Somerville, NJ: Edison Media Research/New York, NY: Mitofsky International [producers], 2004. Ann Arbor, MI: Inter-university Consortium for Political and Social Research [distributor], 2005. They write:

> "The statewide samples were selected in two stages. First, a probability sample of voting precincts within each state was selected that represented the different geographic areas across the state and the vote by party. Second, within each precinct, voters were sampled systematically throughout the voting day at a rate that gave all voters in a precinct the same chance of being interviewed. The national sample is a subsample of the statewide sample precincts. Pre-election telephone interviews were conducted in 12 states with large populations of absentee and early voters and in Oregon, where voting is conducted entirely by mail. The samples for the telephone interviews were selected using random-digit dialing (RDD) in these 12 states. Absentee or early voters were asked the same questions asked at the polling place on election day."

There has been a great deal of confusion about the number of respondents in the national poll. The Election night CNN Web site reported 13,047 respondents; the next day that number changed to 13,660 respondents. The true number, however, is what we report: 11,719 Election Day voters and 500 absentee and early voters.

The main confusion arises from the way the NEP handled the 500 interviews done by telephone before Election Day with those who voted early or by absentee ballot. The national exit poll participants surveyed at the polls on Election Day answered questions from 1 of 4 different surveys. However, the 500 telephone respondents surveyed earlier were given a very long interview that asked every question that appeared on each of the four surveys, and so NEP counted them as 2000 respondents.

152. Drawn largely from Warren J. Mitofsky and Murray Edelman, "Election Night Estimation: The Morris H. Hansen Lecture," *Journal of Official Statistics* 18 (2002): 165–79.

153. David Broder, *Behind the Front Page: A Candid Look at How the News is Made* (New York: Simon & Schuster 1987), p. 253.

154. Albert H. Cantril, *The Opinion Connection: Polling, Politics, and the Press.* (Washington, D.C.: Congressional Quarterly Press, 1991), chapter 3, "Why All Polls are Not Equal," 142.

155. George C. Edwards III and Stephen J. Wayne, *Presidential Leadership: Politics and Policy Making*, 5th ed. (New York: St. Martin's Press 1999) p. 215.

156. From Jonathan Fuerbringer, "Shares Rally as Investors Welcome Election's End," *New York Times*, November 4, 2004: "The stock market rallied at the opening bell yesterday as investors expressed relief . . . that President Bush looked set to return to the White House for a second term. . . . Spurred in part by expectations that Mr. Bush would continue a pro-business agenda, the three main stock market gauges moved up sharply, by 1.5 percent or more, just after trading began. But traders in government bonds—worried that less would be done to narrow the federal budget deficit—pushed down bond prices from the moment it became evident that Mr. Bush would win the crucial state of

Ohio. . . . The price of crude oil, after spending one day below $50 a barrel, jumped 2.5 percent, to $50.88. . . . While investors seemed certain of the election outcome yesterday, on Tuesday they appeared to be misled by the exit polls that quickly began to circulate on Web sites. The early exit polls, which put Mr. Kerry in the lead nationally and in crucial states, led to a sell-off in the afternoon. . . . The stock market response yesterday to the Bush victory was easily seen in one of the market sectors that analysts said the president would favor, drug makers. The stock of Merck jumped 4 percent, while Pfizer climbed 2.6 percent. . . ."

157. Paul B. Carroll and Dianne Solis, "Zedillo's Apparently Clean Win at Polls Diminishes Threat of Mexican Unrest," *Wall Street Journal*, August 23, 1994.

158. Rebeca Rodriguez, "U.S. Political Consultants Signed to Conduct Exit Poll in Mexico," Knight Ridder Newspapers, June 16, 2000.

159. Molly Moore and John Anderson, "Mexican Power Shift Stirs Wide Celebration; Fox Election Victory Called 'Historic Turning Point,'" *Washington Post*, July 4, 2000, Final Edition.

160. John Plunkett, "Broadcasters Hail Success of Joint Poll," *Guardian* (London), May 6, 2005.

161. See Martin Plissner, "Exit Polls to Protect the Vote," *New York Times*, October 17, 2004. "Last fall, an American firm, whose polling clients have included Al Gore and John Edwards, was hired by some international foundations to conduct an exit poll in the former Soviet republic of Georgia during a parliamentary election. On Election Day, the firm, Global Strategy Group, projected a victory for the main opposition party. When the sitting government counted the votes, however, it announced that its own slate of candidates had won. Supporters of the opposition stormed the Parliament, and the president, Eduard A. Shevardnadze, later resigned under pressure from the United States and Russia."

162. Two exit polls were conducted in Ukraine: One, by a Ukranian group, SOCIS, put Yushchenko ahead by 49% to 46%. An exit poll conducted under a Western-funded program, funded in part by the United States, gave Yushchenko 54% of the vote to Yanukovych's 43%. (source: "Storm of Protest at Ukraine Result: Opposition Leader's Call to Defy Security Forces," CNN.com, November 22, 2004 (http://www.cnn.com/2004/WORLD/europe/11/22/ukrainenew/). In testimony to the House International Relations Committee, Ambassador John Tefft gave slightly different numbers, but it's not known from where he got those numbers.

163. Sen. Richard Lugar (R-Ind.), "Ukraine's Election: Next Steps," testimony before the House International Relations Committee, December 7, 2004.

164. Ambassador John Tefft, Deputy Assistant Secretary for European and Eurasian Affairs, "Ukraine's Election: Next Steps," testimony before the House International Relations Committee, Washington, D.C., December 7, 2004, http://www.state.gov/p/eur/rls/rm/39542.htm.

165. See http://www.mitofskyinternational.com.

166. Ken Warren, *In Defense of Polling* (New York: Westview Press, 2003), 165–69.

167. Ken Warren, in discussion with the authors, March 20, 2005.

168. These eleven are classified as battleground states based on their being on at least two of three prominent lists: Zogby, MSNBC, and the *Washington Post*. Another sometimes-mentioned state, Oregon, did not have a comparable exit poll because voting in the state is conducted by mail. (These twelve states did, in fact, turn out to be the most competitive in the election; in no other state was the winning margin less than 7%.)

169. In the pollster lexicon and protocols, the official count is correct by definition, whether or not the official count conforms to votes cast. If Democrats get 5% fewer votes than the exit polls predict, pollsters say either that there is a "Democratic overstatement," or that the poll has a "Democratic bias."

170. Martin Plissner, "In Defense of Exit Polls: You Just Don't Know How to Use Them," slate.com, November 4, 2004.

171. Jack Shafer, "Exit-Poll Charade: Why Slate is Posting the Exit-Poll Numbers," slate.com, November 2, 2004.

172. Richard Morin, "New Woes Surface in Use of Estimates," *Washington Post*, November 4, 2004.

173. Freeman had sixteen CNN exit-poll pages stored in his computer memory from the evening of Election Day, and in each case, Simon's figures are identical to Freeman's. The numbers are also roughly consistent with those released elsewhere.

174. The BBC's Rob Watson put it this way: "The accepted wisdom is that whoever wins two out of the three states of Ohio, Pennsylvania, and Florida will win the election." Real Clear Politics, a political analysis Web site, posted the following on October 28, 2004: "Conventional wisdom for months, including RCP's, had been that whoever won two of the 'big three' Ohio, Pennsylvania, and Florida would almost certainly become president," realclearpolitics.com.

175. For a brief overview on the statistical impact of stratification and clustering, see: "Sample Size and Design Effect:Introduction and Review," Gene Shackman, *Survey Research Methods Section Newsletter* (January 2003). For a more thorough explanation of stratification, see G. Henry, *Practical Sampling*, Applied Social Research Methods Series, volume 21 (Newbury Park, CA: Sage Publications, 1990); and W. Kalsbeek and G. Heiss, "Building Bridges Between Populations and Samples in Epidemiological Studies," *Annual Review of Public Health* 21 (2000): 147–169. Also available at http://www.sph.unc.edu/chsr/Dissemination/Arph_sub.htm.

176. Statisticians have no way to calculate in advance how much clustering will increase the margin of error on a survey. It is a function of the degree of homogeneity of people within clusters. Because we don't have Mitofsky's data, we cannot calculate it precisely now. Statisticians involved in the 1996 exit poll estimated, however, that clustering in that survey resulted in a 30% increase in the margins of error as compared to a simple random sample of voters. The 1996 state exit polls involved roughly the same number of precincts (1,468) as the 2004 exit polls (1,480). See pg. 72 of Daniel M. Merkle and Murray Edelman, "A Review of the 1996 Voter News Service Exit Polls from a Total Survey Error Perspective," in *Election Polls, the News Media and Democracy*, ed. P. J.

Lavrakas and M. W. Traugott (New York: Chatam House, 2000), 68-92. Number of precincts from the NEP Information page: http://www.exit-poll.net/faq.html#a7.

177. The Pew Research Center for People and the Press report "Perceptions of Partisan Bias Seen as Growing—Especially by Democrats," January 11, 2004, found that 42% of Republicans believe that news coverage of the campaign is biased in favor of Democrats, whereas only 30% of Democrats believe that news coverage is biased in favor of Republicans. As the title indicates, however, perception of partisan bias is growing even more rapidly among Democrats, and by now this gap may have closed further, or even disappeared.

178. Blumenthal posted a large, brightly colored logo, but exit pollster Daniel Merkle, who was a member of the NEP, told us, "The logos were used no more prominently in 2004 than they have been in elections since 1990, and the logos on the questionnaire in 2004 were in black and white as they always have been, not in color."

179. Pew, "Perceptions," 77.

180. 2005 e-mail correspondence with authors.

181. The Pew Research Center for the People and the Press, "Polls Face Growing Resistance, But Still Representative Survey Experiment Shows," released: April 20, 2004 http://people-press.org/reports/display.php3?ReportID=211.

182. S. L. Popkin and M. P. MacDonald, "Who votes?" (1998) Blueprint: Ideas for a New Century 1:28-29 (1998)

183. Merkle, Daniel M. and Murray Edelman, "A Review of the 1996 Voter New Service Exit Polls from a Total Survey Error Perspective," *Election Polls, the News Media and Democracy*, ed. P. J. Lavrakas, M. W. Traugott, 68–92 (New York: Chatham House).

184. Daniel M. Merkle, Murray Edelman, K. Dykeman, and C. Brogan, "An Experimental Study of Ways to Increase Exit Poll Response Rates and Reduce Survey Error." Paper presented at the fifty-third annual conference of the American Association of Public Opinion Research, St. Louis, Missouri, May 14–17.

185. Christopher Edley Jr., Philip A. Klinkner, Jocelyn M. Benson, and Vesla M. Weaver, "Democracy Spoiled: National, State, and County Disparities in Disfranchisement through Uncounted Ballots," Harvard University Civil Rights Project, 2002.

186. Special Investigations Division, Committee on Government Reform, "Income and Racial Disparities in the Undercount in the 2000 Presidential Election," U.S. House of Representatives (July 2001).

187. Richard Morin, "Surveying the Damage—Exit Polls Can't Always Predict Winners, So Don't Expect Them to," *Washington Post*, Sunday, November 21, 2004.

188. This data was made available in Edison/Mitofsky.

189. As discussed earlier in this chapter, an exit poll, like any other survey, can be method-ologically flawed. We mentioned the Mason-Dixon exit poll that predicted a landslide victory for Douglas Wilder in a 1990 Virginia gubernatorial race that was, in fact, very close. A study found that the discrepancy stemmed from the use of face-to-face inter-views rather than anonymous questionnaires, apparently some white Democratic vot-ers were reluctant to admit to interviewers that they were voting against Wilder.

Other problems can arise from non–Election Day voting. This problem surfaced in 1982 when exit polls wrongly predicted Democrat Jerry Brown had won over Republican Pete Wilson for United States Senator from California and that Democrat Tom Bradley had beaten Republican George Deukmejian for governor. Both predictions were wrong because of an extraordinarily large number of Republican absentee ballots.

Some of the unexplained discrepancies in New Hampshire are mentioned by Richard Morin and Claudia Deane in "A Snowy Graveyard For Pols And Polls," *Washington Post*, Monday, January 26, 2004:

"In 1992, Voter Research and Surveys' exit poll showed George H. W. Bush beating Buchanan by a relatively narrow six points, only to have Bush finish 16 points ahead on election night. 'I've never done anything that bad,' lamented Warren Mitofsky, then head of VNS and co-director of the current news media exit poll consortium."

The *New York Times*, February 29, 1996, provides the simple facts of the 1996 Arizona Republican presidential primary in the article "3 Networks Admit Error in Arizona Race Reports."

CHAPTER 5: THE INAUGURATION EVE EXIT-POLL REPORT

190. "Evaluation of Edison/Mitofsky Election System 2004," prepared by Edison Media Research and Mitofsky International for the National Election Pool (NEP), January 15, 2004, http://www.exit-poll.net/election-night/EvaluationJan192005.pdf.

191. "Evaluation of Edison/Mitofsky," p. 31.

192. Within Precinct Disparity (WPD) is an average of the difference between the leading candidates' percentages in the exit poll and the actual vote for those sample precincts. The signed (+ or -) WPD gives the direction of this disparity; in this book, a positive WPD represents a disparity in which Bush did better in the official count than he did in the exit poll; a negative WPD represents a disparity in which Bush did worse in the official count than he did in the exit poll. (Edison/Mitofsky reverses the signs: negative WPE is positive WPD, and vice versa.

193. "Kerry Claims Victory after Redskins' Loss," Associated Press, October 31, 2004.

194. U.S. Count Votes' National Election Data Archive Project Analysis of the 2004 Presidential Election Exit-Poll Discrepancies: Response to the Edison/Mitofsky Election System 2004 Report. Released March 31, 2005, Updated April 12, 2005. Authors and Endorsers: Ron Baiman, University of Illinois at Chicago, Kathy Dopp, USCountVotes, President, Steve Freeman, University of Pennsylvania; Brian Joiner, University of Wisconsin; Victoria Lovegren, Case Western Reserve University; Josh Mitteldorf, Temple University; Campbell B. Read, Southern Methodist University; Richard G. Sheehan, University of Notre Dame; Jonathan Simon, J.D. Alliance for Democracy; Frank Stenger, University of Utah; Paul F. Velleman, Cornell University; and Bruce O'Dell, USCountVotes, Vice President. www.uscountvotes.org. The paper is available online at: http://www.uscountvotes.org/ucvAnalysis/US/Presidential-Election-2004.pdf.

A four-page response to Edison/Mitofsky, laying out some of these points had been released by US Count Votes on January 28, 2005, (available online at: http://electionar-chive.org/ucvAnalysis/US/USCountVotes_Re_Mitofsky-Edison.pdf).

195. Mystery Pollster, April 8, 2005 post, http://www.mysterypollster.com/main/2005/01/the_reluctant_b.html. Like other apologists for the election, Blumenthal goes back and forth from arguing that "to continue to see evidence of vote fraud in the 'unexplained exit-poll discrepancy' . . . borders on delusional" (November 17, 2004) to arguing "not that [disproportionate response] is likely, but only that it is possible" (January 21, 2005 and again April 8, 2005.)

196. "US Count Votes' Analysis of the 2004 Presidential Election Exit-Poll Discrepancies," 10.

197. For this analysis, we assume that there are an average of 90% Bush voters in the 80% to 100% Bush precincts, and an average of 70% Bush voters in the 60% to 80% Bush precincts, and so on. For the mathematics behind these calculations, see pages 23–24 of US Count Votes' April 12, 2005 analysis.

198. "US Count Votes' Analysis of the 2004 Presidential Election Exit-Poll Discrepancies," 12

199. Edison/Mitofsky, 42.

200. Edison/Mitofsky provides three different measures of WPE (WPD). Two of them—"Model WPE" and "VNS WPE"—are calculated by removing the four most outlier precincts (those where the discrepancy was the greatest) and then averaging the WPE values for the precincts that remain. "Model WPE" is the measure that NEP tracked on their election-night Decision Summary screen, which is what the networks use to project state winners. "VNS-WPE" (VNS stands for Voter News Service, the predecessor to NEP), which was included so as to be able to compare 2004 WPE with WPE in prior elections, also excludes extreme precincts but uses a different averaging formula. According to Edison/Mitofsky, IM (Input Management) WPE is similar to Model WPE, but the extreme outlier precincts have not been removed.

Throughout this chapter, we use IM WPE (IM WPD) as the basis for our variance analysis. Among the WPE measures, IM WPE is the only complete set. Even if Edison/Mitofsky had some good reason to set aside outlier precincts for other analyses, outliers are the first place to look for fraud.

All of the Edison/Mitofsky WPD measures have a flaw: WPD should be calculated as a ratio rather than as a differential. Elizabeth Liddle, a British doctoral student doing work for Mitofsky International, produced a paper showing that under certain conditions, constructing WPD as a differential could produce some strange arithmetic artifacts. If voters favoring one candidate did in fact disproportionately refuse to participate in the poll, which is the official explanation for the exit-poll discrepancy, then the WPD would seem artificially higher in precincts where the split was close to 50-50 as compared with precincts where one candidate predominates. Those interested in a more thorough mathematical explanation should go to http://www.geocities.com/lizzielid/ WPDpaper.pdf <http://www.geocities.com/lizzielid/WPEpaper.pdf>.)

Unfortunately, without the data, the numbers cannot be backed out and transformed, so we cannot know the extent of the effect, or if in fact there is any effect at all.

Liddle and others, notably Blumenthal, have used this observation to argue that the exit polls cannot be used to demonstrate fraud, and that we should therefore look elsewhere for evidence. But, if anything, it indicates just the reverse. First, the effect is not large. Second, artificially high WPD in close precinct races does not indicate artificially high WPD in close state races. The fact that Ohio was close in the aggregate does not imply that its precinct tallies were, on average, closer than other states. Third, it suggests that the extreme WPDs in Bush strongholds are that much more extreme.

It is highly doubtful that this mathematical artifact affects any finding presented in this book. In all likelihood, every finding we present is meaningful and statistically significant despite noise in the data. The most likely implication of the flawed calculation is that some patterns cannot be detected because of bad numbers. The cleaner the data set, the more patterns that can be discerned, and the more clearly they can be discerned.

Rather than allowing this flaw to be used to dismiss inquiry into the exit poll discrepancy, we must recognize it as yet one more reason why the data must be made available to independent researchers.

201. Edison/Mitofsky, 31.

202. But this WPD figure understates the magnitude of the discrepancy, because WPD is not distributed evenly. As indicated in table 5.4, WPD varies considerably from state to state. The number of precincts NEP polled in each state was a function of the competitiveness of the contests, state demographic mix, and precinct size, rather than the state population, so thirty-eight precincts were polled in South Dakota (population 750,000) and only twenty-nine precincts were polled in New York (population 19,000,000). Because of this, South Dakota's WPD of -4.2 carried more weight in the national average than New York's 11.4. In general, the discrepancy tended to be more extreme in the larger states, where more votes were at stake. Because some of the largest states—notably New York, California, and Ohio—have very high WPDs, extrapolation of state WPD weighted by state electorate reveals a nationwide discrepancy of 7.1 percentage points.

203. Edison/Mitofsky, 42.

204. Ibid.

205. The voter call-line was 1-866-MY VOTE 1, and the Web site, http://www.msnbc.msn .com/id/6364287/.

206. Edison/Mitofsky, 4.

207. Russ Baker, "Election 2004: Stolen or Lost," tompaine.com Posted on January 7, 2005, http://www.tompaine.com/articles/election_2004_stolen_or_lost.php. See also, Freeman's reply: "Exit-Poll Problems: A Reply To Russ Baker," Steven Freeman, January 21, 2005, http://tompaine.com/Archive/others/exit_poll_problems_a_reply_to_russ_baker.php.

CHAPTER 6: HOW DID AMERICA REALLY VOTE?

208. 11,719 Election Day voters and 500 absentee and early voters

209. The graphic was still the same when last accessed in March 2006.

210. On November 9, 2004, the MIT-CalTech Voting Technology Project, "Voting Machines and the Underestimate of the Bush Vote," issued a paper which erroneously used NEP's adjusted data to validate the process. (In other words, they used data in which the count is assumed correct to prove that the count is correct!) Nevertheless, even though this data had been adjusted to conform to the count, the authors found:

"Overall, the final exit polls, as reported by cnn.com, estimated that President Bush had Election Day support from 49.8% of the electorate, compared to the 51.1% he received from the tallied votes. The polls were off from the official returns by 1.3%. In typical public opinion polls, such a difference would be within the poll's "margin of error." However, with the unusually large number of observations in the Election Day exit poll—over 76,000 [the actual number was 114,559]—this difference is well outside the margin of error. The exit-poll numbers and the official returns are significantly different, in a statistical sense. Depending on which numbers one chooses to trust, the poll is either too pro-Kerry or the official results are too pro-Bush." (pages 1–2)

211. After the election, several people posted analyses along these lines on the web. The one that we built upon here was by Alex Satanovsky, "Some observations of the 2004 election" November 4, 2004. See http://inn.globalfreepress.com/modules/news/article.php?storyid=1039.

212. Greg Mitchell, "Daily Endorsement Tally: Bush Has a Big Day, but Kerry is Still Eking Out a Win," *Editor & Publisher*, November 1, 2004.

213. Greg Mitchell, "Daily Endorsement Tally: Kerry Picks up 30 Papers, Widens Lead," *Editor & Publisher*, October 17, 2004.

   Many of the editorials backing Kerry denounced the incumbent in unusually harsh language. The *Miami Herald* accused Bush of "narrow partisanship." Up the coast, the Daytona paper cited his "embarrassing performance." The *Sacramento Bee* said, "The nation has paid a steep price for Bush's arrogance—mounting deficits and debt at home, loss of standing and effectiveness abroad." As Greg Mitchell points out, "newspaper picks in presidential races may not count for very much, but they do mean something. Surveys by *E&P* and others in previous years showed that roughly 5 to 10% of voters (or more) felt that editorials had some influence when they cast their ballots. In a battleground state that's not insignificant." "Daily Endorsement Tally: Editorial Endorsements Run Away from Bush: Thirty-six Papers Supporting Bush in 2000 Endorse Kerry in 2004 Race. Just Six Former Gore Endorsers Embrace Bush," *Editor & Publisher*, October 26–27, 2004.

214. Ford Fessenden, "A Big Increase of New Voters in Swing States," *New York Times*, September 26, 2004.

215. From a speech at the American Enterprise Institute in December 2001.

216. See for example Matt Bai, "Who Lost Ohio," *New York Times* magazine, November 21, 2004. Bai recounts the final twenty-four hours of the 2004 presidential campaign from inside the pro-Kerry organization America Coming Together in Ohio. See also www.washingtonpost.com/wp-dyn/articles/A23754-2004Nov3.html.

217. Marisa Katz, "Off Base," *New Republic*, September 13, 2004, https://ssl.tnr.com/p/docsub.mhtml?i=express&s=katz091304.

218. Fessenden, "A Big Increase of New Voters."

219. *Democracy at Risk: The 2004 Election in Ohio*, Section II, Executive Summary, 2. Report available online at http://www.democrats.org/a/2005/06/democracy_at_ri.php.

220. Democracy at Risk, Section VI, 9.

221. For example, see Pew Center for Research on People and the Press, "Pre-Election Polls Largely Accurate: Lessons from Campaign '04", November 23, 2004.

222. Guy Molyneux, "The Big Five-Oh," *The American Prospect*, October 1, 2004.

223. John Zogby, "Mea Culpa: I Am a Pollster, Not a Predictor," Zogby International Press Release, November 8, 2004. "Surprising to me, and rather significantly," says Zogby, "President Bush was just re-elected with a majority of the vote by an electorate that still gave him a negative job performance rating and felt the country was headed in the wrong direction."

224. An incumbent president ran as a candidate in the following eight elections: 1956, 1964, 1972, 1976, 1980, 1984, 1992, and 1996. "The average percentage going to challenger candidates across these eight races is 88%. Hence, our decision to apply a 90% rule to allocating the truly undecided vote to John Kerry. (We allocated 'refusers' among early voters separately, giving 52% of these to Bush and 48% to Kerry, in conformance with early voters who reported their vote choice.) Thus, of the 3% who were undecided or refused to name their vote preference in our final poll, we allocated 74.25% to Kerry and 25.75 to Bush." Lydia Saad, Gallup Poll Blog, November 1, 2004, http://poll.gallup.com/BLOG/default.aspx?a=11012004.

225. "Nearly One in Ten U.S. Adults Use Wireless Phones Exclusively and Landline Displacement Expected to Grow," Harris Interactive news release, June 27, 2005.

226. Pew Center for Research on People and the Press, "Pre-Election Polls Largely Accurate: Lessons from Campaign '04," November 23, 2004. Pew credits NEP as the source for this data. Given the sum totals, this must be "corrected" data, adjusted so as to conform to the overall count. Responses to the question were not listed on the CNN Web site.

227. Gallup answers questions about their polls and methodologies on their Gallup Poll Blog: http://gallup.com/election2004/BLOG/.

228. *USA Today*, October 2004, http:www.usatoday.com/news/graphics/electionquiz/flash.htm. Gallup gives young voters extra points to help make up for questions 3 and 6, although Teixeira, in "Donkey Rising," finds that this is insufficient.

229. Michael W. Traugott and Clyde Tucker, "Strategies for Predicting Whether a Citizen Will Vote and Estimation of Election Outcome," Public Opinion Quarterly 48, no. 1 (1984): 330–43.

230. "Likely Voters IV—The Gallup Model," Mystery Pollster, October 27, 2004:
    "According to Gallup's David Moore, they aim this year to select a pool of likely voters equal to 55% of their adult sample—their estimate of the appropriate "turnout ratio" likely in this election. In practice, the percentage that scores a perfect 7 out of 7 typically comes very close to 55%. If it ever goes over, they will tighten the scoring of the last ques-

tion about likelihood to vote (giving a point to those who answer 8–10, for example, instead of 7–10), so that likely voters will always be some combination of sixes and sevens this year. The one hitch is that they usually have more than enough sixes to bring the total size of the likely voter pool to 55%. So Gallup weights down the sixes to make the weighted value of the likely voters equal to 55%."

231. For the model mathematics, see "Polling for Errors? Do Pre-Election Telephone Polls Track—and Legitimize—Corrupted Election Tallies through Flawed Methodologies? An Analysis of the 2004 U.S. Presidential Election and the Pre-Election Polls" by Steve Freeman, University of Pennsylvania Center for Organizational Dynamics, Working Paper #06-05: July 11, 2005.

232. Soto, "Why You Should Ignore the Gallup Poll," http://www.theleftcoaster.com/archives/002806.html.

233. Ruy Teixeira, "Donkey Rising: Gallup Poll Racially Biased," October 19, 2004, http://www.emergingdemocraticmajorityweblog.com/donkeyrising/archives/000808.php.

234. Numbers here are drawn from unadjusted election night exit-poll data collected by Jonathan Simon (Freeman 2004, Simon and Baiman 2005). Adjusted exit-poll data comes from the CNN election 2004 Web site.

235. Mystery Pollster, "Likely Voters VII: CBS/NYT" October 29, 2004. "Virtually all of the national surveys use some form of cut-off procedure to define likely voters. Respondents are either classified as likely or unlikely voters. There is one notable exception: The CBS/*New York Times* poll, whose likely voter model involves weighting respondents by their probability of voting."

236. John Zogby, "It Is Not an 11 Point Race," *The Financial Times*, September 7, 2004. Zogby also criticized *Time* for using similarly Republican-heavy samples.

CHAPTER 7: RESPONSIBLE JOURNALISM VERSUS CONSPIRACY THEORY

237. Martin Plissner, "In Defense of Exit Polls: You Just Don't Know How to Use Them," slate.com, November 4, 2004; Jack Shafer, "The Official Excuses for the Bad Exit-Poll Numbers Don't Cut It," slate.com, November 5, 2004.

To hear Lenski of Edison Media talk about it, the whole election brouhaha of 2004 can be blamed on the people who leaked the exit-poll information and on the outlets (Slate, drudgereport.com, wonkette.com, dailykos.com, mydd.com, et al.) that tossed the raw data out for consumption. Joe Lenski, quoted in the *Los Angeles Times* November 4, 2004 asserted: "I'm not designing polls for some blogger who doesn't even understand how to read the data. It's like if you were graded by your readers on the first draft of your article."

238. Jim Rutenberg, "Report Says Problems Led to Skewed Surveying Data," *New York Times*, November 5, 2004. The *Times* also ran a series in which Richard J. Meislin, *Times* editor of news surveys and election analysis, answered questions on exit polls and election results. In that piece, he deflected many questions such as I have raised here with the equally uninformative announcement that the people, "who did them acknowledged

yesterday that there had been more problems than were initially revealed to their news media customers. See Jim Rutenberg's excellent article today."

239. Freeman's original report is posted on his Web site, www.appliedresearch.us/sf and at electionintegrity.org.

240. *Baltimore Sun*, November 5, 2004.

241. *Washington Post*, November 11, 2004.

242. *Nightline*, "Conspiracy Theory," January 19, 2005.

243. See http://moritzlaw.osu.edu/blogs/tokaji/2005/01/mea-culpa-rejected.html.

244. See http://uscountvotes.org/index.php?option=com_content&task=view&id=74&Itemid=43.

245. Jacques Steinberg, "Study Cites Human Failings in Election Day Poll System," *New York Times*, January 20, 2005.

246. MIT-CalTech Voting Technology Project, "Voting Machines and the Underestimate of the Bush Vote," November 9, 2004.

247. See http://www.vote.caltech.edu/media/documents/Addendum_Voting_Machines_Bush_Vote.pdf.

248. See http://abcnews.go.com/Technology/WhosCounting/.

249. J. A. Paulos, email correspondence with authors.

250. Russ Baker, "Election 2004: Stolen or Lost" TomPaine.com Posted on January 7, 2005. http://www.tompaine.com/articles/election_2004_stolen_or_lost.php.

    Freeman's reply: "Exit-Poll Problems: A Reply To Russ Baker," Steven Freeman, January 21, 2005. http://www.tompaine.com/articles/exit_poll_problems_a_reply_to_russ_baker.php http://www.tompaine.com/articles/letters_debating_exit_polls_part_2.php

251. Robert Parry, "Upside-Down Media," February 18, 2006, www.consortiumnews.com.

CHAPTER 8: THERE CAN BE NO MOVING ON

252. November 5, 2004 Doug Halonen, "GOP Wants News Organizations to Abandon Exit Polls," TV Week, November 5, 2004.

253. Presentation to the American Statistical Association's Philadelphia Chapter, October 14, 2005.

254. See, for example, Nancy Tobi of Democracy for New Hampshire, "What's wrong with the Holt Bill? Part 1" http://www.democracyfornewhampshire.com/node/view/2040 and "What's wrong with the Holt bill? Part 2" http://www.democracyfornewhampshire.com/node/view/2103.

255. Zogby Interactive, www.zogby.com, "Likely Voters 12/1/04 thru 12/3/04 MOE +/- 2.0 pct pts." "Question #11. Concerns have been expressed by some observers of the election that problems with counting the votes may have affected the results and deserve further investigation. Do you think these concerns are . . . Very valid: 725 (28.5%); Somewhat valid 357 (14.0%); Mostly invalid 615 (24.2%); Not at all valid 794 (31.2%); Not Sure 55 (2.2%); Total 2547 (100%)."

256. Jim Schiller, *The 1997 Indonesian Elections: Festival of Democracy of Costly Fiction?* Centre for Asia Pacific Initiatives, University of Victoria, Occasional Paper #22, May 1999.

257. DeHaven-Smith, xi-xii.

258. The election dispute of 1800 was followed by the 12th Amendment to the Constitution, and the dispute of 1876 spawned Title III of the federal code.

259. DeHaven-Smith, xv.

APPENDIX A: GERMAN EXIT POLLS

260. Source: Election data: http://www.bundeswahlleiter.de/ (English: http://www.bundeswahlleiter.de/wahlen/e/index_e.htm). Prognoses are those of Forschungsgruppe Wahlen, which has been conducting exit polls for ZDF, one of the two main German television stations. Other television stations employ other exit-polling firms, two of which are "infratest-dimap" and "Forsa." These predictions are, likewise, with rare exception within 1% of the final result (and also of each other.) When one polling company was off by 1.5% for one of the major parties in a recent election, this "large" difference was a big surprise for the public as well as for the researchers/pollsters.

In sharp contrast to the opacity of NEP practices, the German exit pollsters fully disclose on their Web sites not only the prognosis made as the polls close, but that of every subsequent iteration of the data at intervals ranging from about twenty minutes to an hour. Like NEP, they also correct the data based on actual counts from polled precincts, but their processes are perfectly transparent, and the original uncorrected numbers remain available for anyone to see at any time. Their complete data sets can be accessed through the Central Archive for Empirical Social Studies of the University of Cologne. Thanks to Dr. Andreas M. Wuest, Dr. Michael Morrissey, Kurt Gloos, and Lars Vinx for their help in compiling these data.

261. The FDP Freie Demokratische Partei (liberals) is aligned with the Christian Democratic Party, and the Social Democratic Party (SPD) is aligned with the Greens. PDS (socialists) and Republikaner (extreme right) are not in any coalition.

APPENDIX B: HOW SMALL SAMPLES CAN ACCURATELY PORTRAY LARGE POPULATIONS

261. The clustering adjustment is used in trying to predict the vote in a state from a sample of voters that is not selected completely at random from across that state. But here we are asking a different question: "What is the probability that the exit poll results would differ from the official tallies within those same polled precincts?" This is how we calculate Within Precinct Disparity, and clustering does not enter into this calculation.

262. The polling margin of error is calculated from the formula: $1.96 * \sqrt{\frac{p(1-p)}{N}}$ where p is the candidate's percentage of the vote (48.7%), and N is the sample size (3,845). The 1.96 multiplier corresponds to a 95% confidence interval. In this case: $\sqrt{\frac{p(1-p)}{N}} = .008$. The resultant 95% margin of error for Ohio is (1.96 * .008) or +/- 1.6%.

Further Readings

IMPORTANT OFFICIAL DOCUMENTS

Preserving Democracy: What Went Wrong in Ohio. January 5, 2005, Status Report of the House Judiciary Committee Democratic Staff (Republicans on the committee refused to participate). Often referred to as the Conyers Report. Available online at www.house.gov/judiciary_democrats/ ohiostatusrept1505.pdf, or through Academy Chicago Publishers (Anita (ed.) (2005), "What Went Wrong In Ohio: The Conyers Report on the 2004 Presidential Election with Introduction by Gore Vidal)

Edison Media Research and Mitofsky International (2005), "Evaluation of Edison/Mitofsky Election System 2004 prepared by Edison Media Research and Mitofsky International for the National Election Pool (NEP)." January 19, 2005 http://www.exit-poll.net/election-night/EvaluationJan192005.pdf

Democratic National Committee (DNC) report, "Democracy at Risk: The 2004 Election in Ohio." June 22, 2005. Available at http://www.democrats.org/a/2005/06/democracy_at_ri.php

United States Government Accountability Office, Elections: Federal Efforts to Improve Security and Reliability of Electronic Voting Systems Are Under Way, but Key Activities Need to Be Completed. Report to Congressional Requesters, September 2005. Available online at www.gao.gov/new.items/d05956.pdf

A compendium of documents is available in one volume from The Free Press (www.freepress.org): Did George W. Bush Steal America's 2004

Election? Ohio's Essential Documents, by Bob Fitrakis, Harvey Wasserman and Steve Rosenfeld (767 pages).

ELECTION FRAUD AND VOTE SUPPRESSION

The Free Press — Independent News Media — http://www.freepress.org/. Especially the columns of Bob Fitrakis & Harvey Wasserman, in the words of Jesse Jackson, " the Woodward & Bernstein of the 2004 Election"

Bradblog, http://www.bradblog.com/. Stories are not always well vetted, but Brad is usually among the first to post the most important breaking election and voting rights news, and uses lots of links to original sources.

Greg Palast, *Armed Madhouse* (New York: Dutton, 2006).

FLORIDA 2000

Martin Merzer and the Staff of the *Miami Herald, The Miami Herald Report: Democracy Held Hostage* (New York: St. Martin's Press, 2001).

National Opinion Research Center, "NORC Florida Ballots Project." Available at www.norc.uchicago.edu/fl/index.asp. This data is also summarized in an article by Professor Walter R. Mebane, Jr. of Cornell University, "The Wrong Man Is President! Overvotes in the 2000 Presidential Election in Florida," appearing in *Perspectives on Politics*, September 2004.

John Nichols, *Jews for Buchanan* (New York: The New Press, 2001).

Greg Palast, *The Best Democracy Money Can Buy* (New York: Plume, 2004).

Lance deHaven-Smith, *The Battle for Florida: An Annotated Compendium of Materials from the 2000 Presidential Election* (University of Florida Press, 2005).

Jeffrey Toobin, *Too Close to Call: The Thirty-six-day Battle to Decide the 2000 Election* (New York: Random House, 2001).

VOTING TECHNOLOGY AND ELECTION ADMINISTRATION

Blackboxvoting.org. Bev Harris has been the leading investigator of the Voting Machine industry and abuses in Election Administration. See also her book: *Black Box Voting: Ballot Tampering in the 21st Century* (Renton, WA: Talion Publishing, 2003).

Aviel D. Rubin, *Brave New Ballot* (New York: Morgan Road Books, 2006). Rubin has been one of the most important voices documenting vulnerabilities of electronic voting machines. See his site http://avirubin.com/.

Verified Voting Foundation, an uncompromisingly non-partisan agency dedicated to educating the public on the need for reliable and publicly verifiable elections. http://www.verifiedvotingfoundation.org

POLLING, ESPECIALLY EXIT POLLING

Ken Warren, *In Defense of Public Opinion Polling* (Cambridge, Mass: Westview Press, 2003).

Asher Herbert, *Polling and the Public: What Every Citizen Should Know*, 6th ed. (Washington, DC: Congressional Quarterly Press, 2004).

Despite our many reservations about Mystery Pollster, Mark Blumenthal's Web site is one of the best day-to-day sources of information on polls and polling: www.mysterypollster.com.

The Gallup Organization, the Gallup Editors' Blog poll.gallup.com/BLOG provides extensive insights into the mechanics of polls and polling.

RESEARCH AND DATA ARCHIVING

The National Election Data Archive is the new name of USCountVotes (http://uscountvotes.org).

Exit-poll data is stored and made available (without precinct or county identification) through the University of Connecticut's Roper Center a major center for polling data and reports of public opinion. www.ropercenter.uconn.edu

This same exit-poll data is also available through Survey Research Center at the University of Michigan's Institute for Social Research. www.isr.umich.edu/src

LEGISLATION AND POLITICAL ACTION

Verifiedvoting.org, sister organization to the Verified Voting Foundation is an uncompromisingly non-partisan lobbying group championing reliable and publicly verifiable elections in the United States.

VotersUnite! is a national non-partisan organization dedicated to fair and accurate elections. It focuses on distributing well-researched information to elections officials, elected officials, the media, and the public; as well as providing activists with information they need to work toward transparent elections in their communities. The John Gideon, the Executive Director, sends out a Daily Voting News email. www.votersunite.org.

VoteTrust national network of state-based organizations working for secure, accurate and transparent elections. http://www.votetrustusa.org/

John Conyers has provided federal level leadership in championing voting rights. His web page: http://www.house.gov/conyers/

THE MEDIA AND ITS SHORTCOMINGS: AWARENESS ABOUT ELECTION REPORTS AND READINGS

To understand better what news is reported and not reported and why. Project Censored reports on news that goes largely unreported and annually produces a book of the most important "censored" stories. (The stolen election was #3 in 2005.) See the story by Dennis Loo, a Sociologist at California State Polytechnic University, "No Paper Trail Left Behind: the Theft of the 2004 Presidential Election" by Dennis Loo, Ph.D. www.projectcensored.org/newsflash/voter_fraud.html.

Mark Crispin Miller has written brilliantly on the shortcomings of the media in his book, *Fooled Again: How the Right Stole the 2004 Election, and Why They'll Steal the Next One Too (Unless We Stop Them)*. (Basic Books, 2005) and his *Harper's* article: "None Dare Call It Stolen: Ohio, the election, and America's servile press," August 2005, excerpt available online at www.harpers.org/ExcerptNoneDare.

Robert Parry, who broke many of the Iran-contra stories in the 1980s as a reporter for the Associated Press and/or *Newsweek*, now writes for www.consortiumnews.com and has been following Republican election scandals since the 1980s.

Truthout.org, a news digest website with a few of its own columnists that passes along important information.

In These Times magazine, www.inthesetimes.com, has published extensively on this issue, including "Ghosts in the Voting Machines," by Joel Bleifuss and http://www.inthesetimes.com/site/main/article/ghosts_in_the_voting_machines/, and "A Corrupted Election" by Steven Freeman and Josh Mittledorf, http://www.inthesetimes.com/site/main/article/a_corrupted_election/, which was honored by Project Censored as the number 3 most underreported story of the year.

Additional supporting documents and analysis of material in the book can be found on Freeman's website, www.electionintegrity.org.

Acknowledgments

Many people helped in the research and writing of this book.

Jonathon Simon saved the CNN screen shots that were the critical initial data that pushed us into this research. Had it not been for his alertness and quick thinking on election night, the 2004 exit-poll discrepancy well might have vanished with the 1:03 a.m. Web site updates.

Joe Libertelli and Michael Green provided feedback on papers and chapter drafts throughout this process. Others including John Allen Paulos, Fritz Scheuren, Michael Hout, Andrew Gellman, Marc Sapir, Melissa Gonzales, Quintus Jett, Jeremy Firestone, Sandy Rothenberg, Johnnie Pourdehnad, Jacqui Posey, Steve Brant, Steve Cobble, Lilian Friedberg, Leanne Tobias, Claudia Slate, Jim Bever, Steve Hockema, Marc Bogonovich, Ian Lindblom, Stephanie Eckman, Joel Schwartz, and Julie Busby provided feedback or general help at various points.

University of Pennsylvania professors Jonathan Baron, Elaine Zanutto, and Larry Brown, provided valuable technical assistance. Jack Nagel, Steven F. Goldstone Endowed Term Professor of Political Science and Associate Dean for Graduate Studies at the School of Arts and Science, and Michael Delli Carpini, Dean of the Annenberg School of Communications provided both encouragement and perspective on their disciplines. As always, the Penn Reference Librarians exceeded all reasonable expectations. And we owe a great debt to doctoral students Sabyasachi Guharay and Andrei Villarroel who helped enormously to advance our work with generous applications of their knowledge and intelligence.

Thanks to the many people wrote in with support and suggestions on early papers; special thanks to Kaja Rebane, Michael Lubin, and Maria Reeves for suggestions of extraordinary perceptiveness and creativity. Special thanks also to David Griscom, Paul Lehto, and James Q. Jacobs for tenacious work in documenting fraud.

Rep. John Conyers (D.-Mich.) and his staff were unfailingly helpful and conscientious as they dedicated countless hours investigating the allegations. Special appreciation to Ted Kalo, the judiciary committee Minority General Counsel, who adeptly communicated our findings to the committee and has helped us both to understand and to fight a perplexing lack of interest in Washington and the media.

Bob Fitrakis and Harvey Wasserman, who have published more solid reporting on problems in the Ohio election than all the mainstream media combined, were helpful in many ways. Cliff Arnebeck, an attorney with the Massachusetts based Alliance for Democracy, who testified at the Conyers hearings alerted us to many of the Ohio electoral abuses, and David Cobb, the Green Party presidential candidate, provided his perspective on what happened in Ohio during both the election and the recount. Authors Robert Koehler, Martin Merzer, Greg Palast, Robert Parry, Mark Seibel, and Steve Rosenfeld provided valuable insights and information. Mark Crispin Miller has done that and more, serving as a beacon in the fog of recent election coverage.

For expertise on voting technology we owe a debt of gratitude to Bill Rouveral, the inventor of voto-matic (the predecessor to modern punch-card voting); Bev Harris, of BlackBoxVoting.org; David Dill, Stanford University professor and founder of VerifiedVoting.com; and Avi Rubin, computer science professor at Johns Hopkins University and an expert in computer security. We owe a special debt to Barbara Simons, the co-chair of ACM's (Association for Computing Machinery) U.S. Public Policy Committee (USACM) who has answered every question we threw at her about electronic voting.

We appreciate the help provided by Charles Stewart III of the Caltech-MIT/Voting Technology Project (VTP), who was gracious both in issuing an addendum acknowledging their error, and in introducing us to VTP researchers. And thanks to Bob Lee, the Philadelphia County Voter Registration Administrator, who showed us the city's voting operations and gave us an election officer's perspective.

We would like to thank all the people involved in the USCountVotes effort, including Bruce O'Dell, Kathy Dopp, Ron Baimon, Robert Klauber, Vicki Lovegren, Brian Joiner, and Paul Velleman who have given countless hours to challenging task of analyzing, explaining, and publicizing the statistical inconsistencies in the 2004 exit polls, and the election in general.

A very heartfelt thanks goes out to Josh Mitteldorf, to whom we owe more than anyone outside of those directly involved with the book's production. In February 2005, Josh co-wrote a critique of the official exit-poll report for *In These Times* that earned an award from Project Censored as one of the most important "censored" stories of the year. Since then, Josh has provided almost every kind of help imaginable including, but not limited to statistical and analytical counsel, graphic design, and chapter reviews.

Paul Johansen, the vice president of the American Statistical Association's Philadelphia Chapter, did a wonderful job organizing the fall 2005 meeting in which Warren Mitofsky and Steve Freeman gave presentations. Several other Philadelphians, especially Stephanie Singer, Jim Murphy, Vince Salandria, Tom Guggino, and Dava Guerin were all immeasurably helpful in preparing that discussion.

For help in understanding election polling practices in general, we are grateful to John Zogby, Scott Keeter of the Pew Research Center, Dan Merkle, Murray Edelman, and, especially, Ken Warren, who gave us the big picture as well as the details, and the analytics as well as the practical aspects of the art.

Even though we were in an adversarial position, Warren Mitofsky has graciously answered many questions and agreed to speak at length with us, and always with charm and good humor. We thank him and two people who have been working with him, Elizabeth Liddle and Mark Lindeman, for their willingness to share what they can.

We thank Brian Cook and Adam Staley Groves, at *In These Times*, for their work fact checking, and to Phoebe Hwang and Jon Gilbert at Seven Stories Press for their work compiling our many adjustments to the manuscript.

And we offer our gratitude to Seven Stories publisher Dan Simon and literary agent Diana Finch. Both have contributed greatly to the writing of this book. It would not exist without them.

Individually, we offer the following acknowledgements.

Steve Freeman:

I appreciate greatly the support and companionship of friends, family, colleagues and coworkers. Thanks to Becky Collins, Elaine Calabrese, and Carolyn Julye of the University of Pennsylvania's Center for Organizational Dynamics for their help with manuscripts, and, most of all, to the center's director Larry Starr, whose practical wisdom and dedication to free inquiry have been a source of both support and inspiration.

I thank my mother, Sylvia, for her support throughout this period, like every other period of my life. Thanks to my children, Burton and Laura, just for being who they are, and, most of all, to my wife Aurora Casta. I could not possibly have conducted this research without her sacrifice and love.

Joel Bleifuss:

I give sincere thanks to all my colleagues at *In These Times*. And I could not have worked on this book without the support from my family, Teresa Prados and Adrian, Diego and Eloy Bleifuss Prados, who have been there for me throughout.

Index

ABOUT THE AUTHORS

STEVEN F. FREEMAN holds a Ph.D. from MIT's Sloan School of Management and an M.S. in Social System Science from the University of Pennsylvania's Wharton School. Since 2000, he has held several academic positions at the University of Pennsylvania, where he currently serves as Visiting Scholar and a member of the teaching faculty of the Graduate Program of Organizational Dynamics in the School of Arts and Sciences. In addition to his regular courses, he teaches workshops for graduate students on research methods and survey design (a domain that includes polling). He has also taught on the faculty at the Wharton School, and at the Universidad de San Andreas in Argentina and the Central American Institute of Business Administration (INCAE) in Costa Rica, where he has conducted management courses for private and public sector leaders and faculty workshops on research methods. He is the recipient of four national research awards for outstanding scholarship from the Academy of Management.

JOEL BLEIFUSS is editor of *In These Times*. An investigative reporter and columnist, he has had more articles cited as one of the "Top Censored Stories" of the year by Project Censored than any other journalist. His articles have appeared in the *New York Times*, *Utne Reader*, the *Philadelphia Inquirer*, and *Dissent*, among many others.